Rawls's Egalitarianism

This is a new interpretation and analysis of John Rawls's leading theory of distributive justice, which also considers the responding egalitarian theories of scholars such as Richard Arneson, G. A. Cohen, Ronald Dworkin, Martha Nussbaum, John Roemer, and Amartya Sen. Rawls's theory, Kaufman argues, sets out a normative ideal of justice that incorporates an account of the structure and character of relations that are appropriate for members of society viewed as free and equal moral beings. Forging an approach distinct amongst contemporary theories of equality, Rawls offers an alternative to egalitarian justice methodologies that aim primarily to compensate victims for undeserved bad luck. For Rawls, the values that ground the most plausible account of egalitarianism are real equality of economic opportunity combined with the guarantee of a fair distribution of social goods. Kaufman's analysis will be of interest to scholars and advanced students of political theory and political philosophy, particularly those working on justice, and on the work of John Rawls.

ALEXANDER KAUFMAN is Associate Professor of political science at the University of Georgia. His research explores the relation of central values of the democratic political tradition to issues in contemporary politics. His work examines the meaning and policy implications of the notions of freedom and equality that are centrally emphasized in the democratic tradition. Kaufman's research investigates these issues in the context of projects that examine the justification of the welfare state and the nature of egalitarian justice.

Rawls's Egalitarianism

ALEXANDER KAUFMAN
University of Georgia

CAMBRIDGE
UNIVERSITY PRESS

University Printing House, Cambridge CB2 8BS, United Kingdom

One Liberty Plaza, 20th Floor, New York, NY 10006, USA

477 Williamstown Road, Port Melbourne, VIC 3207, Australia

314-321, 3rd Floor, Plot 3, Splendor Forum, Jasola District Centre, New Delhi - 110025, India

79 Anson Road, #06-04/06, Singapore 079906

Cambridge University Press is part of the University of Cambridge.

It furthers the University's mission by disseminating knowledge in the pursuit of education, learning and research at the highest international levels of excellence.

www.cambridge.org
Information on this title: www.cambridge.org/9781108453035
DOI: 10.1017/9781108554138

© Alexander Kaufman 2018

This publication is in copyright. Subject to statutory exception and to the provisions of relevant collective licensing agreements, no reproduction of any part may take place without the written permission of Cambridge University Press.

First published 2018
First paperback edition 2020

A catalogue record for this publication is available from the British Library

ISBN 978-1-108-42911-5 Hardback
ISBN 978-1-108-45303-5 Paperback

Cambridge University Press has no responsibility for the persistence or accuracy of URLs for external or third-party internet websites referred to in this publication, and does not guarantee that any content on such websites is, or will remain, accurate or appropriate.

For Nomi, Jonah, Dafna, and Mira

Contents

Acknowledgments	*page* viii
List of Abbreviations	ix
Introduction	1

Part I Justification

1	Rawls's Practical Conception of Justice: Opinion, Tradition, and Objectivity in Political Liberalism	23
2	Stability, Fit, and Consensus	47
3	Rawls and Ethical Constructivism	75
4	A Satisfactory Minimum Conception of Justice: Reconsidering Rawls's Maximin Argument	108

Part II Democratic Equality

5	The Difference Principle: Cohen's Ambiguities	133
6	Justice as Fairness and Fair Equality of Opportunity	156
7	Democratic Equality	187
8	Ideal Theory and Practical Judgment	218
9	Poverty, Inequality, and Justice	232

References	253
Index	263

Acknowledgments

While writing this book, I received invaluable comments and criticisms from many people. I would particularly like to thank Richard Arneson, Daniel Brudney, Evan Charney, Adam Cureton, Keith Dougherty, Michaele Ferguson, Samuel Freeman, Jon Garthoff, Robert Grafstein, Edward Halper, Martin van Hees, Sean Ingham, Jamie Mayerfeld, David Reidy, Richard Tuck, Clark Wolf, and several anonymous reviewers. The arguments in this book were also powerfully affected by conversations with Seyla Benhabib, Evelyn Brodkin, Ronald Dworkin, Jon Elster, Christine Korsgaard, Martha Nussbaum, and John Roemer.

My greatest debt, however, is to John Rawls, whose work provides a uniquely rich foundation for the study of distributive justice.

Article versions of four of the chapters in this volume were previously published. A version of Chapter 1 was published as "Rawls's Practical Conception of Justice: Opinion, Tradition and Objectivity in Political Liberalism," *Journal of Moral Philosophy*, Volume 3:1 (March 2006): 23–43. A version of Chapter 2 was published as "Stability, Fit, and Consensus," *Journal of Politics*, Volume 71:2 (April 2009): 533–43. A version of Chapter 3 was published as "Rawls and Kantian Constructivism," *Kantian Review*, Volume 17:2 (July 2012): 227–56. A version of Chapter 4 was published as "A Satisfactory Minimum Conception of Justice: Reconsidering Rawls's Maximin Argument," *Economics and Philosophy*, Volume 29:3 (November 2013): 349–69.

Abbreviations

Works by John Rawls are abbreviated as follows:

DJ   "Distributive Justice," in Peter Laslett and W. G. Runciman (eds.), *Politics, Philosophy, and Society* (Oxford: Blackwell, 1967). Reprinted in Samuel Freeman (ed.), *John Rawls: Collected Papers* (Cambridge, MA: Harvard University Press, 1999), pp. 130–53.

JAF *Justice as Fairness: A Restatement* (Cambridge, MA: Harvard University Press, 2001).

JF   "Justice as Fairness," *Philosophical Review* 67/2 (1958): 164–94. Reprinted in Samuel Freeman (ed.), *John Rawls: Collected Papers* (Cambridge, MA: Harvard University Press, 1999), pp. 47–72.

KC   "Kantian Constructivism in Moral Theory," *Journal of Philosophy* 77 (1980): 515–72. Reprinted in Samuel Freeman (ed.), *John Rawls: Collected Papers* (Cambridge, MA: Harvard University Press, 1999), pp. 303–58.

ODPE "Outline of a Decision Procedure for Ethics," *Philosophical Review* 60/2 (1951): 177–97. Reprinted in Samuel Freeman (ed.), *John Rawls: Collected Papers* (Cambridge, MA: Harvard University Press, 1999), pp. 1–19.

PL   *Political Liberalism* (New York: Columbia University Press, [1993] 1996).

TCR "Two Concepts of Rules," *Philosophical Review* 64/1 (1955): 3–32. Reprinted in Samuel Freeman (ed.), *John Rawls: Collected Papers* (Cambridge, MA: Harvard University Press, 1999), pp. 20–46.

TJ   *A Theory of Justice* (Cambridge, MA: Harvard University Press [1971] 1999).

Introduction

This study focuses on John Rawls's complex understanding of egalitarian justice. Rawls addresses this subject both in *A Theory of Justice* and in many of his articles published between 1951 and 1982. In these works, he argues for a view that is distinct from the leading contemporary theories of equality – equality of resources, equality of access to advantage, equality of opportunity for welfare, and equality of capabilities. In particular, Rawls offers an alternative to approaches to egalitarian justice that aim primarily to compensate victims for undeserved bad luck. The values that ground the most plausible account of egalitarianism, Rawls argues, are real equality of economic opportunity combined with the guarantee of a fair distribution of social goods.

Rawls's conception of egalitarian justice, particularly as developed in the argument for *democratic equality* in Chapter 2 of *A Theory of Justice*, has exerted a significant influence on contemporary egalitarian thought. The egalitarian theories of Richard Arneson, G. A. Cohen, Ronald Dworkin, Martha Nussbaum, John Roemer, and Amartya Sen – to name only the most salient contributors to this literature – all respond in various ways to arguments that Rawls develops in that chapter. Rawls's view, moreover, offers resources to address controversies that have emerged in this literature regarding responsibility, the genuineness of choice, and adaptive preferences. Luck egalitarians such as Arneson, Cohen, and Dworkin argue that egalitarian concerns regarding fairness must be tempered by an equal concern with responsibility. In their accounts, egalitarian justice is concerned primarily to compensate for inequalities in well-being for which it is inappropriate to hold the person responsible. Elizabeth Anderson, Samuel Scheffler, Timothy Hinton, and others have responded that such imputations of responsibility will necessarily involve disrespectful and paternalistic judgments regarding the person's use of his or her freedom. In addition, Matt Mattravers and Alexander Kaufman have argued, theories that aim to hold persons responsible for their disadvantage require accounts of free and genuine choice that – in turn – require resolution of a number of intractable metaphysical questions. Rawls's view, however, sets out an approach to responsibility that establishes the basis for a reasonable balance between concerns regarding responsibility and freedom by ensuring fair equality of opportunity and a fair basic structure of society and then treating outcomes as a matter of pure procedural justice. Since Rawls's view does not aim to compensate persons for undeserved well-being deficits, it does not require an account of the genuineness of choice. Similarly, since Rawls's conception does not treat the individual's preferences as the decisive criterion of well-being, the account of just relations generated under that conception is less likely than welfarist accounts to be skewed by adaptive preferences.

Rawls's potential contribution to contemporary egalitarian thought, however, has been obscured by numerous confusions regarding both the content and the justification of his theory. In the contemporary literature, it is not uncommon to find views attributed to Rawls that his work flatly contradicts. For example, it is routinely asserted that Rawls's maximin argument requires redistribution to maximize the share of goods held by the least advantaged members of society. Similarly, it is widely assumed that the difference principle derives its justification directly from the maximin argument. Pluralist commentators claim that Rawls would endorse stringent limits on the content of public discourse in order to suppress challenges to liberal consensus.[1] Another category of commentators argues that Rawls's later work abandons his earlier ambition to identify and specify the objective requirements of distributive justice and instead recommends accommodation to the views of the majority.[2] Stated without qualification, all of these views – and many others routinely attributed to Rawls – are false. During the four decades since the publication of *A Theory of Justice*, error has been overlaid upon error to produce a generally accepted account of the nature of Rawls's views that Rawls would not recognize.

In order to discuss the contribution that Rawls's work might make to contemporary egalitarian thought, then, it is first necessary to address various misunderstandings and confusions regarding his argument and views. In particular, a reader requires a clear and undistorted understanding of Rawls's approach to political justification in order to assess the persuasiveness of Rawls's substantive arguments regarding egalitarian justice. Part I of this book therefore attempts to clarify central aspects of Rawls's argument relating to the issues of objectivity, stability, constructivism, and rational choice under uncertainty. Only after Rawls's views regarding these issues are presented clearly can the reader assess Rawls's contribution to egalitarian thought. The purpose of the book is thus dual. First, I aim to correct misunderstandings that have obscured the potential of Rawls's conception of equality to contribute to contemporary egalitarian thought. Second, I aim to develop the implications of Rawls's conception of egalitarian justice for contemporary debates regarding egalitarian justice and antipoverty policy.

This dual focus – on issues of justification and substance – directs attention to one of Rawls's most significant contributions: his account of moral and political justification. While some contemporary commentators have argued that Rawls's early work is inattentive to challenges to the project of theorizing justice posed by pluralistic disagreement about the nature of the good, Rawls focuses on these challenges at every stage of his career and develops a powerful and persuasive response to moral skepticism. Far from assuming away problems of pluralistic disagreement, Rawls focuses much of his attention on the problem of achieving consensus on even the most fundamental questions relating to justice.

In order to address this problem, Rawls seeks to identify the possible grounds of moral justification and to identify "possible bases of agreement where none seems possible" (TJ 509). Rawls concedes that "[w]e must recognize the possibility that there is no way to get beyond a plurality of principles" (TJ 36). Nevertheless, Rawls argues persuasively that (1) certain weak assumptions about the nature and requirements of justice (e.g., justice should be impartial) are widely shared – at least among citizens of democratic societies, and (2) a careful argument from these weak and widely shared premises has the potential to ground judgments that can constitute the focus of consensus, even among people who disagree about the nature of the good.

Doubts about the possibility of justifying normative claims, even seemingly attractive propositions, are pervasive in the contemporary theoretical literature. This skeptical orientation has undermined confidence in the possibility of generating a justifiable egalitarian agenda. Rawls's response to these doubts thus continues to be highly relevant to contemporary discourses regarding distributive justice and constitutes perhaps his most significant contribution.

Rawls's sophisticated approach to justification, moreover, enables him to offer a subtle response to the question of whether – and to what degree – choice justifies otherwise unacceptable inequality and deprivation. Ronald Dworkin argues that an acceptable account of egalitarian justice must hold the individual responsible for the consequences of his or her choices and must therefore refuse to compensate persons for resource deficits that are the result of choice rather than bad brute luck.[3] Rawls's theory, Dworkin argues, is weakened by its failure to hold individual sufficiently responsible for their choices.

Rawls's theory, however, reflects a concern with responsibility quite similar to the view that Dworkin proposes. Rawls's theory is – as he emphasizes – designed to realize pure procedural justice. Within institutions characterized by pure procedural justice, "what a person is entitled to depends on what he does" (TJ 74). Rawls's theory, that is, aims to ensure to each person equal opportunity to compete for advantage within fair economic institutions. The person's just share is determined entirely by what the person has "done in good faith in the light of established expectations" (TJ 76). Rawls thus holds each individual responsible for generating their own fair share of social goods in precisely the manner that Dworkin recommends.

Rawls nevertheless argues for an important qualification of the view that genuine choice justifies unequal holdings. In particular, Rawls's view requires that no choice that a person can make can justify certain extreme levels of inequality and deprivation. As I suggest in Chapter 6, Rawls's argument on this issue provides a particularly powerful counter to Dworkin's position because Dworkin, like Rawls, offers a constructivist approach to justice that is designed to neutralize the influence of arbitrary factors (in particular, bad brute luck) on life chances. In requiring the provision of assistance in extreme cases of choice-generated inequality and deprivation, I argue, Rawls shows himself to be more consistent than Dworkin in the treatment of bad brute luck.

The remaining sections of this introduction describe the basic elements of Rawls's accounts of justice as fairness and political liberalism in order to create a context for the chapters that follow. In the following sections, I will (1) describe the overall character and structure of Rawls's arguments; and (2) highlight issues that will be examined in greater detail in later chapters.

A Theory of Justice

In *A Theory of Justice*, Rawls describes an approach to political reasoning that he calls "due reflection" and employs this approach to argue for an account of a fair choice position from which reliable judgments of justice may be formed. Rawls's argument derives much of its shape and structure from its roots in his approach to justification. This subsection will describe Rawls's approach to justification before providing an account of the substance of his theory.

Justification

Justification, Rawls argues, is a matter of the mutual support of many considerations, "of everything fitting together into one coherent view" (TJ 507). In particular, an acceptable theory must fit with and organize our considered judgments of justice. Considered judgments are judgments made under conditions favorable to the exercise of the sense of justice and therefore exhibiting none of the familiar defects of reasoning. These conditions include access to full information, adequate time for reflection, the absence of stress or other influences that might distort judgment, and independence from the influence of existing dogma or ideological doctrine. Judgments affirmed under these conditions express settled convictions such as the rejection of slavery and of religious intolerance. These judgments, Rawls argues, may be viewed as provisional fixed points (TJ 18) that an account of justice must fit – fixed because they are judgments in which we have confidence, but provisionally fixed because no judgment at any level of generality can plausibly be viewed as definitive.

Considered judgments operate at different levels of generality. Persons form considered judgments about the nature of justice itself (e.g., the kinds of considerations that are relevant to judgments of justice), about specific issues (e.g., slavery, religious persecution), and about specific aspects of policy (e.g., whether affirmative action is required to correct damage caused by racial discrimination). During the reflective process that Rawls calls "due reflection," the person models in the form of a decision procedure considered judgments regarding the kinds of restrictions that it seems reasonable to impose on judgments of justice. The resulting decision procedure, which Rawls calls the *original position*, plays a central role in Rawls's justification of his theory. Two considered judgments, the first requiring that persons should not be able to tailor principles to their own case and the second requiring that judgments of justice should not be grounded in considerations that are irrelevant from the standpoint of justice (TJ 16–17), justify the most salient feature of the original position: persons are to choose principles as though they were behind a veil of ignorance that deprives them of information regarding their interests, talents, and abilities, about the nature of the society in which they live, and about any information that is irrelevant (to judgments of justice) from the moral point of view.

After generating an account of this decision procedure, the person employs the procedure to select principles of justice. The principles selected must then be tested to determine whether, when they are applied to specific issues and policy questions, the results match our specific considered judgments regarding these issues. Initially, Rawls expects that there will be discrepancies. If so, the person must consider and revise her considered judgments and/or the account of the decision procedure. If a description of the decision procedure can be devised that yields principles that match the person's adjusted considered judgments, then the person has achieved *reflective equilibrium* – her principles and judgments coincide. Political principles that match our considered judgments in reflective equilibrium, Rawls argues, can be characterized as objective – they are the principles that we would want everyone, including ourselves, to follow.[4]

Justice as Fairness

A conception of justice is necessary, Rawls argues, to regulate the most basic social institutions in order to determine the division of the advantages generated by social cooperation. An acceptable conception of justice must regulate the effects of the basic structure of society – the major social institutions that determine the division of advantages from cooperation – on the life chances of citizens in order to ensure that the burdens and benefits of cooperation are distributed fairly. In particular, an acceptable conception must ensure that the basic structure does not favor starting positions defined in terms qualities of individuals that are distributed in a way that is "arbitrary from a moral perspective."

A Theory of Justice

In *A Theory of Justice*, Rawls argues for two specific principles to regulate the basic structure. These principles require that:

1 Each person is to have an equal right to the most extensive total system of equal basic liberties compatible with a similar system of liberty for all.
2 Social and economic inequalities are to be arranged so that they are both:
   a to the greatest benefit of the least advantaged, and
   b attached to offices and positions open to all under conditions of fair equality of opportunity. (TJ 266)

Rawls provides arguments to justify acceptance of these principles in both Chapters 2 and 3. While Rawls, in fact, states that the argument presented in Chapter 2 merely provides an explication of the second principle that supplements and supports the formal argument developed from the standpoint of the original position, the line of reasoning developed in Chapter 2 clearly contains an independent argument regarding the nature of an acceptable conception of distributive justice – an argument that reflects an important strand of Rawls's reasoning. It is important, then, to take account of the informal argument presented in Chapter 2 as well as the formal argument presented in Chapter 3 when assessing the structure of Rawls's justification of his theory. The informal argument of Chapter 2 works from specific considered judgments regarding arbitrariness and the inviolability of the person, while the formal argument of Chapter 3 employs the original position to identify principles that rational choosers would select from the standpoint of a fair decision procedure.

The Informal Argument

The argument of Chapter 2 assumes that persons who accept the considered judgment that justice requires respect for the inviolability of the person will accept the first principle and, therefore, focuses on the justification of the second principle. In developing this informal justification, Rawls does not employ the original position to structure the argument. Rather, he argues directly from the considered judgments that (1) arbitrary factors should not determine life chances and (2) acceptable principles of justice are the principles that free and equal people would choose for themselves. If it is assumed that the principles regulating the distribution of goods must be acceptable to all persons viewed as free and equal, Rawls argues, then it is reasonable to assume that all inequalities permitted by the principles must satisfy *two conditions* – first the inequalities must reasonably be expected to be *to everyone's* advantage; and second the inequalities must be attached to *positions and offices open to all* (TJ 53). Rawls's informal justification for the second principle generates an account of acceptable principles to regulate the distribution of goods by examining three conceptions of distributive justice that combine possible elaborations of these two conditions: (1) natural liberty, (2) liberal equality, and (3) democratic equality (TJ 57–73)

Natural liberty interprets "to everyone's advantage" to require satisfaction of the *principle of efficiency*, and interprets "open to all" to require that *careers are open to talents* (TJ 57–63). As Rawls notes, many possible arrangements of the basic structure satisfy the principle of efficiency, and that principle provides no basis for singling out one of these possible distributions as just. The requirements of the principle could not, for example, rule out arrangements including serfdom or apartheid as unjust. Natural liberty therefore supplements the principle of efficiency by requiring that careers must be open to talents. This additional condition, however, simply requires that all must have the same legal rights of access to social positions. As Rawls notes, this added requirement would view as just conditions in which the distribution of social goods is determined by endowments such as inherited wealth and social position. Natural liberty, Rawls concludes, is unacceptable as a conception of distributive justice because it would treat as just arrangements in which factors that are arbitrary from the moral point of view determine or strongly affect the distribution of social goods.

Liberal equality continues to interpret *to everyone's advantage* to require satisfaction of the principle of efficiency, but interprets *positions open to all* to require satisfaction of the principle of *fair equality of opportunity* (TJ 63–65). Fair equality of opportunity requires that those with similar abilities and skills should have similar life chances. This principle thus aims to neutralize completely the influence of social endowments on the opportunities available to each individual. Under liberal equality, therefore, a just society is a meritocracy. While liberal equality offers a more attractive account of distributive justice than natural liberty, liberal equality still permits the distribution of social goods to be determined by the natural distribution of abilities and talents. Liberal equality thus continues to allow a factor that is arbitrary from the moral point of view to determine the nature of a just distribution and does not, therefore, constitute an acceptable conception of distributive justice.

Democratic equality addresses this problem by continuing to interpret "positions open to all" to require fair equality of opportunity, but interpreting "to everyone's advantage" to require satisfaction of *the difference principle* (which requires that "the higher expectations of those better situated are just if and only if they work as part of a scheme which improves the expectations of the least advantaged members of society") (TJ 65–73). Democratic equality therefore avoids allowing the distribution of social goods to be determined by either (1) inherited social position or (2) inherited natural abilities. Rather, democratic equality combines (1) a principle designed to neutralize the influence of social endowments on the distribution of goods by ensuring equal opportunity with (2) the difference principle, which is designed to ensure that after equal liberty and equal opportunity have been ensured, inequalities in the distribution of social goods fall within a range that is consistent with fairness.

The Formal Argument

In the second (formal) argument for the two principles, Rawls argues that it is rational for persons reasoning about justice under the constrained conditions of the original position to employ a maximin rule of choice – a rule that instructs the chooser to select that option that secures the "most satisfactory minimum" state of affairs (TJ 132–39). While the maximin rule is not an appropriate guide for all, or even most, choices under uncertainty, Rawls argues that it is the appropriate rule to regulate judgments in the original position because of (1) the informational constraint imposed by the veil of ignorance and (2) two additional features of that choice position. First, Rawls argues, if potential losses and gains are both unlimited, it is rational to be more concerned to avoid the worst possible outcomes than to insist upon preserving the possibility of the greatest possible gains. Second, rational choosers will insist upon ruling out completely certain unacceptable outcomes. If, for example, slavery is a real possibility – as it must be for persons behind a veil of ignorance – and if a person can eliminate that possibility *simply* by choosing a principle forbidding slavery; then, Rawls argues, any rational person would insist upon the choice of that principle.

It is important to emphasize that the "satisfactory minimum" sought by the choosers is not a minimum income or bundle of primary goods. Rather, Rawls argues that the "satisfactory minimum" that choosers will attempt to secure constitutes "an adequate minimum conception of justice" (TJ 153) – that is, the conception that provides the most satisfactory minimum guarantee of protections of their fundamental interests by regulating the "two coordinate roles" of the basic structure (JAF 48): (1) securing equal basic liberties and (2) regulating background institutions to secure social and economic justice in the distribution of goods. In particular, Rawls argues, the choosers will choose a conception that (1) minimizes invasions of fundamental liberty interests, (2) promotes equal opportunity to develop and exploit their talents, and (3) mitigates the inequalities that continue to exist in a social order that ensures equal opportunity.

Rawls argues that the principles of justice as fairness provide the most adequate minimum guarantee relating to the *first* role of the basic structure by showing that the principles minimize the "strains of commitment" (TJ 153–54). Any principles of justice chosen will cause some tensions (strains of commitment) between members of society and the social institutions that enforce the requirements of justice. Some just principles of distribution may be unrealizable because of this kind of tension. The parties must, therefore, consider what it would be like to keep the agreement (to respect the principles of justice chosen) if they were assigned the worst social position. If they imagine that, in such a case, they would wish that they had chosen different principles, then they have overtaxed their ability to commit.

Perhaps the greatest strain on commitment, Rawls argues, occurs when a person or group must accept an invasion of their basic rights so that another person or group may benefit. No other theory of justice rules out such a possibility as unequivocally as justice as fairness (because Rawls's theory makes the inviolability of the person a foundational guarantee). Thus, Rawls's two principles are more likely than any other approach to justice to minimize the strains of commitment. Note that Rawls's argument really amounts to the claim that his principles protect fundamental *liberty interests* more securely than any other principles of justice.

Rawls argues that the principles of justice as fairness provide the most adequate minimum guarantee relating to the *second* role of the basic structure by showing that the principles ensure that members of a society regulated by justice as fairness receive a larger share of the primary good of self-respect (and therefore – when this share is combined with the guarantees of equal opportunity and fair compensation – a larger overall share of primary goods) than they would under any other conception of justice (TJ 154–57). In particular, the least advantaged social position in a society under the two principles will, Rawls argues, be less unacceptable than under any other conception of justice because the public commitment to reciprocity embodied in the two principles reflects a joint intention to "abstain from the exploitation of the contingencies of nature and social circumstance" (TJ 156). In affirming a conception of justice embodying this intention, "persons express their respect for one another in the very constitution of their society" (TJ 156). Thus, "public recognition of the two principles gives greater support to men's self-respect" (TJ 155), most particularly in the case of the least advantaged.

Note that if both of Rawls's arguments (the formal and informal arguments) are persuasive, then reasonable and rational persons will endorse the same principles of justice on the basis of (1) fully informed arguments grounded in our considered judgments and (2) arguments developed from the standpoint of the original position. Thus, our principles and our (considered) judgments coincide, and we are in reflective equilibrium. The combined arguments of Chapters 2 and 3 of *A Theory of Justice* are thus designed to establish that Rawls's two principles correspond to the considered judgments of a reasonable and rational person in reflective equilibrium.

Political Liberalism

In *Political Liberalism*, John Rawls modifies his theory in order to generate an account of justice that could provide a basis for consensus in societies divided by disagreements regarding basic religious, philosophical, and moral views. A politically liberal theory aims to gain the reasoned, informed, and willing support of persons who disagree fundamentally regarding basic values by identifying grounds for consensus located in the ideas and values of the political culture. A politically liberal conception of justice constructed through a procedure that builds from basic and shared ideas and values to principles that express the practical implications of those values, Rawls argues, can constitute the basis for such a consensus.

Rawls attempts to generate an account of the theoretical basis for consensus among members of a pluralistic society by developing and extending his earlier account of political justification. As in his earlier account of due reflection, Rawls aims to identify the bases of agreement by grounding his argument in basic and shared ideas. If a conception of justice can be worked up from basic ideas that are affirmed by all reasonable members of society, and if that conception serves effectively as the basis of consensus, then the conception will constitute the focus of an overlapping consensus of reasonable conceptions of the good. As the focus of such a consensus, the conception will be the subject of *willing and informed affirmation* of all reasonable members of society; and the conception will be *stable* in the sense that the desire to sustain a just society under that conception will dominate the incentive to undermine the society by free-riding on the willingness of others to act justly.

This shift in Rawls's concern – from the construction of a conception of justice that articulates the sense of justice of a reasonable person to the specification of a conception that can constitute the focus of overlapping consensus – requires reconsideration of several aspects of Rawls's approach. In *A Theory of Justice*, individuals ground their moral reflections in considered judgments of justice, while in *Political Liberalism* citizens ground their political reflections in ideas latent in the public political culture; and in *A Theory of Justice*, moral agents seek to attain a perfectly general reflective equilibrium regarding judgments of justice, while in *Political Liberalism* citizens aim to construct a conception of justice that can be the focus of consensus of a certain type.

In developing his argument, Rawls introduces and elaborates three ideas that are essentially connected to the politically liberal character of his conception. First, Rawls describes the subject of a theory of political liberalism as *a political conception of justice*. A *political* conception is a view that is *freestanding* because it is worked up from ideas implicit in the public political culture that are affirmed by all reasonable persons. The argument for such a theory aims to avoid reliance upon substantive philosophical, religious, or moral assumptions that require the acceptance of special doctrines that are not widely accepted within the public culture. Second, Rawls argues that the conception generated through such a reflective process may constitute the *focus of an overlapping consensus*. Because the conception is worked up from shared ideas and relies only upon premises that are implicit in the political culture and widely shared, the arguments for the conception rely upon no assumptions that could be rejected by a reasonable person. The argument for the conception is thus developed in a manner that has the potential to persuade any reasonable person that the conception is reasonable. Finally, the conception can be justified to all citizens based upon *public reason* – arguments from reasons and ideas implicit in the public political culture.

While Rawls's later work modifies a number of aspects of his analytic approach, it is important to note that Rawls's accounts of justification and theory acceptance remain essentially consistent. The standard for the justification of a political judgment in late Rawls remains the test of due reflection – would a reasonable and rational person, on due reflection and in reflective equilibrium, accept the claim that the judgment is reasonable. In addition, Rawls continues to employ a form of constructivism to identify and justify the principles of an acceptable conception of justice. Finally, Rawls continues to work within the framework of ideal theory – his arguments are designed to generate an account of justice for a well-ordered society of persons effectively motivated by the sense of justice.

Outline of Chapters

Before Rawls's contribution to egalitarian thought can be presented clearly, a number of issues relating both to Rawls's approach to justification and the substance of his theory must be addressed. Part I of the book focuses on issues relating to justification. Modifications of Rawls's approach in articles and books published after 1982 have led commentators to claim that political liberalism (1) is unattractively accommodationist and yet also (2) imposes unacceptable restrictions on contributions to public discourse. I examine these concerns in Chapters 1 and 2. The complexity of Rawls's account of constructivism and its relation to his general account of justification in ethics have led commentators to question Rawls's account of both the theoretical foundation and the practical application of his constructivist argument. I address these issues in Chapters 3 and 4. Part II focuses on the substance of Rawls's account of democratic equality. The difference principle of justice has been the subject of many critiques, and I discuss one of the most influential of these critiques in Chapter 5. The purpose of this chapter is not merely to clear away confusions but also to clarify the meaning of the difference principle and its function within Rawls's theory. The remaining chapters examine the requirements of Rawls's account of distributive justice that go beyond the requirements of the difference principle. These chapters are designed both to develop an account of Rawlsian distributive justice that goes beyond conventional accounts and – in the process – to suggest the nature of the contribution that Rawls's theory can make to the current egalitarian literature. In the remainder of this section, I summarize the main ideas of each chapter in the context of my argument.

Justification

Chapter 1: Objectivity

Rawls argues that a politically liberal conception of justice can provide the basis of a reasoned, informed and willing political agreement by locating grounds for consensus in the fundamental ideas and values of the political culture. Critics urge, however, that such a conception of justice will be designed merely to appeal to the situated views of actual citizens. In order to evaluate this concern, I suggest in Chapter 1, it is necessary to focus on the approach to justification that grounds Rawls's argument. A conception of justice is justified, Rawls asserts, if it is supported by arguments grounded in shared ideas that are sufficiently persuasive to convince all reasonable persons that the conception is reasonable. Rawls argues that the two principles that constitute his politically liberal conception satisfy this standard: they are the principles that reasonable citizens of modern democratic cultures *should* choose *on due reflection* – that is, after reflecting fully upon their considered judgments regarding justice under conditions conducive to sound reflection. Since the choice of the two principles is grounded in due reflection, rather than in an appeal to situated opinions, I argue that the criticism fails.

Chapter 2: Stability

In *Political Liberalism*, Rawls develops a distinct account of the stability of a conception of justice. According to this account, a conception of justice is stable if it is possible for the holders of diverse reasonable views about the good to affirm the conception on due reflection. If persons affirming diverse and conflicting reasonable conceptions of the good can affirm a political conception of justice on due reflection, then – Rawls argues – that conception is capable of constituting the focus of a stable overlapping consensus within a pluralistic culture. A number of commentators, however, argue that Rawls's approach secures affirmation by limiting the scope of political deliberation, removing controversial issues from democratic debate, or socializing citizens to accept liberal assumptions. In Chapter 2, I argue that these objections seriously mischaracterize Rawls's theory. Rawls's account of stability, I argue, is designed neither to restrict debate nor to socialize the participants in that debate.

Chapter 3: Constructivism
Rawls's account of ethical and political constructivism is perhaps his most striking contribution to ethics. The clearly defined structure of Rawls's political constructivism and the transparency that such a structure produces, Rawls suggests, constitute significant virtues for an account of political reasoning for societies characterized by pluralistic disagreement. The constructivist representation of moral judgments formed in the context of a concretely described decision procedure and informed by a general knowledge of facts about human society has, however, led to the perception among many commentators that Rawls's constructivism is grounded in specific factual information or in principles or values that are not principles or values of justice. Thus, G. A. Cohen claims Rawls's constructivism is "fact-infested"[5] and, in addition, grounds its judgments in strategic and other considerations that are irrelevant to justice, while Aaron James asserts that Rawls assumes that constructivist moral judgment is authoritative only when "grounded in independent judgments about what kind of social practices exist and what kinds of agents participate in them."[6] Both of these views, I argue, misrepresent the character of Rawls's account of constructivism.

Chapter 4: The Maximin Argument
In *A Theory of Justice*, John Rawls argues that it is possible to describe an appropriate initial situation from which to form reliable judgments about questions of justice.[7] This initial situation, which Rawls calls

the "original position," models the practical implications of fundamental and shared intuitions regarding justice, in particular intuitions concerning the role that considerations regarding fairness, impartiality, and the avoidance of arbitrariness should play in grounding judgments of justice. Once these intuitions are modeled faithfully, Rawls argues, the structure of the resulting choice problem dictates that rational persons occupying the original position should apply a maximin rule of choice in choosing principles of justice to regulate their joint social relations. Critics, however, argue that (1) Rawls's argument relies upon an implausible approach to choice under uncertainty, (2) persons employing a maximin rule of choice would not necessarily choose Rawls's two principles of justice, and (3) the maximin rule is not the most attractive decision rule that is available under conditions of uncertainty. Chapter 4 argues that these critiques of Rawls's argument suffer from a shared defect: each assumes incorrectly that the maximin rule of choice directs choosers to secure for themselves and the persons they represent the largest possible (1) share of income and wealth or (2) bundle of primary goods. As a result, these critiques generally conflate the satisfactory minimum sought under the maximin rule with the assistance provided to the least advantaged under the difference principle. It is the purpose of this chapter to distinguish clearly between these two ideas and, as a result, to demonstrate that the leading critiques of the maximin argument reflect a misunderstanding of the character of Rawls's theory.

Democratic Equality

The difference principle is not the most fundamental element of Rawls's second principle of justice – in fact, it is lexically subordinate to the principle of fair equality of opportunity. Nevertheless, the greatest part of the critical literature on Rawls focuses on the difference principle. Part II begins by focusing on the most influential of these critiques.

Chapter 5: The Difference Principle

Gerald Cohen's later work criticizes John Rawls's theory of justice for tolerating "deep inequalities" in cases in which permitting selfish maximizing behavior by the more fortunate generates benefits for the least advantaged members of society. Rawls's argument justifying these inequalities, Cohen argues, introduces two ambiguities into his theory relating to (1) the degree to which permissible inequalities must be *necessary* in order to satisfy the difference principle and (2) the proper definition of the basic structure of society. Once the ambiguities in Rawls's argument are resolved, Cohen argues, it is clear that the difference principle justifies little or no inequality in incomes. Chapter 5 argues that Cohen's critique is grounded in a confused reading of that principle. On one hand, the difference principle does not require that inequalities must be "necessary" in order to benefit the least advantaged; on the other hand, the difference principle does not license unrestrained selfish maximizing behavior.

Chapter 6: Fair Equality of Opportunity

Rawls's principle of fair equality of opportunity requires the guarantee of equal prospects of success to all persons with similar levels of talent and ambition. Policies designed to deliver on this guarantee must attempt to ensure that members of all sectors of society should have "the same prospects of success regardless of their initial place in the social system" (TJ 63). Satisfaction of this guarantee would require significant social policies designed to ensure equal access to education and equal opportunity to acquire knowledge, skills, and employment. This requirement is assigned lexical priority over the difference principle and thus defines the fundamental character of distributive justice in Rawls's theory. Rawls's conception of equality is thus characterized primarily by its commitment to securing conditions of genuine equal opportunity in which persons may live together as equals, and not – as some commentators suggest – by a commitment to the redistribution of income or resources.

Chapter 7: Democratic Equality

Democratic equality is the conception of distributive justice that is realized through the joint implementation of the principle of fair equality of opportunity and the difference principle. While the two principles are ranked in lexical order, Rawls emphasizes that the principles operate as a unit. That is, each principle interacts with and qualifies the character and proper operation of the other principle. Interaction between the two principles ensures that (1) implementation of the principle of fair equality of opportunity does not establish a meritocracy and that (2) the joint operation of the principles provides the basis for a form of social life in which social institutions are constituted in a manner than abstains from the exploitation of the contingencies of nature and social circumstance. This chapter examines the character and requirements of the conception of distributive justice realized through the joint implementation of these two principles.

Chapter 8: Ideal Theory
In *A Theory of Justice*, Rawls develops an account of justice designed to regulate the basic institutions of a *well-ordered* society – a society in which the behavior of all members is effectively motivated by the sense of justice, so that "everyone is presumed to act justly" (TJ 8). Rawls thus develops his arguments from the assumption of strict compliance. This development of the argument in the form of ideal theory is justified, Rawls argues, because ideal theory "provides...the only basis for the systematic grasp of [the] more pressing" issues of social justice (TJ 8). Amartya Sen, however, argues that Rawls's reliance upon an ideal theoretic approach introduces several problems into his argument. Most significantly, Rawls's choice to develop his argument while working from the assumptions of ideal theory leads him to develop an account of justice designed to identify a *single* set of institutions that most closely fits the considered judgments of reasonable members of society. In this chapter, I argue that Rawls's approach is both more flexible and more practical than Sen suggests.

Chapter 9: Practical Application
Application of the principles that constitute justice as fairness to specific social institutions and circumstances will ground significant substantive judgments regarding institutions and policy. This chapter examines the nature of the judgments that the principles would justify in the context of the social conditions currently existing in the United States. Such a focus illustrates both (1) the potential of justice as fairness to contribute to egalitarian thought and (2) the manner in which the principles provide a framework rather than a blueprint.

Rawls's account of egalitarian justice thus addresses the concern – expressed by Scheffler and others – that an acceptable account of egalitarian justice must go beyond an account of justice in distribution, and set out a normative ideal of justice that incorporates an account of the structure and character of an egalitarian society. In particular, the function of the second principle in transforming social goals and social understandings of the meaning of success ensure that all persons are guaranteed equal citizenship, not merely equal opportunity to leave others behind in a zero-sum form of economic competition. Thus, Rawls's theory, as Scheffler notes, "shows how ... a plausible form of distributive egalitarianism can be anchored in a more general conception of equality as a social and political ideal."[8]

Notes

1. See Mouffe (1996), pp. 245–56; Wenar (1995); Wingenbach (1999).
2. See Alejandro (1988); Baier (1989); Hampton (1989); Kukathas and Pettit (1990); Raz (1990); Estlund (1998).
3. See Dworkin (2000).
4. Rawls distinguishes between *narrow reflective equilibria* deriving from deliberations that do not question the deliberator's basic value premises and *wide reflective equilibria* that derive from the consideration of "alternate conceptions of justice and the force of various arguments for them." Only the second kind of equilibrium, Rawls asserts, contains judgments that are of concern to political and moral philosophy. Reflection that does not reassess and reevaluate the set of ideas taken initially and provisionally as fixed points will not, in Rawls's view, produce judgments that are relevant to the construction of a theory of justice. An account of justice may therefore be viewed as acceptable if it matches our considered judgments in *wide* reflective equilibrium.
5. Cohen (2008), p. 287.
6. James (2005), p. 282.
7. Rawls defines the original position as an "initial status quo which insures that the fundamental agreements reached in it are fair" (TJ 15).
8. Scheffler (2010), p. 199.

PART I
Justification

1 Rawls's Practical Conception of Justice
Opinion, Tradition, and Objectivity in Political Liberalism

How is it possible for reasonable persons who hold inconsistent and even conflicting religious, philosophical, and moral views jointly to affirm a conception of justice that supports toleration, democracy, and distributive justice? John Rawls argues that political liberalism can provide a basis for consensus supporting just democratic institutions, despite the pluralistic disagreement that characterizes modern democratic societies, because of the theory's *practical* character and aims. Political liberalism is to provide a basis for "reasoned, informed and willing political agreement" (PL 9) by identifying grounds for consensus located in the fundamental ideas and values of the political culture. Thus, the theory "starts from within a certain political tradition," and its content "is expressed in terms of certain fundamental ideas seen as implicit in the public political culture of a democratic society" (PL 13–14).

If this approach is successfully executed, the resulting political theory is likely to have several attractive features. Such a theory will be grounded in ideas that are widely shared and will be likely to bear in a nontrivial way upon actual concerns and controversies within the culture. In addition, a theory derived from ideas implicit in a political culture addresses communitarian criticisms of Rawls's earlier work. A conception of justice worked up from ideas implicit in a historically situated culture can no longer be criticized as presupposing a conception of the self as radically unsituated.[1] Similarly, it is implausible to argue that a theory derived from ideas that structure the political practices of an existing society fails to provide the necessary basis for the "willing identification" of members of the community.[2]

A politically liberal approach to political reflection, in addition, links Rawls's account of the substantive requirements of justice with his account of political justification in the context of pluralistic moral disagreement. In the context of politically liberal theory, due reflection is designed both (1) to enable deliberators to generate an acceptable account of what justice requires and (2) to ensure that the resulting account may be the focus of consensus. In particular, politically liberal due reflection generates its account of the requirements of justice through the elaboration of fundamental ideas that are widely shared among members of the political culture, even those who hold inconsistent and even conflicting religious, philosophical, and moral views. In working from weak and widely shared ideas, Rawls's method is designed to identify "possible bases of agreement where none seem to exist" (TJ 509). In political liberalism, then, the reflective approach that articulates the substance of justice is designed to ensure that the substance of the conception will be collectively acceptable.

Rawls's recently practical approach, however, suggests two new theoretical concerns regarding Rawls's project. First, the approach might appear to require a significant modification of the account of political reasoning developed in *A Theory of Justice*. There Rawls argued that political reasoning should be grounded in considered judgments that are accepted as provisional fixed points and should work from these considered judgments, through a process of self-examination and revision, to a final reflective equilibrium that incorporates or addresses all theory-based objections. Considered judgments regarding fairness and the inviolability of the person, Rawls argued, ground the idea of the original position (in which persons are deprived of information regarding their natural and social endowments) as a fair choice procedure. Political principles that would be chosen in the original position – and which therefore match our considered judgments in wide reflective equilibrium – can be characterized as objective.[3] Moreover, if these principles were accepted as stating objective propositions about the nature of just practices and institutions, it seemed natural to infer that these principles stated moral truths.

Rawls's practical conception of justice, however, disowns "claims to universal truth, or claims about the essential nature and identity of persons."[4] It might appear, therefore, that Rawls's recent work reflects a dramatic retreat from the philosophical ambition of his approach to political reasoning in *A Theory of Justice*. Many commentators, in fact, argue that Rawls's political liberalism is designed merely to ensure political stability by appealing to the situated views of actual citizens.[5] In order to secure a consensus among these citizens, it is argued, the theory must make any concessions necessary to assure that each citizen will find the theory acceptable.[6] The second theoretical concern suggested by Rawls's practical approach involves the fundamental ideas that Rawls claims are implicit in a democratic political culture. How are these ideas to be identified? What would constitute a satisfactory demonstration that the three ideas that Rawls emphasizes are uniquely characteristic of such a culture? Is it plausible to suggest that any *single* set of ideas could adequately embody the character of a political culture in this way?

The proper response to these concerns, I argue, must focus on the normative character of Rawls's argument at all levels of generality. Even the claim that certain fundamental ideas are implicit in a democratic culture is normative, and not merely descriptive. That is, the claim is not that each reasonable member of such a culture in fact currently recognizes the fundamental status of these ideas. Rather, Rawls argues that if each member reflected carefully and fully upon his or her political beliefs and convictions, he or she should judge, in reflective equilibrium, that this set of ideas (or a set belonging to a narrow class of sets; see PL 164) in fact embodies the values that he or she views as fundamental.[7]

An examination of Rawls's method of identifying this set of fundamental ideas will therefore clarify both (1) the nature of Rawls's justification for selecting this particular set of ideas as implicit in democratic political culture and (2) the degree to which Rawls's political conception of justice retains or abandons his earlier aspirations for objectivity in political reasoning. I will argue that the reduced level of philosophical ambition in Rawls's recent work is more apparent than real. Rawls's early work was less ambitious in its claims, and his recent work less accommodationist in its qualifications of those claims, than has been generally appreciated.

In the first section, I argue that Rawls's account of practical political deliberation does, in fact, offer a plausible approach to the task of specifying the fundamental ideas that characterize a democratic political culture. In the second section, I reject the claim that a conception of justice that disowns claims to universal truth is necessarily lacking in philosophical ambition.

Fundamental Ideas

In order to derive a conception of justice from ideas implicit in the public political culture, Rawls must first identify the relevant set of ideas. Rawls argues that three basic ideas are implicit in a democratic culture: (1) society as a fair system of cooperation over time, (2) citizens as free and equal persons, and (3) a well-ordered society (PL 14). Many commentators, however, remain skeptical of Rawls's claim that critical reflection can reliably identify fundamental ideas that embody the character of a democratic political culture.

Critics urge that Rawls's set of fundamental ideas "would be rejected by many individuals and groups who form important elements of that culture."[8] Indeed, "the men who drafted the U. S. Constitution" would have been unlikely to embrace this set of ideas.[9] Moreover, it is argued, "people in modern pluralist societies" simply do not share a *single* set of political beliefs and convictions.[10] Privileging *one* particular set of value premises would mask "quite legitimate disagreement concerning what *in fact* is most fundamental" to the tradition.[11] If the members of a culture did, in fact, converge upon a single set of fundamental political ideas, it would still be implausible to suggest that they would all share Rawls's particular conception of those ideas.[12] Finally, it is argued, Rawls's political constructivism is not the method best suited to the task of constructing a politically stable theory of justice; a method more adequate to this task, moreover, will not support Rawls's account of the fundamental values implicit in a democratic culture.[13]

These critical arguments assume that Rawls's set of fundamental ideas must be (1) designed merely to ground consensus by appealing to the actual opinions of citizens of a democratic political culture and (2) extracted exclusively from the explicit content of the existing political tradition. If these assumptions were correct, critics would be justified in highlighting sources of potential and actual dissent from Rawls's account of the fundamental ideas implicit in the public political culture or in the pluralistic variety of public opinion; the mere fact of such dissent would constitute a decisive objection to Rawls's argument.

In this section, I argue that these critical arguments mischaracterize Rawls's argument. In particular, practical political deliberation is not limited to appeals to public opinion or to ideas explicitly contained within the political tradition. Rather, such deliberation must involve wide-ranging reflection regarding the substantive merits of moral arguments.

Fundamental Ideas and Public Opinion

Rawls explicitly rejects the view that an acceptable political theory must be constructed from the situated views of members of society. It would be "political in the wrong way," Rawls argues, simply to look to existing comprehensive doctrines and draw up a political conception "that strikes a kind of balance of forces" (PL 39).[14] Rawls, in fact, offers an account of theory acceptance that establishes quite different criteria of acceptability: "a political conception of justice, to be acceptable, must accord with our considered convictions...[in] 'reflective equilibrium'" (PL 8). The question is not, therefore, whether the conception conforms to our current views but whether the conception faithfully articulates our considered judgments after due reflection (PL 28; see TJ 42–43). Moreover, *due reflection* is a demanding requirement. In the process of such reflection, we are to examine our considered judgments in light of a consideration of "alternate conceptions of justice and the force of various arguments for them" (PL 384n16)[15] and to revise and adjust our convictions to incorporate or respond to any relevant criticisms and insights.[16]

But how are we, on due reflection, to determine which convictions require revision? Rawls specifies a standard of acceptability: is the judgment supported by reasons "sufficient to *persuade* all reasonable persons that it is reasonable...under conditions favorable to due reflection" (PL 119, emphasis mine)? Rawls defines a reasonable person as one who is ready "to abide by [fair terms of cooperation] willingly, given the assurance that others will likewise do so" (PL 49). Moral judgments that can be justified to all such reasonable persons as reasonable, Rawls argues, are objectively justified. Rawls's criterion for the objectivity of political convictions thus clarifies the nature of the standard to which the convictions grounding an acceptable political conception must conform: they must be supported by reasons that are sufficient to persuade "reasonable and rational persons, who are sufficiently intelligent and conscientious in exercising their powers of practical reason, and whose reasoning exhibits none of the familiar defects of reasoning" (PL 119). Arguments offered in support of the conception should not, therefore, be designed to address the concerns of situated persons whose beliefs and convictions may be unexamined or merely partially rationalized. Rather, these arguments must be designed to persuade possessors of relatively unflawed critical faculties with broad and unbiased perspectives.

Modification of the Decision Procedure

The claim that many members of the culture might refuse to acknowledge Rawls's set of fundamental ideas as reflective of their political convictions does not, therefore, constitute a serious objection to Rawls's account, since Rawls does not intend that these ideas should simply correspond to citizens' situated views. A second and related criticism, however, offers what might seem to be a more plausible argument. This argument asserts that *political liberalism* modifies Rawls's account of reflection in the original position. According to this view, Rawls's current account requires that the conclusions of deliberators in the original position be evaluated in a second stage to determine whether they could serve as the basis for an overlapping consensus. If the principles chosen in the original position could not ground such a consensus, the principles must be adjusted to achieve a better fit with citizens' situated views.[17] If this view were correct, then an acceptable political theory *would* need to appeal to citizens' situated views in order to survive the second stage of deliberation.

Jürgen Habermas, a leading proponent of this view, argues that two-stage deliberation is required by the logic of Rawls's account.[18] If the principles chosen in the original position were to fail to ground an overlapping consensus, Rawls concedes, modification of those principles would be necessary in order to secure stability (PL 65–66).[19] In order to provide a forum in which such changes could be achieved, Habermas argues, Rawls's account appears to require a second stage of deliberation in which deliberators would "attempt to anticipate in reflection the direction of *real discourses* as they would probably unfold under conditions of a pluralistic society."[20] Habermas thus suggests that two-stage deliberation is logically required by Rawls's claim that the principles of justice must ground a stable overlapping consensus.

Before addressing Habermas's specific claims, it is important to emphasize that Rawls's concession is neither extraordinary nor problematic.[21] If reasonable deliberators judge, in reflective equilibrium, that acceptable principles of justice must provide the focus for an

Fundamental Ideas 29

overlapping consensus, then principles that fail to provide such a focus are unacceptable and are in fact objectively unjust. Since the principles chosen are unacceptable, they must be replaced or changed. Rawls's concession that "acceptable changes" in such principles will be necessary is therefore simply the natural and necessary implication of his argument. But does the necessity of modifying the principles of justice require the introduction of a two-stage account of deliberation that modifies the chosen principles to reflect the direction of real discourses in a pluralistic society?

Rawls does not think so. In fact, Rawls addresses and explicitly rejects the two-stage reading. It is precisely "putting people's comprehensive conceptions behind the veil of ignorance," Rawls argues, that "*enable*[*s*] *us* to find a political conception of justice that can be the focus of an overlapping consensus" (PL 25n27, emphasis mine). The connection between the various situated comprehensive conceptions and the principles of justice selected is secured *entirely* by the elaboration of fundamental ideas that are "drawn from the public political culture of a democratic society" (PL 25n27) and "implicitly recognized" (PL 8) by all reasonable members of that society. In choosing principles of justice in the original position, "we leave aside how people's comprehensive doctrines connect with the content of the political conception of justice and regard that content as arising from the various fundamental ideas" (PL 24–25n27).

Rawls reaffirms his rejection of this notion of two-stage deliberation in his "Reply to Habermas," explicitly distinguishing the notion of overlapping consensus contemplated in political liberalism from the "idea of consensus that comes from everyday politics" (PL 389). In the latter, "the politician tries to put together a coalition or policy that all or a sufficient number can support," whereas in the former, the political conception offered as the focus of consensus "can be justified... without looking to, or trying to fit, *or even knowing what are*, the existing comprehensive doctrines" (PL 389, emphasis mine).

Rawls's political conception of justice can serve as the focus of consensus, he argues, *not* because it is tailored to fit the various comprehensive views held by members of society but because "it tries to put no obstacles in the path of all reasonable doctrines... *by eliminating from this conception any idea that goes beyond the political, and which not all reasonable doctrines could reasonably be expected to endorse*" (PL 389, emphasis mine). That is, the connection between the political conception and the views of persons who affirm reasonable doctrines is secured entirely through the elaboration of shared fundamental ideas in a manner that makes no appeal to premises that could not be accepted by each holder of a reasonable doctrine. If the political conception in fact elaborates only shared ideas without appealing to premises unacceptable to holders of reasonable doctrines, then, Rawls argues, the political conception will constitute the focus of an overlapping consensus because it avoids "any idea that goes beyond the political, and which not all reasonable doctrines could reasonably be expected to endorse" (PL 389).

Rawls thus extends the approach to justification that he set out in *A Theory of Justice*. In the earlier work, Rawls argued that the justification of an account of justice should work from "shared and preferably weak conditions" to conclusions that "match our considered judgments" in reflective equilibrium (TJ 18). Political liberalism offers an interpretation of that approach designed for a democratic society characterized by reasonable pluralism. By working only from the basic ideas – premises that Rawls believes are so fundamental to the character of a democratic culture that they are shared by all reasonable members of a democratic society characterized by reasonable pluralism – political liberalism can work to conclusions that "reasonable and rational persons would eventually endorse... under conditions favorable to due reflection" (PL 119).

It is important to emphasize, moreover, that Rawls's notion of due reflection provides precisely the deliberative forum that Habermas suggests is missing from Rawls's framework. Habermas argues that such a forum is necessary in order to provide a context in which the principles chosen in the original position may be reconsidered in light of information regarding the direction of *real discourses* under conditions of a pluralistic society. But Rawls's framework requires that any concerns or objections raised in the course of such real discourses must be considered during due reflection. If those concerns ground persuasive objections to the principles chosen in the original position – or to Rawls's account of the structure of the original position, itself – then the theory must be revised to reflect the substance of the objections. Rawls's account of political deliberation therefore incorporates information regarding real discourses without requiring the introduction of a second stage of deliberation in the original position.

Fundamental Ideas 31

Yet Rawls does distinguish between two stages in the *exposition* of his account of political liberalism. Some commentators urge that this distinction constitutes evidence that Rawls does, in fact, contemplate two stages of deliberation in the original position.[22] Why does Rawls distinguish between stages in the exposition of his argument, and what are the implications of making such a distinction? Rawls makes this distinction in order to emphasize the division of labor between Parts I and II of *Political Liberalism*. In Part I, which presents the first stage of the exposition, Rawls *specifies and defends* the principles of justice that could provide a basis for stable cooperation among citizens who are deeply divided by conflicting moral, philosophical, or religious doctrines.[23] Rawls argues that it is possible for citizens who are divided in this way to affirm one set of principles of justice, or a class of sets that vary within a narrow range (see PL 164), if that set (or class of sets) is worked up from ideas implicit in the public political culture. Rawls particularly emphasizes the centrality of theory *construction* in *securing* consensus: "[t]he *reason* such a conception may be the focus of an overlapping consensus of comprehensive doctrines is *that it develops the principles of justice from public and shared ideas*" (PL 90, my emphasis).

It is important to note that the goal of generating principles that can serve as the focus of overlapping consensus is therefore central to the *first stage*, as well as the second stage, of the exposition. There is no preliminary stage in which principles are worked up without regard to the fact of reasonable pluralism.

In Part II, which presents the second stage of the exposition, Rawls elaborates the conception of justice derived in Part I to describe those features of a well-ordered society that would allow it to establish and preserve consensus.[24] The argument of Part II is particularly important because Rawls argues that the aim of his theory is to provide "a basis of reasoned, informed and willing consent" (PL 9). Rawls can only claim that his theory is practical in this sense if he can argue plausibly that political liberalism *can* "gain the support of an overlapping consensus of reasonable religious, philosophical, and moral doctrines in a society regulated by it" (PL 10).

Rawls attempts to meet this burden of persuasion by attempting to show that the political conception of justice is compatible with the forms of reasonable comprehensive views that would be endorsed on due reflection by citizens of pluralistic democracies. In order to defend this claim, Rawls offers an argument that examines the possibility of realizing an overlapping consensus under very special circumstances. In particular, Rawls argues that holders of all reasonable comprehensive conceptions *in a well-ordered society* could affirm the political conception as compatible with their comprehensive views.[25] Rawls discusses relations in a well-ordered society, rather than in actual and nonideal conditions, because he wants to examine the reasons to affirm or reject the political conception that would motivate holders of various comprehensive views who were *effectively motivated by the desire to identify and act from principles of justice because they are just*.

Rawls focuses on persons who are motivated in this way – who are in Rawls's terms *fully autonomous* (see PL 77) – because fully autonomous persons, in considering whether to accept a conception of justice, would focus exclusively on whether the conception in fact embodied the practical implications of their basic ideas of justice. In particular, their deliberations would be undiluted by concerns regarding the pursuit of unjust advantage. In focusing on the views of persons who are fully autonomous, then, Rawls focuses his analysis on the considerations that are of particular relevance for a theory designed to identify the practical implications of basic political ideas.

Unless an overlapping consensus could be achieved under such ideal conditions, Rawls argues – if psychological or collective action problems would predictably undermine efforts to sustain an overlapping consensus, even among the fully autonomous – such a consensus could not be achieved under the less than ideal conditions that characterize actual societies. The purpose of Rawls's discussion of overlapping consensus is, therefore, to demonstrate the feasibility of the political conception, not to concede the necessity of tailoring that conception to accommodate the views of various comprehensive doctrines.[26]

In order to develop his argument for the feasibility of an overlapping consensus in a well-ordered society, Rawls examines a series of model cases "that illustrate the different ways in which a political conception can be related to comprehensive doctrines" (PL 169). The holder of a comprehensive liberal view, for example, could regard that view "as the deductive basis of the political conception and in that way continuous with it" (PL 169). The holder of a comprehensive utilitarian view might find the political conception acceptable because it makes assumptions about "the bounds on complexity of legal and institutional rules as well as the simplicity necessary for guidelines in public reason" (PL 170) that are consistent with utilitarian views on these matters. The most problematic case involves the holder of a comprehensive religious doctrine who insists that ensuring the resolution of some fundamental question according to the requirements of her doctrine "justifies civil strife" (PL 152). We can, Rawls suggests, at least minimize the incompatibility between this comprehensive view and the political conception by denying, not the truth of the doctrine, but the claim that civil strife is justified: "we say of the rationalist believers that they are mistaken in denying the fact [of reasonable pluralism]" (PL 153). If, by respecting such limits on discourse with the rationalist believer, we secure overlapping consensus, Rawls suggests, the consensus will be "for the moment at least, reasonable" (PL 153). If reasonable and rational holders of these various comprehensive views, deliberating in a well-ordered society, could judge that the political conception is compatible with their comprehensive views, Rawls argues, the theory is not utopian.

It is important, however, to emphasize the limited scope of Rawls's argument. He recognizes that citizens of nonideal societies are not necessarily fully autonomous. Thus, while Rawls offers the political conception as a resource from which an overlapping consensus for a nonideal society could be constructed, he does not argue that such a conception would necessarily gain the support of citizens of nonideal societies who are not fully autonomous. He argues rather that the political conception could be the focus of an overlapping consensus among fully autonomous persons in a well-ordered society, and is therefore compatible with the comprehensive views that would be held by citizens of pluralistic democracies.

Ideas External to the Tradition

But doesn't Rawls's account of theory acceptance appeal to a standard of justification independent of the culture's tradition; and isn't such an appeal inconsistent with the claim that a practical account of justice is located *within* a particular political tradition (PL 13–14)? Rawls claims that his criterion for theory acceptance is, in fact, consistent with the practical character of his political theory. I will argue that Rawls sustains this claim, and that the rationale that he offers suggests important insights regarding Rawls's understanding of the relationship between justification and theoretical objectivity.

When we deliberate about political questions, Rawls claims, we begin with a set of considered judgments that we view as provisional fixed points. If Rawls has correctly identified the set of fundamental democratic ideas, then the provisional fixed points from which members of a democratic culture begin will be the set of ideas that Rawls has suggested. It is important to stress, however, that while their deliberations *begin* with a set of fundamental ideas, the members are not limited to arguments grounded in this set, nor are they limited to appeals to *any* canonical account of the core ideas of the political culture.[27] The deliberators are free to assess and revise any and all notions received from their tradition, including interpretations of fundamental ideas (e.g., liberty, equality, due process).[28]

But can deliberators "located within a tradition" plausibly be expected to reassess the tradition itself? Aren't politically liberal deliberators in fact required to relativize their judgments to the culture in which they are located?[29] The short answer to the latter question is *no*. The individual "look[s] to the public culture as the shared fund of implicitly recognized basic ideas and principles" (PL 8) in order to generate the substance of a theory of justice. But in order "to be acceptable," the theory must accord, not with some canonical statement of cultural norms and values, but "with our considered convictions, *at all levels of generality*, on due reflection...[in] 'reflective equilibrium'" (PL 8, emphasis mine). During due reflection, the person "can revise [any of her] existing judgments...even the judgments we take provisionally as fixed points" (TJ 18; see PL 399).

Rawls, in fact, specifically distinguishes between narrow reflective equilibria deriving from deliberations that do not question the deliberator's basic value premises,[30] such as the set of fundamental ideas, and wide reflective equilibria that derive from the consideration of "alternate conceptions of justice and the force of various arguments for them" (PL 384n16). Only the second kind of equilibrium, Rawls asserts, contains judgments that are of concern to political and moral philosophy.[31] Thus, deliberations that do not reassess and reevaluate the set of ideas taken initially and provisionally as fixed points will not, in Rawls's terms, produce judgments that are relevant to the construction of a theory of justice, even a politically liberal theory.

The set of fundamental ideas must, therefore, be as much a product as a ground of political deliberation. A central aspect of due reflection involves the refining of the original, provisionally fixed, set of fundamental ideas into a final set of ideas capable of grounding an acceptable theory. During reflection, the provisionally fixed set of ideas is revised to reflect, among other things, a reflective understanding of the role that such a set of basic ideas will play as the ground of public agreement. The process is thus recursive. Deliberation begins with a set of ideas, and reflects back on them in order to generate a more satisfactory set.

Simone Chambers neglects precisely this aspect of Rawls's argument in suggesting that, because Rawls requires an account of "deliberation about the premises from which choices are made, political liberalism must make citizens the final court of appeal in questions of justice."[32] Even if Rawls is correct in arguing that the basic democratic ideas are latent in the culture, Chambers suggests, not every idea that is latent in a political culture deserves our allegiance. Slavery, serfdom, and class hierarchy are all ideas that have been latent in political cultures. In order to justify the claim that the political conception is founded on an objective order of reasons and therefore objective, then, Rawls needs to justify acceptance of the basic political ideas that ground his theory. Since his theory fails to provide such a justification, Chambers claims, Rawls is forced to make citizens the final court of appeal. Chambers has failed to notice, however, that Rawls's account of due reflection is offered expressly to address the need to justify acceptance of the basic ideas. Since Rawls supplies a forum for the necessary deliberation, Chambers's reconstructive argument is unnecessary.

The structure of Rawls's argument therefore defines a specific relationship between the content of a democratic political tradition and the individual's practical political deliberations. Each deliberator must attempt to define the best account of justice, making use of the best available theoretical resources, and revising where necessary to address or incorporate critical insights. Thus, due reflection begins with partially reflective considered judgments regarding the fundamental ideas that are characteristic of a democratic culture, and will work toward a fully reflective set of ideas that are characteristic of such a culture.

The notion of a democratic political culture, then, is not a constraint upon deliberation, but a resource from which to build an acceptable political theory, and an ideal to regulate political deliberation. In fact, as should now be evident, political deliberation can *begin* with almost any set of initial ideas contained within a democratic political culture. If the deliberation is genuinely reflective; if reflection works as Rawls says it does; and if each deliberator has access to similar conceptual resources; then each reasonable deliberator will end up with a set of ideas that constitutes the most satisfactory reflective interpretation (from the standpoint of a deliberator affirming her particular comprehensive conception) of the fundamental ideas implicit in the culture of a modern democratic culture, regardless of the contents of the deliberator's initial set of considered judgments. Since Rawls assumes that reasonable pluralism is a permanent feature of democratic public culture, he acknowledges that even reasonable and rational citizens in reflective equilibrium may fail to converge upon one unique set of fundamental democratic ideas; but his argument suggests that the considerations favoring a politically liberal account of those ideas – deriving from the deep commitment of the tradition of democratic thought to the values of fairness, liberty, and equality – are sufficiently strong so that such reasonable and rational citizens would have compelling reasons to converge upon a class of politically liberal sets of ideas "that vary within a more or less narrow range" (see PL 164).

Criticisms of political liberalism that merely point to potential or actual inconsistencies between Rawls's set of fundamental ideas and the explicit norms or beliefs of a particular democratic tradition, therefore, reflect a misunderstanding of Rawls's methods and goals. Practical reflection works from the ideas implicit in a political culture, but is not limited by that material when critical insights must be addressed or incorporated. The claim that Rawls's concerns regarding stability have led him to propose an accommodationist theory, then, are unpersuasive.

Justice and Truth

In a related criticism, commentators argue that Rawls's attempt to "separate general truth-claims from the elucidation of our shared understandings"[33] leads to a "parochial"[34] and unsatisfactory approach to political theorizing. Rawls, it is argued, must at least assert the truth of the propositions that provide the normative foundation for his political conception.[35] In fact, it is asserted, Rawls's avoidance of truth claims involves a misunderstanding of the proper function of philosophy.[36]

Normative Foundations

Even a political conception of justice that aspires to provide the basis for reasoned agreement among persons who hold conflicting religious, philosophical and moral views must, critics argue, assert the truth of certain foundational propositions.[37] In particular, a politically liberal conception of justice must assume the truth of the claim that the views of each member of society deserve equal respect. Unless a foundational claim of this type is accepted as true, David Estlund argues, the political conception of justice cannot ground obligations and justify the use of coercive force.[38]

In fact, William Galston and Jean Hampton note, Rawls *is* prepared to insist upon such a claim: he specifically asserts that a just society must employ coercion in order to protect the principle of toleration – the principle that the views of each member of society deserve equal respect.[39] "Here is an idea," Hampton observes, "over which he is prepared to fight."

While Rawls may be "prepared to fight" in support of this idea, however, he refuses to characterize it as "true." Rather, Galston and Hampton claim, Rawls assumes that this idea is the subject of consensus.[40] But, Hampton argues, there is no consensus in favor of the claim that a just society must respect principle of toleration. It is precisely because there is no such consensus, in fact, that political philosophers have an obligation to assert that the claim is true and "to persuade opponents of that idea to change their minds."[41]

Rawls, however, neither assumes the existence of consensus nor abandons the task of persuasion. Far from assuming that an overlapping consensus requiring toleration actually exists among the situated views of ordinary persons, Rawls assumes only that reasonable and rational persons in reflective equilibrium would affirm the idea of toleration. Rawls, in fact, offers his work in an effort to *persuade* each reader that justice requires the acceptance of fundamental claims requiring toleration and equal concern and respect.

But, Estlund argues, the central problem with political liberalism's refusal to assert the truth of its fundamental premises is that the theory relies upon a purely formal standard of theory acceptance: political liberalism's fundamental premises are acceptable because an insular group (the "reasonable") would accept those elements of the theory as reasonable. If Rawls asserted that acceptance by such an insular group established the *truth* of the theory, then, Estlund claims, his theory would "provide a fine answer to the question" of what makes the reasonable the right group to determine the contents of our account of justice.[42] Since Rawls refuses to make such a claim, however, he has not explained why acceptability to some other insular group (e.g., the Branch Davidians) should not constitute an equally valid standard of theory acceptance.

Estlund, however, argues from an incomplete description of Rawls's account of theory acceptance. That account requires not merely that a proposition must be *accepted* by all reasonable persons as reasonable, but that it must be so accepted *on due reflection*; and due reflection is not a merely formal standard. In due reflection, the person works from a set of considered judgments regarding justice which are viewed as "provisional fixed points which we presume any conception must fit" (TJ 18) to the choice of a set of principles of justice. She then evaluates the principles in light of her initial premises.[43] If the principles are in some way inconsistent with her set of considered judgments, the analysis "work[s] from both ends" (T J 18): the person reassesses both her premises and her judgments until "[her] principles and [her] judgments coincide" (TJ 18). Finally, after achieving a narrow equilibrium derived from the analysis of the initial set of considered judgments, due reflection broadens the analysis by taking into account "all possible descriptions to which one might plausibly conform one's judgments" (TJ 43), so that the deliberations accord due weight to *all* relevant considerations.

When this process is carried out by *reasonable* persons "whose reasoning exhibits none of the familiar defects of reasoning," Rawls argues, the resulting judgments are *objective*–that is, "actually founded on an order of reasons" (PL 119). While Rawls does not claim that the output of such deliberation is "true," then, he does claim that it "objective"; and it is objective precisely because the persons conducting the deliberation are "reasonable." Reasonableness, therefore, is not merely an identifying characteristic of an arbitrarily chosen insular group, but rather a quality that characterizes the actual deliberations and grounds the objectivity of the resulting judgments. Thus Rawls does not, as Estlund assumes, provide a merely formal standard of theory acceptance. His standard requires that the theory must be accepted *for the right reasons* – reasons that establish the objectivity of the judgment accepting the theory. Since acceptability, in Rawls's account, is not determined merely by a formal test (whether it would be accepted by an insular group), Estlund's objection fails.

The Proper Task of Philosophy

Nevertheless, critics assert, Rawls's avoidance of truth claims reflects a misunderstanding of the proper task of philosophy. In fact, it is argued, that task includes "*giv[ing] expression* to important conflicts in society about the ideals of social life"; and it is therefore "quite appropriate for political philosophy to advance its claims by appealing to the truth of its conclusions."[44] In fact, Galston argues, an approach that separates the elucidation of shared political understandings from the idea of truth improperly abandons "the philosophical quest for the grounds of action."[45] The lack of philosophical ambition manifest in political liberalism, Kukathas and Pettit conclude, "is a far cry from the bravura of the earlier Rawls."[46]

Rawls does not, however, avoid the task of giving expression to conflict about the ideals of social life. His theory, for example, develops forcefully the argument that "even the welfare of society cannot override" respect for fundamental rights (TJ 3). This claim conflicts sharply with consequentialist theories that privilege wealth maximization or other efficiency goals over rights.

Rawls refuses to assert that this claim is "true," however, because "there is no shared public basis to distinguish the true beliefs from the false" (PL 128). That is, if we accept the premise that human reason, in its normal operations, results in "a plurality of reasonable yet incompatible comprehensive doctrines" (PL xviii), then the claim that elements of one such doctrine or theory are "true" can be no more than an unproved assertion from the point of view of other reasonable persons and other reasonable comprehensive views. The assertion that a moral or political proposition is true or false thus "goes beyond the bounds of a political conception of justice" (PL 114). Rawls's practical conception of justice for this reason "does without the concept of truth" (PL 94).

Political liberalism does not, however, do without the concept of political convictions that are "actually founded on an order of reasons," and therefore objective (PL 119). Political liberalism simply rejects the notion that objective convictions must be "true...of an independent order of values" (PL 114). That is, Rawls rejects the notion that such convictions describe facts about the world, so that "the knowledge given" by applying such convictions is "something like perception."[47] Rather than being "controlled by the facts"[48] in this way, Rawls argues, objective convictions are those supported by reasons that are sufficiently compelling to persuade all reasonable persons that the conviction is reasonable.[49] Thus, as discussed in the first section, Rawls's criterion for objectivity tests the persuasiveness of the reasons offered in support of the conviction. Since an objective conviction must be supported by a justification that in fact *persuades* reasonable persons, the necessary justification must either constitute or rely upon a shared public basis for distinguishing persuasive from unpersuasive justifications. Thus, Rawls's account of objectivity requires that a shared public basis for distinguishing objective from nonobjective convictions can be identified or constructed. Rawls's account of objectivity does not, therefore, go beyond the limits of a political conception of justice. Rather, it is because he believes that a practical account of objectivity will provide a shared basis for the task of realizing agreement in the face of reasonable pluralism that Rawls develops such an account.

But if Rawls's approach does without the notion of truth, what criterion is available to test the persuasiveness of the reasons offered to justify political convictions? In *A Theory of Justice*, Rawls argued that objectivity could be achieved by taking up an "appropriate[ly] general point of view" (TJ 452–53). While the original position "defines" this point of view, the original position itself merely constitutes a representation of the considered judgments of a reasonable person in reflective equilibrium.[50] Thus, the objective reasons that would be endorsed from an appropriately general point of view are in fact reasons that match the deliberator's considered judgments in reflective equilibrium. Since reflective equilibrium is defined as the fit between reasons, convictions, or principles and "our considered convictions ... on due reflection" (PL 8),[51] an order of reasons that persuades all reasonable persons on due reflection is simply an order of reasons that matches the considered judgments of such persons in reflective equilibrium. In both accounts, therefore, objective reasons or convictions are those that match the considered judgments of reasonable and rational deliberators in reflective equilibrium.

It is important to emphasize the close fit between the theoretical aspirations of *A Theory of Justice* and *Political Liberalism*. In both works,

Rawls argues for a conception of justice that is objective, not true. Rawls highlights this point in *Political Liberalism;* but it is important to note that *A Theory of Justice* also argues for the objectivity, and not the truth, of the output of the original position deliberations (TJ 452–53). Moreover, Rawls's criterion of objectivity in *Political Liberalism* is consistent with the account of objectivity in *A Theory of Justice*: in both works, reasons or convictions are objective if they match the deliberator's considered judgments in reflective equilibrium.

Rawls's concerns regarding stability have not led him to propose a conception of justice that is lacking in philosophical ambition. Rather, Rawls's arguments are grounded in demanding criteria of objectivity. Rawls's account of objectivity, moreover, performs an important role in securing the possibility of fit between the political conception of justice and the views of reasonable citizens of a well-ordered society. Rawls argues that such citizens, on due reflection, could reasonably judge that (1) the fundamental ideas which ground political liberalism are compatible with the values contained within their various comprehensive doctrines and that (2) political liberalism constitutes the most satisfactory interpretation of the fundamental ideas. Such citizens would, therefore, have sufficient justification to "embed their shared political conception in their reasonable comprehensive doctrines" (PL 392; see 387) and to privilege requirements of the political conception over the requirements of other values contained in their doctrine. While the deliberations of situated citizens will not necessarily mirror the deliberations of reasonable citizens of a well-ordered society, Rawls is optimistic that his practical account of objectivity, by working from fundamental ideas implicit in the common political culture, can provide reasonable situated citizens with a shared basis for the task of realizing overlapping consensus in the face of reasonable pluralism.

Conclusion: Continuity in Rawls's Philosophical Project

While Rawls offers a defensible account of objectivity in theory construction, does his practical goal of specifying a political conception capable of serving as the focus of an overlapping consensus constitute a retreat from the broader ambitions of *A Theory of Justice*? How broad, in fact, were the ambitions of that earlier work? Justice as fairness, Rawls argued, was designed to provide "a better account of [the] structure" of the sense of justice. Rawls was quite modest about the contribution of his theory to this project: "if we can characterize one (educated) person's sense of justice, we might have a good beginning" (TJ 44). Far from offering a definitive and universal theory, Rawls admitted uncertainty about the generality of his conclusions: it is unclear, Rawls concedes, "whether the principles that characterize one person's considered judgments are the same as those that characterize another's." Moreover, Rawls offered his work as an exploratory contribution to the study of human moral faculties, and remained open to the possibility that no completely systematic account might be satisfactory: "[i]f men's conceptions of justice finally turn out to differ, the ways in which they do so is a matter of the first importance" (TJ 44).

Thus, Rawls offered his work as merely "a guiding framework designed to focus our moral sensibilities" (TJ 46). In his earlier theory, as in his recent work, Rawls privileged the goal of providing a basis for reasoned and willing agreement: "[i]f the scheme as a whole seems on reflection to clarify and order our thoughts, and if it tends to reduce disagreements and to bring diverse convictions more in line, then it has done all that one may reasonably ask" (TJ 46).[52]

Rawls's work continues to be motivated by the aspiration to identify the structure of the sense of justice. Once this dominant motivation is recognized, it is clear that Rawls's principal philosophical opponents are not only utilitarians, but also moral skeptics and intuitionists who argue that "the complexity of the moral facts defies our efforts to give a full account of our judgments." The only response to such a denial, Rawls recognizes, "consists in presenting the sort of constructive criteria that are said not to exist" (TJ 35). Rawls's accounts (current and past) of practical deliberation are ambitious attempts to present such constructive criteria.

As Rawls's understanding of his subject has evolved, he has chosen to highlight different aspects of practical reasoning. Nevertheless, Rawls's theoretical aspirations have remained remarkably consistent. In both the early and later works, Rawls aims to (1) clarify the structure of the sense of justice, (2) focus moral and political discussion, (3) provide a defensible account of objectivity in political reasoning, and (4) identify the bases for reasoned agreement.

While Rawls continues to maintain that practical deliberation reasons from the individual's set of considered judgments, his recent work provides the clarification that those judgments are informed, but not determined, by the culture and tradition in which they were formed. Rawls, nevertheless, continues to maintain that we have the capacity and the obligation to assess and, if necessary, revise and abandon any or all of the cultural ideas with which we begin our deliberations. Recognition of the fact of reasonable pluralism, therefore, does not lead Rawls to adopt the view that a conception of justice should be designed to achieve consensus by appealing to the situated views of citizens. Rather, Rawls continues to argue that an acceptable conception of justice must match our considered judgments in reflective equilibrium. Rawls's recent work therefore constitutes an extension of, rather than a retreat from, his project of providing a defensible account of objectivity in political reasoning.

Notes

1 Sandel ([1982] 1998).
2 Taylor (1989), p. 165.
3 In *A Theory of Justice*, Rawls describes objective principles as "the principles that we would want everyone (including ourselves) to follow were we to take up together the appropriate general point of view" (TJ 453). Since our considered judgments in reflective equilibrium define and constitute the "principles that we would want everyone...to follow," the point of view achieved in reflective equilibrium is presumably "appropriate[ly] general," and the principles that we endorse in wide reflective equilibrium are therefore objective.
4 Rawls (1985), p. 388.
5 See Estlund (1998); Kukathas and Pettit (1990); Raz (1990); Baier (1989); Hampton (1989); Alejandro (1988).
6 See Hill (1994), p. 343.
7 It is important to emphasize that Rawls does not *predict* that all reasonable persons will accept this set of ideas. In fact, he concedes that "it is inevitable and often desirable that citizens have different views as to the most appropriate political conception" (PL 227). Rather than a prediction, Rawls offers an *argument* that the politically liberal class of sets of ideas provides the most satisfactory interpretation of the fundamental ideas that constitute the political culture of modern democracies.
8 Galston (1989), p. 712; see Doppelt (1989); Hampton (1989), p. 813; Klosko (1994), p. 1893; O'Neill (1988), pp. 708–9.
9 Galston (1989), p. 713.
10 Young (1995), pp. 185, 189–90; see Doppelt (1989), pp. 842–43.
11 Doppelt (1989), p. 842.

12 Hampton (1994), pp. 198–99; see Klosko (1997), p. 638; Scheffler (1994), p. 13.
13 Klosko (1997), pp. 637–38; see Habermas (1995), pp. 109–31.
14 "We do not look to the comprehensive doctrines that in fact exist and then draw up a political conception that strikes a kind of balance of forces between them... To do so would make [the political conception] political in the wrong way" (PL 39–40).
15 Similarly, in *A Theory of Justice*, considered judgments are to be examined in light of "all possible descriptions to which one might plausibly conform one's judgments" (TJ 49).
16 "The test is that of reflective equilibrium: how well the view as a whole articulates our more firm considered convictions of political justice, at all levels of generality, after due examination, *once all adjustments and revisions that seem compelling have been made*" (PL 28, emphasis mine).
17 Klosko (1993), p. 350.
18 Habermas (1995).
19 "What if it turns out that the principles of justice as fairness cannot gain the support of reasonable doctrines, so that the case for stability fails? Justice as fairness as we have stated it is then in difficulty. We should have to see whether acceptable changes in the principles of justice would achieve stability; or indeed whether stability could obtain for any democratic conception" (PL 65–66).
20 Habermas (1995), p. 121.
21 The concession that if the principles chosen in the original position failed to ground an overlapping consensus, "acceptable changes in the principles of justice" would be necessary in order to secure stability.
22 Klosko (1997, 1994).
23 "The first three lectures set out the first stage of the exposition" of Rawls's response to the question "how is it possible that there can be a stable and just society whose free and equal citizens are deeply divided by conflicting and even incommensurable religious, philosophical, and even moral doctrines." This first stage justifies the selection of "principles of justice that specify the fair terms of cooperation among citizens and specify when a society's basic institutions are just" (PL 133).
24 "The second stage of the exposition... considers how the well-ordered democratic society of justice as fairness may establish and preserve unity and stability given the reasonable pluralism characteristic of it" (PL 133–34).
25 "The second stage of the exposition... considers how the *well-ordered democratic society* of justice as fairness may establish and preserve unity and stability... to see how a well-ordered society can be unified and stable, we introduce... the idea of an overlapping consensus" (PL 133–34,

emphasis mine). "[A] main aim of PL is to show that the idea of a well-ordered society in *Theory* may be reformulated so as to take account of the fact of reasonable pluralism" (PL xliii).

26 "Any realistic idea of a well-ordered society may seem to imply that some [compromise of the political conception compelled by circumstances] is involved. Indeed, the term "overlapping consensus" may suggest that. We must show, then, that this is not the case" (PL 169).

27 "Although in order to get started various judgments are viewed as firm enough to be taken provisionally as fixed points, there are no judgments on any level of generality that are in principle immune to revision." Rawls ([1975] 1999), p. 289. "[T]he key background ideas are themselves in need of justification. We accept them, and they are justified, in light of other things we believe in wide reflective equilibrium." Daniels (1996), p. 154.

28 When we seek to achieve reflective equilibrium, our deliberations include "our considered convictions at all levels of generality; *no one level, say that of abstract principle or that of particular judgments in particular cases, is treated as foundational*" (PL 8n8, emphasis mine). "[W]e may [on reflection] reaffirm our particular judgments and decide instead to modify the proposed conception of justice with its principles and ideals...It is a mistake to think of abstract principles and general conceptions as always overriding our more particular judgments" (PL 45). Wide reflective equilibrium involves the consideration of all of "the leading conceptions of justice found in our political tradition (including views critical of the concept of justice itself)" (JAF 31).

29 See Kukathas and Pettit (1990), pp. 144–45; Raz (1990), p. 8. Both Raz and Kukathas and Pettit claim that Rawls's practical approach to theorizing about justice works from the assumption that ideas implicit in the political culture should be accepted uncritically as the foundation of political analysis. Raz (8) argues that Rawls's analysis works from "the fact that certain beliefs form the common currency of our public culture." Rawls's practical approach, Raz argues, "does not seek deep foundations for these beliefs; it concerns itself neither with their justification nor with its absence" (8).

30 That is, equilibria that derive from the consideration merely of "descriptions to which one might conform one's judgments...which more or less match one's existing judgments" (TJ 43).

31 "Wide and not narrow reflective equilibrium (in which we take note only of our own judgments) is plainly the important philosophical concept" (PL 384n16). See TJ 43; Rawls (1975), p. 289.

32 Chambers (1996), p. 71.

33 Galston (1989), p. 725.

34 Baier (1989), p. 171.
35 Galston (1989); Hampton (1989); Raz (1990).
36 Kukathas and Pettit (1990), pp. 142–50.
37 See Hampton (1989); Raz (1990).
38 Estlund (1998), p. 262.
39 Hampton (1989), p. 813; see Galston (1989), p. 721.
40 "[I]f there were an overlapping consensus on [this idea] (as he believes), our society would have the foundations necessary for genuine philosophizing." Hampton (1989), p. 813. The justification of this proposition, as an element of the political conception, "lies in its fidelity to the shared understandings of the culture." Galston (1989), p. 719.
41 Hampton (1989), p. 813.
42 Estlund (1998), p. 261.
43 We assess "whether applying these principles would lead us to make the same judgments...which we now make intuitively and with the greatest confidence" (TJ 17).
44 Kukathas and Pettit (1990), pp. 149–50.
45 Galston (1989), p. 725.
46 Kukathas and Pettit (1990), p. 150.
47 Williams (1985), p. 149.
48 Williams (1985), p. 141.
49 "To say that a political conviction is objective is to say that there are reasons...sufficient to convince all reasonable persons that it is reasonable" (PL 119).
50 "We can check an interpretation of the initial situation, then, by the capacity of its principles to accommodate our firmest convictions...[A] description of the initial situation that both expresses reasonable conditions and yields principles which match our considered judgments duly pruned and adjusted...I refer to as reflective equilibrium" (TJ 18).
51 In *Political Liberalism*, Rawls argues that an "order of reasons" is objective if the reasons offered are sufficiently compelling to persuade "all reasonable persons...under conditions favorable to due reflection" (PL 119).
52 See the corresponding language in *Political Liberalism*: "if [the political conception] has narrowed the gap between the conscientious convictions of those who accept the basic ideas of the constitutional regime, then it has served its purpose" (PL 156).

2 | Stability, Fit, and Consensus

A conception of justice is stable, John Rawls argues, if it is capable of gaining the willing support of persons who disagree fundamentally regarding basic values, and if that willing support is sufficiently deeply rooted to motivate those persons to resist normal tendencies to privilege their particular interests over the requirements of justice. In particular, Rawls argues, *justice as fairness* – the conception of justice that he defends in both *A Theory of Justice* and *Political Liberalism* – is a stable conception because it is capable of gaining such willing and deeply rooted support. Rawls argues that the two principles of justice that constitute that conception – principles that require the guarantee of (1) the most extensive scheme of equal basic liberties compatible with equal liberty for all and (2) social arrangements in which social and economic inequalities are (a) reasonably expected to be to everyone's advantage and (b) attached to positions open to all (TJ 53) – will be capable of gaining the willing support of the holders of the diverse conceptions of justice that are held by members of western democratic societies. It is possible, Rawls argues, for those affirming – for example – the conflicting liberalisms of Kant and Mill, the nonliberal views of Burke, moral skepticism, and doctrines based on religious authority to affirm these two principles of justice as consistent with and extensions of their moral conceptions of the good (PL xxxix). The two principles of justice as fairness, he argues, are therefore capable of constituting the focus of a stable overlapping consensus within a pluralistic political culture.

Satisfaction of the stability requirement – in Rawls's view – constitutes an essential part of the justification of a conception of justice. That is, Rawls argues that an acceptable justification of a proposed conception of justice must provide persuasive arguments to support the claim that the proposed conception is capable of constituting the focus of a stable overlapping consensus. This requirement reflects Rawls's concerns regarding the conditions under which the use of coercive force can be justified. The implementation of the requirements of a conception of justice will necessarily involve the use of coercive force, and – Rawls argues – the exercise of coercive force by the state can be justified only if the fundamental elements of the constitution that authorizes the exercise of that force are justifiable to all citizens on terms that they can reasonably be expected to accept. If the employment of the conception of justice to regulate social relations is to be justified, then, it must be possible to demonstrate to each holder of a reasonable comprehensive view that she has adequate grounds for viewing the content of that conception as consistent with or extensions of their moral conceptions of the good. The stability requirement is thus an important element of the account of moral and political justification that Rawls generates in order to address the challenges to the project of theorizing justice posed by moral skepticism and pluralistic disagreement about the nature of the good.

Theorists who reject the view that Rawls's conception of justice could constitute the focus of an overlapping consensus, however, argue that Rawls underestimates the depth of the disagreement that exists within pluralistic societies. In *A Theory of Justice*, it is asserted, Rawls implausibly assumed general acceptance of a Kantian conception of the person. Even in *Political Liberalism*, in which Rawls emphasizes the significance of pluralistic disagreement, Rawls assumes that members of pluralistic societies will be *reasonable*, for the most part, where the term "reasonable" implies acceptance of liberal principles of toleration. The later Rawls, according to this view, remains insensitive to the real depth of pluralistic disagreement and of the theoretical challenges raised by this deep disagreement.

This alleged obtuseness in the work of the foremost contemporary liberal theorist of justice has, moreover, been taken to reflect the incapacity of liberal theory generally to address the social and theoretical problems raised by pluralism. Not only, it is argued, does liberal theory lack the conceptual resources to address problems raised by pluralistic disagreement, but also liberal theorists like Rawls remain insensitive to the depth and significance of these problems.

Far from ignoring these problems, however, Rawls made the issue of stability the principal focus of his account of political liberalism precisely because of his concern with problems raised by pluralistic disagreement. It was his judgment that the account of stability in Part III of *A Theory of Justice* was unrealistic, Rawls emphasizes, that led him to modify the account of justice presented in that work (PL xviii). Rawls's account of stability in *A Theory of Justice* relied upon the assumption that all persons would view *the realization of their natures as free and equal* as a good that is (1) essential to their well-being and (2) at least equal in priority with *all* other fundamental moral concerns.[1] Rawls later judged that such an assignment of priority would not necessarily be generally accepted by members of a society characterized by reasonable pluralism, in particular by persons who accept doctrines based upon religious authority.

In order to address this concern, *Political Liberalism* develops a distinct account of stability. According to this account, a conception of justice is stable if it is possible for the holders of diverse and possibly conflicting reasonable views about the good willingly to affirm the conception as expressing the deepest social values embodied in their diverse value theories (PL 38–40, 140ff.). Rawls describes a conception of justice that can be affirmed in this way as the focus of an overlapping consensus of reasonable comprehensive views. Rawls's political conception of justice is to constitute such a focus because it identifies grounds for willing agreement located in fundamental ideas implicit in the political culture. Rawls's political liberalism, then, views stability as a matter of the fit between a conception of justice and a plurality of comprehensive doctrines.

While Rawls argues that his account of stability is designed to secure the *willing* support of persons who disagree fundamentally, a number of commentators assert that Rawls's approach seems designed to secure stability by restricting the scope of democratic debate or by socializing the views of potential participants in that debate. Political liberalism, according to these arguments, secures stability through implicit or explicit pressure exercised upon citizens by public institutions. In particular, it is argued, political liberalism would (1) exclude "unreasonable" moral doctrines from a just society's overlapping consensus,[2] (2) limit the content of public debate to exclude appeals to religious beliefs or comprehensive moral doctrine,[3] and (3) socialize citizens to accept liberal values.[4] I argue that these objections mischaracterize Rawls's theory. Rawls's account of stability, I argue, is designed neither to restrict debate nor to socialize the participants in that debate. In this chapter, I (1) discuss the status of Rawls's account of stability within his theoretical framework and (2) respond to the objections to that account noted above.

Stability and Justice

In *Political Liberalism*, Rawls treats stability as a matter of the fit between a conception of justice and various comprehensive views regarding the good. But fit with what views; and what kind of fit? Why, finally, is it appropriate to impose such a requirement; why should it not be sufficient for an account of justice to show the support of judgments based upon due reflection that take into account all identifiable relevant considerations?

Fit with What Views?

Rawls examines the possibility of achieving a stable overlapping consensus under very special circumstances. A stable conception, Rawls argues, must demonstrate fit not with the actual situated views of citizens, but with the views of the holders of reasonable comprehensive conceptions *in a well-ordered society*.[5] Members of a well-ordered society, it is important to emphasize, desire to identify and act from principles of justice *because they are just;* their sense of justice effectively determines their practical judgments (see PL 35, 77). A politically liberal conception, then, must demonstrate fit, not with the situated views of members of an actual society, but with an idealized representation of the views of persons whose sense of justice dominates their other motivations.

Many commentators have found this claim to be so counterintuitive that they have insisted that Rawls must mean to require fit with actual situated views.[6] And fit with situated views *would* appear to be the appropriate requirement if Rawls's theory aimed merely to identify the means of persuasion or enforcement necessary to ensure the persistence of a particular form of regime. Under such a view, stability would be regarded as "a purely practical matter," and a conception of justice would adopt stability as a goal in order to ensure regime persistence over time (PL 142).

But Rawls offers a theory of *justice*, not of regime persistence. Unjust regimes may achieve stability and persist over time; but the ability to persist does not make them just. Views that reinforce the stability of unjust or imperfectly just regimes do not provide information relevant to the task of constructing a theory of *justice*. Relevant information can best be obtained by examining those views and judgments in which the sense of justice is clearly expressed.[7] Rawls therefore focuses his analysis on the views of members of a well-ordered society who are reasonable (effectively motivated by the sense of justice) and rational (able to reason clearly and free from the common sources of distortion in reasoning). In requiring that an acceptable conception demonstrate fit with the views of reasonable members of a well-ordered society, then, Rawls simply focuses his analysis on the views and judgments that offer information relevant to the task of constructing a theory of justice.

Rawls's focus upon relations in a well-ordered society also, however, allows him to test the feasibility of the political conception. Such a focus allows him to examine the reasons to affirm or reject the political conception that would motivate holders of various comprehensive views who *were* effectively motivated by the desire to act from principles of justice. Unless an overlapping consensus could be achieved under the ideal conditions of a well-ordered constitutional democracy, Rawls argues, it could not be achieved under the less than ideal conditions that characterize actual societies (PL 35). The purpose of Rawls's discussion of overlapping consensus is, therefore, to demonstrate the feasibility of the political conception, not to concede the necessity of tailoring that conception to accommodate the views of various comprehensive doctrines.[8]

Kind of Fit

A politically liberal conception of justice can secure the willing affirmation of reasonable members of a well-ordered society characterized by reasonable pluralism, Rawls argues, because the conception is worked up from basic and fundamental ideas that are implicit in the political culture (PL 13–14). Fit between the political conception and the various comprehensive views of citizens is secured because the fundamental ideas that ground the conception are shared among citizens and are constitutive of their comprehensive views. But how do citizens understand the relation of fit between their comprehensive views and the content of the political conception? Does Rawls assume a ready correspondence between the comprehensive views of reasonable citizens and the contents of the political culture?

Rawls assumes precisely the contrary. A politically liberal conception of justice is to secure the willing agreement of citizens "when our shared political understandings... break down," and even "when we are torn within ourselves" (PL 44). The political conception attempts to mediate conflict by "connect[ing] conflict with the familiar and the basic" – that is by (1) identifying fundamental political ideas shared by persons whose substantive views regarding policy conflict and (2) elaborating the practical political implications of those ideas. Proponents *and* opponents of affirmative action, for example, may affirm the basic idea that "it should be impossible to tailor [the requirements of justice] to the circumstances of one's own case" (TJ 16). If parties to the controversy can be persuaded that the practical implication of this basic idea is that an account of justice should be constructed from the standpoint of persons who have no knowledge of their particular situated interests, substantial progress toward consensus will have been made.

Willing agreement is achieved, then, by a process of construction from basic ideas that are shared to judgments that will, on due reflection, be affirmed by all reasonable citizens because they express the practical implications of the basic ideas.[9] It is important to note that Rawls claims that citizens will affirm the political conception *on due reflection* (or, equivalently, in reflective equilibrium[10]). Rawls does not, therefore, anticipate spontaneous and unmediated affirmation of the political conception; rather, he argues that affirmation will be the product of a thorough reflective process. *Due reflection*, as Rawls defines it, is a demanding standard. In the course of such reflection, the deliberator is to examine her considered judgments in light of a consideration of "all possible descriptions to which one might plausibly conform one's judgments" (TJ 43, see PL 28), and to revise and adjust her convictions to incorporate or respond to any relevant criticisms and insights.[11]

A reasonable person will accept certain views after due reflection because she believes that they are supported by the most persuasive arguments, and may therefore be characterized as *objective*.[12] As discussed in Chapter 1, Rawls argues that a moral or political conviction is objective if it is supported by reasons "sufficient to persuade all reasonable persons that it is reasonable" (PL 119). Rawls's criterion for the objectivity of political convictions clarifies the nature of the relation of fit that must exist between a stable political conception and the views of reasonable citizens: the conception must be supported by arguments, grounded in ideas that are shared by reasonable citizens, that are sufficient to persuade "reasonable and rational persons, who are sufficiently intelligent and conscientious in exercising their powers of practical reason, and whose reasoning exhibits none of the familiar defects of reasoning" (PL 119) to affirm the conception.

Appropriateness of the Requirement

Why must stability constitute a concern fundamental to political philosophy? Why should it not be sufficient that a conception of justice is supported by the most persuasive arguments based upon an assessment of all identifiable relevant considerations?

The short answer is that Rawls considers stability to be one of the relevant considerations that must be assessed. We must demonstrate that the requirement of fit could be satisfied, Rawls suggests, in order to justify the judgment that the political conception could legitimately be employed to govern relations among citizens.[13] The political conception cannot, therefore, be *justified* unless the possibility of fit of the right kind can be demonstrated.[14]

Demonstrating the possibility of fit constitutes an essential element of the justification of a conception of justice because implementation of the requirements of a conception of justice will necessarily involve the use of coercive force. In a society of free and equal citizens whose views are characterized by reasonable pluralism, Rawls argues, the exercise of coercive force by the state can be legitimate only if the fundamentals of the constitution that authorizes the exercise of that force are justifiable to all citizens on terms that they can reasonably be expected to accept (PL 137). If the employment of the conception of justice to govern social relations is to be *justified*, then, it must be possible to demonstrate to each holder of a reasonable comprehensive view that she has adequate grounds for accepting the authority of the political conception. Thus, the requirement of fit – the requirement that a conception of justice must be capable of achieving the willing support of persons who disagree fundamentally regarding basic values – must be satisfied in order to *justify* the theory, not merely to demonstrate that the theory is capable of persisting over time.

Restricting the Scope of Debate

Political liberalism aims to secure an overlapping consensus among holders of *reasonable* comprehensive doctrines. Yet in defining the views that must be included in an overlapping consensus so stringently, critics claim, political liberalism would restrict public discourse too inflexibly. In particular, political liberalism would limit the class of reasonable views that constitute an overlapping consensus to those which (1) could be affirmed by reasonable persons,[15] (2) are consistent with fundamental liberal commitments,[16] or (3) support a reasonable balance of values.[17]

Views That Could Be Affirmed by Reasonable Persons

In an influential article, Leif Wenar argues that Rawls's standard for the *reasonableness of a* doctrine would exclude the views of "almost all currently recognizable comprehensive doctrines."[18] Rawls's account of political liberalism, Wenar concludes, therefore fails to describe a political conception of justice that is capable of fitting into and being supported by diverse reasonable comprehensive doctrines. Rather, Rawls's political liberalism is "too exclusionary" to be the focus of an overlapping consensus.[19]

Wenar does not claim that Rawls argues explicitly for such an exclusionary standard of reasonableness. Rather, Wenar argues that Rawls's explicit characterization of a reasonable doctrine is formulated so ambiguously that it requires reconstruction; and the most acceptable reconstruction would exclude almost all recognizable comprehensive views. In this subsection, I will argue that Rawls's characterization of a reasonable doctrine is not formulated ambiguously and does not, therefore, require reconstruction. Since Wenar's reconstruction is neither necessary nor consistent with the aims and values of political liberalism, I will argue, Wenar's argument fails.

Rawls's "explicit characterization" of a reasonable comprehensive doctrine, Wenar argues, is too imprecise to "rule out" doctrines "that are clearly unreasonable in Rawls's sense."[20] Rawls's characterization, Wenar claims, states only that a reasonable comprehensive doctrine is an exercise of both theoretical and practical reason, and that it "belongs to and draws upon a tradition of thought and doctrine" (PL 59). Such a characterization, as Wenar notes, would not exclude white supremacism, Muslim fundamentalism, or rational egoism from the class of reasonable views.[21]

While Rawls's explicit characterization is therefore "unsuccessful," there is available "a more attractive interpretative option," which is to define a reasonable comprehensive doctrine as "a comprehensive

Restricting the Scope of Debate 55

doctrine that a reasonable person would affirm."[22] Rawls, Wenar notes, "presents a wealth of material on what makes for a reasonable person."[23] Such persons (1) possess the capacity for a sense of justice and for a conception of the good, (2) are ready to propose and abide by fair terms of cooperation, (3) recognize the burdens of judgment, (4) have a reasonable moral psychology, and (5) recognize the essential elements of a conception of objectivity.[24] Defining a reasonable comprehensive doctrine as a doctrine that a reasonable person would affirm thus provides the basis for a characterization of a reasonable doctrine that is sufficiently precise to exclude white supremacism, Muslim fundamentalism, and many other doctrines from the class of reasonable views.

The problem, in fact, is that the characterization that Wenar's reconstruction makes possible is too precise. A characterization requiring that the holder of a reasonable doctrine must have the third, fourth, or fifth qualities that Rawls attributes to reasonable *persons*, Wenar argues, will exclude "many who could otherwise join a liberal consensus." For example, Wenar claims, "religious doctrines typically deny that the burdens of judgment obtain."[25] If this claim is correct, then – under Wenar's reconstructed characterization of a reasonable comprehensive doctrine – most religious views would fail the test of reasonableness and would be excluded from the overlapping consensus. Similarly, if only views that accept Rawls's account of reasonable moral psychology are viewed as reasonable, then many views that reject such an account – Wenar claims that classic utilitarians, Humeans, and "Hobbes's followers," for example, would fall within this category[26] – will also be excluded from the overlapping consensus.[27]

While Rawls's explicit characterization of a reasonable comprehensive view is unsuccessful because of its lack of precision, Wenar argues, the most plausible reconstruction of this notion "take[s] the full presentation of justice as fairness beyond its self-image as a political conception of justice."[28] Rawls, Wenar concludes, is unsuccessful in his effort to construct a theory that could serve as the focus of an overlapping consensus for the members of a society characterized by pluralistic disagreement.

It is important to emphasize, however, that Wenar's critique of Rawls is persuasive only if Rawls's characterization of a reasonable comprehensive doctrine does require reconstruction. While Wenar's argument depends crucially upon this claim, the justification that he offers for it is brief, cursory, and – I will argue – unpersuasive. Wenar's argument, in fact, relies entirely upon a single passage in which Rawls sets out the "three main features" of a reasonable comprehensive doctrine (PL 59, first full paragraph). This passage states that a reasonable comprehensive doctrine is an exercise of both theoretical and practical reason and that such a doctrine "belongs to and draws upon a tradition of thought and doctrine" (PL 59). Assuming that this passage constitutes Rawls's full account of a reasonable view, Wenar claims that Rawls's characterization would not exclude from an overlapping consensus doctrines "that are clearly unreasonable in Rawls's sense."[29] On the basis of this argument, Wenar concludes that Rawls's characterization of a reasonable view is too imprecise to be successful.

Far from constituting Rawls's full account of a reasonable view, however, the passage that Wenar cites merely introduces an extended discussion in which Rawls develops his characterization of a reasonable view. In the paragraph following the passage cited by Wenar, in fact, Rawls begins to address the concern that Wenar raises regarding the need for a precise standard to define the point at which a doctrine ceases to be reasonable and must be viewed as unreasonable: "We avoid excluding doctrines as unreasonable *without strong grounds based on clear aspects of the reasonable itself*" (PL 59, my emphasis). This passage has two important implications. First, Rawls intends to be very cautious about excluding *any* doctrines as unreasonable. And second, a standard for excluding unreasonable doctrines *can* be generated based upon an analysis of "clear aspects of the reasonable." While the latter phrase might seem obscure, Rawls is simply referring to the sense of *being reasonable* that he has set out as the subject of this section of Lecture II: the notion of *being* reasonable defines "the scope of what reasonable people think can be justified to others" (PL 59).

Rawls proceeds to develop this notion to generate a "standard of reasonableness" (PL 60n13) defining the point at which a doctrine must be viewed as *unreasonable*. Reasonable persons, Rawls argues, will think that it is unreasonable to use state power "to repress comprehensive views that are not unreasonable" (PL 60). This aspect of "being reasonable" is, in fact, "a part of a political ideal of democratic citizenship." The reasonable element in this ideal defines "what free and equal citizens as reasonable can require of each other with respect to their comprehensive views" (PL 62). Such citizens may *not* require of other members of society "anything contrary to what...their representatives in the original position could grant" (PL 62). In particular, no such representative could grant political authority to any person or association "to use the state's police power to decide... basic questions of justice as that person's, or that association's, comprehensive doctrine directs" (PL 62). The use of political power "to insist on [one's] own beliefs" and "to prevent the rest [of society] from affirming their not unreasonable views" is therefore *unreasonable* (PL 61). Comprehensive doctrines "that would suppress, if they could, liberty of conscience and freedom of thought" (PL 64–65), that are prepared "to use the sanctions of state power to correct, or punish, those who disagree" (PL 138), and that "reject one or more democratic freedoms" (PL 64n19) are therefore unreasonable. Thus, the views of a white supremacist who argues that members of racial minorities do not deserve equal treatment under the law, while morally unattractive, remain "reasonable" as long as he merely expresses his views while accepting the authority of civil rights legislation enacted by the majority. If, however, the white supremacist's views require the use of force to coerce persons who disagree with him, then his views are unreasonable.

Consider the status, under this standard of reasonableness, of the views of Wenar's religious believer who "den[ies] that the burdens of judgment obtain."[30] Wenar argues that such a person must deny that the burdens of judgment obtain because a religious doctrine "characteristically presents itself as universally accessible."[31] It is relevant to note, first, that Wenar's argument does *not* establish decisively that such a religious believer must deny that the burdens of judgment obtain. The claim that a doctrine is accessible does not entail that all persons must in fact recognize its accessibility; and adherents of a particular doctrine, in attempting to explain why many persons in fact fail to affirm that doctrine (despite its accessibility), might well accept the burdens of judgment as the most persuasive explanation of that failure. Even if the religious believer *does* deny that the burdens of judgment obtain, however, her views remain "reasonable" under Rawls's standard of reasonableness – and would therefore be included in an overlapping consensus – as long as those views do not require the use of force to coerce persons who disagree with her.

Rawls thus argues for a standard of reasonableness that is (1) sufficiently precise to "rule out" as unreasonable many forms of white supremacism, extreme fundamentalism, and rational egoism, but

(2) not – as Wenar claims – "too exclusionary" to be the focus of an overlapping consensus. Rawls's standard, in fact, will exclude *only* views that require or permit the use of state power to repress the reasonable comprehensive views of others or to invade basic liberties. This account of reasonableness is thus "deliberately loose" (PL 59) because, as Rawls argues, a tighter standard would "[run] the danger of being arbitrary and exclusive" (PL 59). His criterion of reasonableness is therefore designed to give *"rather minimal* conditions appropriate for the aims of political liberalism" (PL 60n13, my emphasis).

Ironically, then, while Rawls's standard of reasonableness is "deliberately loose" in order to minimize the exclusion of doctrines, Wenar's reconstruction of Rawls's standard secures excessive precision in order to maximize the exclusion of doctrines. Wenar's reconstruction is therefore both unnecessary and inappropriate. It cultivates a precision that Rawls deliberately avoids in order to secure a goal of exclusion that Rawls rejects.

Eliminating the Political

Like Wenar, Chantal Mouffe is concerned that the exclusion of unreasonable views from the overlapping consensus is inconsistent with Rawls's desire to construct a political conception of justice. Mouffe argues that Rawls, in fact, employs the distinction between "simple" and "reasonable" pluralism to disguise as the output of impartial moral reflection a political decision to exclude from public debate the views of persons who reject the fundamental commitments of liberalism.

While Rawls argues that an overlapping consensus must be capable of gaining the support of all *reasonable* persons, Mouffe notes, Rawls defines "reasonable persons" as persons "who have an enduring desire to honor fair terms of cooperation."[32] This definition, Mouffe claims, indirectly asserts "that reasonable persons are those who accept the fundamentals of liberalism."[33] Therefore, Mouffe argues, a politically liberal overlapping consensus need only accommodate the views of persons who accept the fundamentals of liberalism; and Rawls's claim that an acceptable conception of justice need only be capable of constituting the focus of an overlapping consensus in a society characterized by *reasonable* pluralism in fact functions to exclude from public discourse views that "would jeopardize the dominance of the liberal principles in the public sphere."[34] Thus, Mouffe concludes, in Rawls's ideal of a well-ordered society, "legitimate dissent would have been eliminated from the public sphere."[35]

This result would, as Mouffe suggests, "indeed [be] worrying"[36] if it were supported by a sound reading of Rawls's argument. But could Rawls, who offers a standard of reasonableness that is "deliberately loose" in order to avoid the danger of "being arbitrary and exclusive" (PL 59), endorse a theory that deliberately excludes from public discourse the views of persons who dissent from liberal values? The short answer is *no*. Mouffe's analysis of Rawls's argument is unsound in two important respects.

First, Mouffe asserts that, since an overlapping consensus aims for the support of reasonable persons, Rawls considers that only the views of reasonable persons (defined as persons who accept the fundamental commitments of liberalism) are relevant to the reasoning that grounds acceptance of the overlapping consensus. This claim, however, distorts Rawls's argument. While the focus of an overlapping consensus is a view that is affirmed by reasonable persons, reasonable persons – in Rawls's account – affirm that view *on the basis of due reflection*. In the course of due reflection, the person (1) examines her considered judgments of justice in light of a consideration of "all possible descriptions [of the sense of justice] to which one might plausibly conform one's judgments" and (2) revises and adjusts her considered judgments to reflect *any* relevant critical insights (TJ 43). Thus, the reflection that grounds acceptance of an overlapping consensus takes into account *all conceivable relevant views*, in particular the objections that may be raised by nonliberal dissenters.

Second, Mouffe incorrectly assumes that Rawls's account of overlapping consensus would require the exclusion from public discourse of views that a political liberal would not consider relevant to the reasoning grounding acceptance of the overlapping consensus. In fact, as discussed above, Rawls's account of overlapping consensus requires that the deliberation grounding overlapping consensus must take into account "all possible descriptions [of the sense of justice] to which one might plausibly conform one's judgments" (TJ 43). In order to determine whether to affirm a conception of justice, a reasonable citizen must, in fact, seek out and assess the most powerful objections to that conception before forming his or her judgments.

Why, then, is Mouffe persuaded that Rawls's account of overlapping consensus would require the exclusion of nonliberal views? Mouffe appears to confuse Rawls's account of (1) *the justification of an overlapping consensus* with his account of (2) *the limits of public reason*. Rawls's account of public reason is separate and distinct from his account of stability and does *not* describe the reasoning process through which the focus of an overlapping consensus is identified and justified. Rather, public reason provides an account of the kind of justifications that reasonable persons *who have already accepted a politically liberal theory as their conception of justice* will view as acceptable reasons to offer to one another as the public basis for policy decisions regarding basic questions of justice. Such reasonable persons, Rawls argues, will judge on due reflection that public deliberations regarding these questions must be supported by a public form of reasoning that all reasonable members of a pluralistic society could reasonably be expected to endorse (PL 218, 225[37]) because deliberations in the public sphere, unlike an individual's reflections regarding the justification of overlapping consensus, should appeal only to values and ideas that all citizens could reasonably be expected to accept and should avoid appeals to comprehensive doctrine that go beyond the bounds of the political conception unless those appeals derive independent and sufficient support from arguments grounded in public reason (PL 223).

While Mouffe's narrow claim that Rawls's account of *stability* restricts the contribution of nonliberals to public discourse fails, then, it might seem that Mouffe's general claim that a politically liberal society will exclude the views of dissenters from public discourse is on firmer ground. In arguing that only certain kinds of justifications should be viewed as appropriate in the public sphere, Rawls's account of the limits of public reason might appear to restrict the contribution of nonliberals to public discourse. Moreover, Rawls concedes that holders of certain comprehensive doctrines within a political culture may "urge far tighter standards of reasonableness" (PL 60n13) than the standard that Rawls develops in *Political Liberalism*. While Rawls's concession here does not affect his account of the sense of reasonableness that is relevant to the definition of a reasonable comprehensive doctrine, it might seem plausible to suggest that the presence of holders of such views in a political culture could complicate the process of public justification – consistent with the requirements of public reason – in a manner that deterred the public expression of some convictions.

Would the limits of public reason, in fact, deter or forbid the public expression of convictions deriving from comprehensive doctrines,

Restricting the Scope of Debate 61

but relevant to public discourse? In order to determine whether, and to what extent, public reason might unacceptably restrict public discourse, it is necessary to establish (1) the precise class of persons who are subject to the limits of public reason, (2) the specific issues that are subject to these limits, and (3) the kind of duty that is imposed by public reason on the average citizen as he or she contributes to public discourse.

Persons Subject to the Limits of Public Reason

The limits of public reason apply directly only to persons "when they engage in political advocacy in the public forum" (PL 252[38]). Such limits thus apply to the reasoning of (1) judges in their decisions, (2) government officials advocating and enacting policy, and (3) candidates seeking public office[39] (see PL 252–53). These limits do not, then, apply directly to ordinary citizens when they (1) discuss and debate political issues among themselves or (2) participate in politically active associations.

Issues within the Scope of Public Reason

The limits of public reason do not apply to all public discussion of political issues, or even to all public discussion of important political issues. Rather, the limits of public reason apply only to a narrow class of issues concerning "matters of constitutional essentials and basic justice" (PL 224). More precisely, the limits of public reason apply only to public discussions relating to "the general structure of government" or "the basic rights and liberties of citizenship" (PL 227). Much, or even most, of the content of everyday public political discourse would therefore be unaffected by the notion of public reason.

Nature of the Duty to Respect the Limits of Public Reason

The limits of public reason thus apply primarily to political officials in their public deliberations regarding constitutional essentials and issues of basic justice. One might, therefore, be tempted to conclude that the idea of public reason is unlikely to justify anything more than nominal limits on the scope of public deliberation. Such an account of the scope of public reason may, however, underestimate its potential impact on public discourse. Rawls argues that ordinary citizens voting in elections in which constitutional essentials or issues of basic justice are at stake should view themselves as subject to the limits of public reason (PL 215). In such cases, Rawls asserts, each citizen occupies the position of legislator and is subject, by extension, to the limits on public justification that apply to elected legislators. Moreover, Rawls argues that citizens should be prepared to explain their votes on such basic issues to each other in terms that respect the full limits of public reason (PL 243).

Would Mouffe therefore be correct to suggest that, at least in the case of the public discussion of matters of basic justice that are subject to a vote, a society that honors the idea of public reason will suppress legitimate dissent? In order to resolve this concern, it is necessary to consider more carefully the nature of the duty to respect the ideal of public reason. Rawls argues that the central requirement of public reason is a sincere judgment: "A citizen engages in public reason... when he or she deliberates within a framework of *what he or she sincerely regards*... as a conception that others as free and equal citizens might also reasonably be expected reasonably to endorse."[40] Far from requiring that participants adhere to codified set of limits on appropriate contributions to public discourse, then, Rawls argues that a person honors the ideal of public reason as long as he or she applies "the criterion of reciprocity"[41] to their contribution to public discourse, where that criterion requires that "we sincerely believe... [and] reasonably think that other citizens might also reasonably accept" the reasons that we offer to justify political actions.[42] As long as a person *sincerely believes* that the reasons that he or she introduces into public discourse – or the doctrine to which he or she appeals in such discourse – are reasons others could share, this passage suggests, their contribution is comfortably within the limits of public reason. The duty to honor public reason is thus a duty to form a sincere judgment, not a duty to honor a canonical set of restrictions on contributions to public discourse. Mouffe's argument that public reason will justify the suppression of dissent, then, appears to exaggerate the limits that public reason would place on public discourse.

Finally, suppose that a person views her comprehensive doctrine as of such overriding importance that, understanding that other citizens cannot reasonably be expected to endorse appeals to this doctrine, she nevertheless bases a public argument regarding an issue of basic justice (that is subject to a vote) on an appeal to the absolute authority of that doctrine. In such a case, the person *does* exceed the bounds of public reason; but this conclusion adds little if anything to the routine intuitive judgment that the person has exceeded the bounds of political civility. In insisting upon the authority of a doctrine that others reasonably reject, such a person expresses a form of disrespect for those other persons that can be readily appreciated without reference to the notion of public reason. The ideal of public reason does not forbid such contributions to public discourse, but it does serve as a reminder that appealing to the absolute authority of a comprehensive view while understanding that others reasonably dissent from that view is obviously uncivil.

A Reasonable Balance of Issues

Like Mouffe, Evan Charney is concerned that Rawls's distinction between reasonable and unreasonable comprehensive doctrines may lead him to exclude an unacceptably large number of views from participation in an overlapping consensus. Charney argues that Rawls, in order to ensure that controversial issues can be resolved in political terms, restricts the *set* of reasonable views to doctrines that are capable of supporting *a reasonable balance of values* on the issues that they raise. Rawls, Charney notes, argues that views that cannot support such a balance "do not accord with public reason."[43]

While Charney recognizes that the claim that a view does not accord with public reason does not necessarily establish that the view is unreasonable, he argues that Rawls's discussion of the issue of abortion supports the claim that Rawls intends to apply this *balance of values* standard to define the boundary between reasonable and unreasonable doctrines. Rawls, Charney asserts, claims that the issue of abortion is connected to three primary political values: (1) respect for human life, (2) the reproduction of human society over time, and (3) the equality of women citizens. Rawls argues that a doctrine that fails to support a balance of these values and, as a result, "exclud[es] th[e] duly qualified right to an abortion in the first trimester" (PL 243) is "to that extent unreasonable" (PL 243).[44] The failure to support a reasonable balance of issues, Charney claims, is thus decisive in Rawls's judgment that the doctrine is unreasonable. It therefore "seems textually unequivocal."[45] that Rawls employs the balance of values test to determine whether a doctrine is or is not reasonable.

Moreover, Charney argues, Rawls must, under this standard, classify as unreasonable a doctrine that does not satisfy this test *whether or not the individual attempts to secure the passage of legislation embodying that view*: "even when an individual does not vote on the basis of her comprehensive views,... by the tenets of political liberalism, her views can still be classed as unreasonable."[46] Since unreasonable views may not constitute a part of an overlapping consensus, Charney concludes, "Rawls's conception of an overlapping consensus points to a rather surprising unity, even homogeneity, of comprehensive views."[47] Like Mouffe and Wenar, then, Charney suggests that Rawls is unsuccessful in his effort to construct a political conception of justice that could secure consensus in a society characterized by even moderately diverse political views.

As in the cases of the critiques offered by Mouffe and Wenar, however, the reader must wonder how Rawls could possibly propose the theory attributed to him. In Charney's account, political liberalism would not include in an overlapping consensus the views of even a reasonable opponent of abortion who "does not believe that [her] view can reasonably be defended by public reason and therefore does not... seek to overturn *Roe v. Wade*."[48] Can Charney's account constitute a faithful interpretation of political liberalism?

The short answer, I suggest, is again *no*. Charney argues that Rawls's discussion of the issue of abortion in Lecture VI of *Political Liberalism* sets out a tightly restrictive account of the boundaries of an overlapping consensus. A closer look at the passage on which Charney bases his argument, however, suggests that the passage is, in fact, *not relevant* to the question of which doctrines may form part of an overlapping consensus. The discussion of abortion is presented in a subsection of Lecture VI with the title: "Apparent Difficulties with Public Reason" (PL 240–47), a subsection that does not discuss issues relating to overlapping consensus. The language that Charney cites, moreover, is offered as an *"illustration"* of the kind of case in which "comprehensive doctrines run afoul *of public reason*" (PL 243, my emphasis). When Rawls writes in this passage that a view that fails to support a reasonable balance of issues is "to that extent unreasonable" (PL 243n32), then, Rawls is simply making the obvious point that a view that does not meet the standard that determines which views "accord with public reason" is, in fact, inconsistent with the limits of public reason. Rawls makes his focus *on the limits of public reason*, and not on the boundaries of overlapping consensus, clear in the very next sentence in which he concludes that, "assuming that this question is either a constitutional essential or a matter of basic justice, *we would go against the ideal of public reason* if we voted from a comprehensive doctrine that denied this right" (PL 244n32, my emphasis). The passage upon which Charney bases his argument has, therefore, no bearing on the issues of stability or the nature of an overlapping consensus and thus provides no support for Charney's argument regarding the boundaries of an overlapping consensus.

Issues Removed from the Public Sphere

Even if political liberalism would not exclude an unacceptably large number of *doctrines* from the overlapping consensus, a number of commentators – in particular, Ed Wingenbach and Patrick Neal – argue that the theory would restrict the *issues* that may be debated in the public sphere. Since Rawls, Wingenbach argues, assumes in his later work that liberal constitutional democracy is "reasonably just" and therefore worth defending, Rawls shifts his attention from questions of distributive justice to the question of how to create a stable democratic society. And, Wingenbach argues, Rawls is prepared to advocate the removal of divisive issues from the political agenda if this is necessary to secure stability.[49]

Moreover, Neal argues, if Rawls succeeded in this effort to exclude divisive issues from the political agenda, he would undermine the role of public discourse as a medium within which political interests constitute themselves. Political stability is, Neal concedes, an important consideration; and if we could be confident that the removal of divisive issues from the agenda served *everyone's* interests, "we might sensibly proceed in the manner that Rawls outlines." But what, Neal asks, if political interests are best understood "as emerg[ing] and constitute[ing] themselves within" the process of political activity? If we accept such a view, then Rawls's approach would seem to risk "closing the channels through which 'free and equal persons' manifest themselves."[50]

While Rawls does write of taking divisive issues off the political agenda (PL 157), however, the interpretation supplied for this language by Wingenbach and Neal distorts Rawls's meaning. Neal bases his argument on language from "The Idea of an Overlapping Consensus" in which Rawls argues that constitutional provisions that secure the basic liberties operate properly in removing from political deliberation issues that should be "take[n] off the political agenda and put...beyond the calculus of social interests."[51] In that essay, however, Rawls is careful to explain that "when certain matters are taken off the political agenda, they are no longer regarded as proper subjects for political decision *by majority or other plurality voting.*"[52] Rawls does not, then, propose that public debate on these issues should be foreclosed, but rather that political decisions regarding these matters must be made by supermajorities (see PL 402). The language on which Neal's argument relies does not, therefore provide a sound basis for the claim that Rawls's approach would "clos[e] the channels through which 'free and equal persons' manifest themselves."[53]

Wingenbach offers an argument similar to Neal's but focusing on language from Lecture IV of *Political Liberalism*.[54] In that lecture, however, Rawls provides precisely the same explanation for the notion of taking matters off the political agenda (see PL 151n16) as in the article cited by Neal. In both the article and the lecture, then, Rawls is simply endorsing the practice of protecting fundamental rights at the constitutional level and requiring supermajority votes to amend the provisions guaranteeing those rights.

Far from wishing to foreclose the question of whether such rights should be protected, moreover, Rawls is quite clear that this question should remain open in a politically liberal society. Citizens of such a society can and should pursue constitutional reform if they judge, on due reflection, that (1) rights protected under the constitution should not receive such legal protection or that (2) the form of protection provided in the constitution is inappropriate. Rawls specifies that citizens in a well-ordered society are to "adjust and revise [the constitution] as changing social circumstances require," in particular "whenever the constitution...[is] in various ways unjust and imperfect" (PL 402). Far from removing issues connected to fundamental rights from the public sphere, then, Rawls acknowledges that "[n]o (human) theory could possibly anticipate...the needed reforms...for improving present [constitutional] arrangements" (PL 401).

Indeed, the charge that Rawls's conception of justice would shackle public discourse in the manner suggested by Neal and Wingenbach fundamentally misinterprets the character of the theory. Rawls argues that citizens of a well-ordered society should "continually" discuss and reassess "questions of political principles and social policy" (PL 400). Rawls, in fact, urges consideration of the widest feasible range of issues and arguments in the ongoing project of constructing a just constitution.

But, Neal and Wingenbach might respond, when Rawls urges citizens to reassess their constitution, he is urging them to make certain that their constitution protects basic liberties *in a manner that satisfies Rawls's first principle of justice*. Since the requirements of that principle define the boundaries of permissible constitutional reform, this objection might continue, Rawls's theory does in fact restrict the scope of public deliberation despite Rawls's calls for continual reassessment of the justice of current constitutional arrangements.

Such an objection, however, underestimates the scope of the reflection that is recommended by Rawls's theory. While Rawls recommends reassessment of the constitution to determine whether its provisions are consistent with the first principle, he also recommends reassessment of the principles chosen in the original position to determine whether those principles constitute an acceptable conception of justice:

That the principles [of justice] are indeed the most reasonable ones is a conjecture... We must check it against the fixed points of our considered judgments at all levels of generality... In either direction, we may be led to revise our judgments. (PL 381)

The principles chosen in the original position are not, therefore, assigned special priority in due reflection. Citizens are to reassess those principles continually, just as they are to reassess every other aspect of the political conception. If they find that the principles that constitute their conception of justice are not supported by the most powerful considerations, then they must "modify [that] conception of justice with its principles... until judgments at all levels of generality are at last in line on due reflection" (PL 45). Rawls, in fact, specifies that citizens are to consider carefully "alternate conceptions of justice and the force of various arguments for them" (PL 384n16). Far from aiming to "coerce our considered convictions," Rawls's account of the choice of principles of justice is simply designed to allow citizens to identify the practical implications of values that they do in fact affirm (PL 45). If Rawls's two principles are, on reflection, found to realize those values imperfectly, then the principles must be amended or replaced.

Socialization

Wingenbach disputes the view that Rawls's theory encourages wide-ranging reflection, arguing that Rawls relies upon socialization "to shape and mold the comprehensive doctrines of members of that society."[55] By "form[ing] the social world in which our character and...conceptions of the good, are first acquired," the political conception defines and shapes citizens' comprehensive views.[56] Citizens who resist this socialization are viewed as threats to stability that "must be contained."[57] Even if political debate is unconstrained, then, citizens of a well-ordered society will lack real freedom to consider alternative political arrangements because they will have been socialized to accept and affirm liberal principles.

While Wingenbach interprets Rawls to require socialization and manipulation, however, the natural interpretation of Rawls's language is much less sinister. In the passage that Wingenbach quotes, Rawls does not argue that the political conception does or should socialize persons to accept any particular theory or ideology. Rather, Rawls argues that in a well-ordered society, the principles of justice, as reflected in the background political culture, "enable us to become free and equal citizens...*and to understand our role as persons with that status*" (PL 41). Rawls thus argues for social institutions that enable citizens *to understand and assess for themselves* their social role and status.

But, Wingenbach might respond, the principles nevertheless socialize citizens to accept liberal worldview and assumptions that ground their social role, in particular the view that citizens should be viewed as free and equal. While the presence of the principles in the background culture might encourage such a view, however, Rawls argues persuasively that other elements of the political culture of a well-ordered society will preclude such socialization. In particular, the publicity condition is designed to ensure that citizens of such a society "are in a position to know and accept the pervasive influences...that shape their conception of themselves...nothing should be hidden" (PL 68). Thus, the relation of citizens to the political culture is designed to be fully informed and reflective rather than automatic and unconscious.

But, Wingenbach will note, Rawls argues that citizens are put in a position "to accept" pervasive influences from the culture; does this language not suggest that Rawls intends that citizens should be socialized? Rawls's account of the basis of this acceptance suggests that the answer to this question is *no*. Citizens' acceptance of the political order, Rawls argues, is based upon due reflection that takes into account all considerations that lead them to affirm the political conception rather than some other conception of justice (PL 67). In particular, due reflection involves the examination of "all possible descriptions [of our sense of justice] to which one might plausibly conform one's judgments" (TJ 43, see PL 28). Rawls thus clearly intends that citizens should be put in a position to form their political views on the basis of fully informed reflection. Far from aiming to socialize citizens' comprehensive views, then, Rawls encourages free, fully informed, and wide-ranging reflection regarding basic questions of value.

But while political liberalism may not *aim* to socialize, Wingenbach might respond, politically liberal institutions and policies will necessarily produce a socializing *effect* on members of a politically liberal society by promoting and endorsing certain liberal values. In particular, Rawls argues that public education in such a society should provide knowledge of "basic rights" such as "liberty of conscience" (PL 199). Even if this knowledge is presented in a neutral fashion, it will be argued, the insertion of this material into the educational curriculum will socialize members of society to accept liberal ideas and will therefore define and restrict the scope of public discourse.

Once this objection is stated clearly, however, it becomes easier to see why the argument should not constitute a decisive objection against political liberalism. Critics such as Wingenbach are primarily concerned to ensure that public discourse remains receptive to claims grounded in diverse value theories. Yet these critics appear to assume that social neutrality regarding rights and liberty of conscience is more likely to foster a diverse public discourse than social endorsement of norms respecting these values. This assumption is not obviously true. If a politically liberal society teaches respect for liberty of conscience effectively, its citizens will respect and be receptive to the moral and political views of all members of society. Citizens of political cultures that do not encourage such respect will, in contrast, be more vulnerable to the appeals of factions that teach intolerance and ideological exclusiveness. It seems reasonable to expect, then, that members of a liberal political culture will be *more* tolerant of and receptive to diversity than members of a culture that is neutral regarding rights and liberty of conscience.

But, it might be objected, a society that encourages toleration will promote an agenda of toleration at the cost of diluting unreserved commitment to religious and other conceptions of the good. According to such a view, the society's commitment to toleration and mutual respect will become an excuse for avoiding deep engagement among persons holding divergent moral, political, or religious views. Such an objection, however, fails to note that in a society that teaches respect for toleration effectively, the contestation of ideas will be encouraged and valued, and all participants will be encouraged to express their views without reservation. Unreserved commitment to various conceptions of the good is in fact likely to receive its most complete public expression in societies that encourage toleration. While a public conception of justice with *any* determinate content, then, is likely to have some influence on the views of persons whose public political life is regulated by that conception, political liberalism serves the goal of open and vigorous public discourse – which, I suggest, motivates Wingenbach's concern regarding socializing effect – more effectively than conceptions of justice that do not require the teaching of liberal values.

Conclusion

Rawls's concern with stability reflects his view that an acceptable theory of justice must be capable of gaining the willing and informed support of persons who disagree fundamentally regarding basic values. Rawls argues that political liberalism is well designed to secure such willing and informed support because the conception identifies grounds for consensus implicit in the public political culture. A number of commentators, however, claim that political liberalism aims to secure stability by restricting the range or content of political debate or socializing citizens to accept liberal values. Moreover, these commentators suggest, Rawls's failure to design a conception of justice that is capable of securing consensus within a pluralistic society reflects the inadequacy of liberal theory, generally, to address the issues raised by the phenomenon of pluralistic disagreement regarding the good.

Conclusion

I have argued that these claims fail. Rather than attempting to restrict debate, remove issues from the public sphere, or socialize citizens' views to ensure agreement, political liberalism attempts to secure consensus through a process that encourages both free public deliberation and fully informed reflection. Critics have not, therefore, demonstrated that political liberalism fails to describe an approach capable of securing the willing support of persons who disagree fundamentally. Far from confirming the inadequacy of liberal theory to address issues related to value pluralism, then, Rawls's theory appears to constitute a resource that may be employed productively to address social questions and problems relating to pluralistic disagreement.

Notes

1 In *A Theory of Justice*, Rawls treated the issue of stability as a matter of the congruence of a sense of justice and the person's good. The sense of justice is congruent with the person's good, Rawls argued, because the development of that sense is essential to the realization of the person's nature as a free and equal person (TJ 501). The person will therefore view the realization of the sense of justice as an essential good, one that "that contains within itself its own priority" (TJ 503).
2 See Charney (1998); Mouffe (1996); Wenar (1995).
3 See Wingenbach (1999); (Neal 1994).
4 Wingenbach (1999).
5 "[T]o see how a *well-ordered society* can be unified and stable, we introduce...the idea of an overlapping consensus" (PL 133–34, emphasis mine). "[A] main aim of PL is to show that the idea of a *well-ordered society* in Theory may be reformulated so as to take account of the fact of reasonable pluralism" (PL xliii, emphasis mine).
6 Klosko (1994); Kukathas and Pettit (1990); Raz (1990); Baier (1989).
7 "[J]ustice as fairness is the hypothesis that the principles which would be chosen in the original position are identical with those that match our considered judgments and so these principles describe our sense of justice" (TJ 42).
8 "Any realistic idea of a well-ordered society may seem to imply that some [compromise of the political conception compelled by circumstances] is involved. Indeed, the term "overlapping consensus" may suggest that. We must show, then, that this is not the case" (PL 169).
9 "[W]e look to the fundamental ideas implicit in the culture and seek to uncover how citizens themselves might, on due reflection, want to conceive of their society as a fair system of cooperation over time" (PL 46).

10 "[A] political conception of justice, to be acceptable, must accord with our considered convictions, at all levels of generality, on due reflection, or in what I have called elsewhere 'reflective equilibrium'" (PL 8).
11 "[T]he test is that of reflective equilibrium: how well the view as a whole articulates our more firm considered convictions of political justice, at all levels of generality, after due examination, *once all adjustments and revisions that seem compelling have been made*" (PL 28, emphasis mine).
12 "Political convictions... are objective – actually founded on an order of reasons – if reasonable and rational persons, who are sufficiently intelligent and conscientious in exercising their powers of practical reason, and whose reasoning exhibits none of the familiar defects of reasoning, would eventually endorse those convictions,... provided that these persons know the relevant facts and have sufficiently surveyed the grounds that bear on the matter under conditions favorable to due reflection" (PL 119, see 110).
13 "[O]ur exercise of political power is only fully proper when it is exercised in accordance with a constitution the essentials of which all citizens as free and equal may reasonably be expected to endorse" (PL 137).
14 For helpful accounts of stability as a condition of the justification of a conception of justice, see Cohen (1993); Freeman (1994); Hill (1994).
15 Wenar (1995), p. 38.
16 Mouffe (1996).
17 Charney (1998).
18 Wenar (1995), p. 59.
19 Wenar (1995), p. 33.
20 Wenar (1995), pp. 35–36.
21 Wenar (1995), p. 36.
22 Wenar (1995), pp. 35–36.
23 Wenar (1995), p. 36.
24 Wenar (1995), p. 37.
25 Wenar (1995), p. 43.
26 Wenar's argument may move too quickly here. Classical utilitarianism, Wenar argues, presents the person as motivated solely by pleasure and pain; such a view must therefore reject Rawls's account of a "reasonable moral psychology" which assigns motivational force to conception-dependent desires. In assessing this argument, it is important to note, first, that a utilitarian need not view the person as motivated *solely* by pleasure and pain. As eminent a utilitarian as John Stuart Mill argued, not that persons are motivated solely by pleasure and pain, but that "when we *do* unmotivatedly desire a thing [that is, our desire does not flow from the acceptance of a duty] we desire it under the idea of it as something pleasant." Skorupski (1989), p. 14. Moreover, even if utilitarian

Conclusion

theory described persons as motivated solely by pleasure, such a view of motivation would not require that conception-dependent desires cannot motivate. A person may derive significant pleasure from acting on principle in order to realize a conception of the good. It is presumably pleasure of this sort to which Mill refers when he writes of "the higher meaning [of happiness]...such as human beings with highly developed faculties can care to have." Skorupski (1989), p. 24. Rawls, in fact, argues that Mill's characterization of the motivation provided by this higher meaning of happiness "is [simply] the desire to act on the difference principle" (TJ 439). Moreover, it would seem that all utilitarians must be motivated by at least one conception-dependent desire – the desire that all persons should resolve practical questions in a manner that maximizes aggregate happiness. Similarly, there is no reason that a Humean general appetite to good might not take the form of an appetite to realize an ideal of the good grounded in moral principles. Finally, since Hobbes describes the desire for individual advantage as the most fundamental human motivation, Wenar concludes that Hobbes must deny that conception-dependent desires can have motivational force. Since the holder of a conception-dependent desire wishes act in accordance with an ideal grounded in reasonable *or* rational principles, however, a reader of Hobbes who is persuaded by Hobbes's arguments and motivated by the desire to implement his theory is, in fact, motivated by a conception-dependent desire.

27 Wenar (1995), p. 50.
28 Wenar (1995), p. 41.
29 Wenar (1995), p. 35.
30 Wenar (1995), p. 43.
31 Wenar (1995), p. 44.
32 Mouffe (1996), p. 249, quoting PL 55.
33 Mouffe (1996), p. 249.
34 Mouffe (1996), p. 249.
35 Mouffe (1996), p. 252.
36 Mouffe (1996), p. 252.
37 See Rawls (1999), p. 155.
38 See Rawls (1999), p. 133.
39 Rawls (1999), p. 133.
40 Rawls (1999), p. 140, my emphasis.
41 Rawls (1999), p. 141.
42 Rawls (1999), p. 137.
43 Charney (1998), p. 107.
44 Charney (1998), p. 107.
45 Charney (1998), p. 107.

46 Charney (1998), p. 107.
47 Charney (1998), p. 108.
48 Charney (1998), p. 107.
49 Wingenbach (1999), p. 220.
50 Neal (1994), p. 106.
51 Neal (1994), p. 106, citing Rawls ([1987] 1999).
52 Rawls (1987), p. 435, emphasis mine.
53 Neal (1994), p. 106.
54 Wingenbach (1999), p. 220.
55 Wingenbach (1999), p. 222.
56 Wingenbach (1999), p. 222, quoting 41.
57 Wingenbach (1999), p. 222.

3 | *Rawls and Ethical Constructivism*

John Rawls's account of ethical constructivism is perhaps his most striking contribution to ethics. The notion of constructivism developed in this account has, in fact, been described as a new possibility in ethical and political theory[1] because it employs antirealist resources to address concerns raised by moral skeptics and pluralist critics of liberalism. A constructivist approach holds that moral propositions are right or justified when they are consistent with acceptable moral principles, and moral principles are acceptable when they are the product of an appropriately designed decision procedure. The structure of an appropriately designed decision procedure embodies weak and widely shared considered moral judgments, and moral reasoning that employs a constructivist procedure thus implements Rawls's notion that moral reasoning should work from "shared and preferably weak conditions" to conclusions that "match our considered judgments"...[in] reflective equilibrium" (TJ 18).

The constructivist representation of moral judgments formed in the context of a concretely described decision procedure and informed by a general knowledge of facts about human society has led to the perception among many commentators that Rawls's constructivism is grounded in specific factual information or in principles or values that are not principles or values of justice.[2] Thus, G. A. Cohen claims Rawls's constructivism is "fact-infested"[3] and, in addition, grounds its judgments in strategic and other considerations that are irrelevant to justice,[4] while Aaron James asserts that Rawls assumes that constructivist moral judgment is authoritative only when "grounded in independent judgments about what kind of social practices exist and what kinds of agents participate in them."[5]

Both of these views, however, misrepresent the character of Rawls's account. Cohen and James, like many other commentators on Rawls's work, seem to assume that a moral judgment in Rawls's account "either articulates a description of some fact or is a disguised version of some alternative use of language."[6] Thus, the confusion in both arguments derives from a failure to take seriously the centrality in Rawls's account of the Kantian intuition that moral judgments are grounded neither in facts nor in independent and preexisting norms or principles, but rather in a process of reasoning.

In examining this strand of Rawls's work, it is important to distinguish his account of constructivism from the substantive accounts of justice that Rawls develops in *A Theory of Justice* and *Political Liberalism*. While Rawls's account of constructivism works from many of the same assumptions that ground his substantive political theory, Rawls's constructivism provides an account of the structure of moral reasoning that is independent of both justice as fairness and political liberalism. Rather than providing or supplementing an account of a substantive moral or political conception, Rawls's constructivism develops an approach to assessing the reasonableness of moral judgments that can be employed *to evaluate* substantive moral conceptions.

It is equally important to distinguish Rawls's earlier account of Kantian constructivism from the account of *political* constructivism that Rawls develops in his later work on political liberalism. *Political* constructivism develops the notion that a procedure that represents intuitive ideas and considered judgments that are shared by citizens of a democratic society can generate principles of justice that can constitute the focus of an overlapping consensus of reasonable views.

In revising his account of ethical constructivism, Rawls detaches his account, at least in part, from its original foundation in Kantian intuitions.[7] He nevertheless continues to ground his account of constructivism in the Kantian insight – which he assumes that reasonable persons who disagree regarding the good could nevertheless affirm on due reflection – that principles of justice are best represented as those principles that free and equal persons could jointly affirm under fair choice conditions. Rawls's work on Kantian constructivism thus develops the foundation for his later attempt to generate a political theory of justice with the potential to provide the basis for realizing consensus, or at least reducing moral conflict, in societies characterized by a pluralistic diversity of moral views.

In this chapter, I will examine the relation between Rawls's constructivism and its foundation in Kantian intuitions. In particular, I will focus on the progressive influence on Rawls's approach of the Kantian intuition that the substance of morality is best understood as constructed by free and equal people under fair conditions and is not determined by appeals to the authority of a preexisting and independent order of values. Rawls's focus on this Kantian intuition, I will argue, motivates the focus on social contract that grounds both his accounts of the original position and of reflective equilibrium. In the first section, I briefly sketch Rawls's general approach to moral justification and the status of constructivism within that approach. In the second section, I examine the progressive influence of Kantian intuitions on Rawls's political thought and account of constructivism, both in his development of ideas from social contract doctrine and in his extension of ideas from "Outline of a Decision Procedure for Ethics." In the third section, I discuss and reject arguments in the current constructivist literature that locate the authority of Rawls's constructivism in facts or in nonmoral values or elements of existing practices. In the fourth section, I examine leading objections to Rawls's constructivist interpretation of Kant. Finally, I conclude by discussing the relation between Kantian constructivism and political constructivism.

Moral Justification

While constructivism constitutes a salient component of Rawls's account of moral justification, it nevertheless represents a subordinate strand of that account. Rawls's most general standard of moral and political justification requires that a moral proposition is justified if and only if it matches the considered judgments of a reasonable and rational person on due reflection in reflective equilibrium. In due reflection, the person reasons from premises that are (1) "widely shared but weak" (TJ 16) and (2) judged to be reliable when viewed from "conditions favorable for deliberation and judgment in general" (TJ 42). Premises that satisfy this standard constitute *considered judgments* "in which our own moral capacities are most likely to be displayed without distortion" (TJ 42). During due reflection, the person "attempts to organize the basic ideas and principles implicit" in his or her considered judgments into a coherent moral or political view (PL 8) and aims to reach a state of reflective equilibrium in which his or her "general convictions, first principles, and particular judgments are...in line" (PL 384n16).

Rawls's account of due reflection in fact extends his earlier efforts – efforts that reflect a number of non-Kantian influences – to describe criteria for evaluating the validity of proposed moral and political judgments. According to the arguments developed in "Outline of a Decision Theory for Ethics," a moral judgment is valid if and only if it would be accepted by competent moral judges, and a principle is valid if and only if it shows "a capacity to hold its own" (ODPE 11) against a subclass of relevant considered judgments. This account of the validity of moral judgments, in its attempt to apply "the relevant requirements of practical reason" (PL 90) to determine which moral judgments best satisfy the criteria of a rational method of ethics, reflects the influence of Henry Sidgwick's *The Methods of Ethics*. Rawls's assumption, in "Two Concepts of Rules," that reflection about questions of justice must identify principles that apply primarily to basic institutions reflects the influence of David Hume's *Treatise of Human Nature* and of Ludwig Wittgenstein's idea of a social practice.[8]

Rawls's reflections regarding the nature of valid moral and political judgments lead him to conclude that such judgments are properly viewed as conclusions derived through the operations of an acceptable deliberative procedure. In developing this view, Rawls is increasingly drawn to the intuition – which he attributes to Kant – that moral reasoning is "part of the general theory of rational choice" (DJ 132)[9] applied to the problem of securing reasonable and mutually justifiable social relations. Once Rawls has reached this conclusion, the idea of social contract – in particular, Kant's account of social contract – plays an increasingly central role in Rawls's account of justification in ethics.

The Kantian Influence

While the influence of Kant is not evident in Rawls's earliest published work (see ODPE, TCR), Rawls begins to refer to the central importance of Kant's thought in "Justice as Fairness," and discussions of the central significance of Kant's thought are increasingly salient in Rawls's work between 1958 and 1980. Rawls is careful, however, to emphasize that his work does not attempt to offer exegesis of Kant's views. Rather, it develops Kantian themes in manner that makes Rawls's work "closer to [Kant's] view than to the other traditional moral conceptions that are appropriate for use as benchmarks of comparison" (KC 305).

Rawls's working out of Kantian themes increasingly affects both his account of justification in ethics and his development of his substantive account of justice during the period between the publication of

"Justice as Fairness" and "Kantian Constructivism in Moral Theory." Most fundamentally, Rawls is influenced by Kant's view that a moral action derives its worth from the principle of volition that motivates the action rather than from any particular end attained.[10] In the first part of the *Groundwork*, Kant argues that "an action from duty has its moral worth *not in the purpose* to be attained by it... but merely [in] the *principle of volition* in accordance with which the action is done" (Kant, 1996, p. 55; G 4.400).[11] In this and similar passages, Kant argues that moral reasoning is characterized not by the pursuit of certain ends or goals, but by the reason for action contained in the underlying principle of volition. The analysis of moral judgment, for Kant, becomes an analysis of noninstrumental principles of volition and arguments constructed from those principles.

If the nature of the reason grounding an act determines its moral quality, then the moral quality of an act can be assessed by determining whether reasonable persons under suitable conditions would have sufficient reasons to consent to the act. Kantian intuitions thus lead Rawls to focus his moral analysis around the notion of rational consent as developed in Kant's theory of social contract. Social contract, Rawls notes in "Justice as Fairness," "does express, suitably interpreted, an essential part of the concept of justice" (JF 71). An examination of the evolution of Kant's progressive influence on Rawls in fact suggests that Rawls's constructivism evolves directly from his interpretation of Kant's theory of social contract and not from an interpretation of the categorical imperative procedure. In addition, Rawls's extension of the Kantian social contract argument provides a basis for the extension of the non-Kantian strand of Rawls's account of justification in ethics developed in "Outline of a Decision Procedure for Ethics." Finally, the notion of a social contract doctrine as a form of rational choice theory suggests to Rawls the idea of employing a hypothetical social contract model as a procedure that specifies the relation between a particular conception of the person and a conception of justice.

Constructivism and Social Contract

Rawls first notes the significance of Kant's theory of social contract for his approach in "Justice as Fairness," where he suggests that "Kant was not far from wrong when he interpreted the original contract merely as an idea of reason" (JF 71). While legal and political obligation do not literally originate in any form of original agreement, social contract constitutes "an ethical idea applicable to social arrangements irrespective of the question of origins" (TJ 223). Just as ideas of reason generally secure the greatest unity and extension for the concepts of the understanding, the idea of social contract can be employed "to clarify the concept of justice" by representing its general unifying ground (JF 59). This view of justice as grounded in the notion of social contract, in fact, follows naturally from Rawls's view that the question of justice "arises once the concept of morality is imposed upon mutually self-interested agents, similarly circumstanced" (JF 59). If justice is a conception that self-interested agents create to regulate their joint interactions, then the metaphor of a contract seems appropriate to represent the kind of jointly acceptable standard for behavior that is required.

In presenting the idea of social contract as a general unifying ground for the concept of justice, Rawls follows Kant's view that the idea of an "original contract" – by which a people "unites into a society" by "establishing a *civil constitution*" (Kant, 1996, p. 290; TP 8: 289) through the exercise of the "general (united) will of the people" (Kant, 1996, p. 295; TP 8: 295) – constitutes "the touchstone of any public law's conformity with right" (Kant, 1996, p. 297; TP 8: 297). Rawls also follows Kant in viewing the idea of social contract as uniquely well-suited for this role *because* it expresses the fundamental idea that is essential to judgments of justice – the idea of fairness (JF 47). As Kant notes, public laws generated by the general will of the people must be "incapable of doing wrong to anyone," since "all decide about all, hence each about himself" (Kant, 1996, p. 295; TP 8.295). It is this aspect of the concept of justice. Rawls argues, that is neglected by utilitarian theory – utilitarianism improperly applies "the principle of choice for one man" to society (DJ 132). Social contract theory, Rawls argues, therefore comes closer than utilitarian theory to expressing an essential part of the concept of justice (JF 71).

Once principles of justice are viewed as the product of joint agreement, the construction of a conception of justice requires precise accounts of (1) fair conditions for agreement and (2) genuine, free, and informed consent. Rawls presents definitive accounts of both of these elements of his theory in *A Theory of Justice*, and commentators have generally assumed that Rawls models the decision procedure that incorporates these elements – the original position – directly upon the categorical imperative procedure. An examination of the development of the Kantian theme of social contract in Rawls's early articles, however, contradicts this standard view. Rawls develops his constructivist approach to justification by working directly from Kant's theory of social contract and only later takes note of the relation between his account and the categorical imperative procedure.

Rawls first offers an account of a contractarian approach to justification in "Justice as Fairness." In this paper, Rawls argues that the choice of acceptable principles of justice may be viewed as the product of willing agreement among rational agents under conditions that meet "the standards which parties could accept as fair" (JF 63). Rawls develops the idea by discussing a hypothetical account of deliberation about justice among rational agents whose allegiance to their existing practices is grounded in the role of those practices in securing their rational advantage (JF 56–60). In the process of deliberation, participants propose principles of justice to regulate current disputes in which they are engaged. A proposed principle becomes binding only of it is acceptable to all participants, and an accepted principle binds all members of society in all relevantly similar future cases. While the participants are thus fully informed regarding their situated interests, Rawls designs the choice situation to prevent cases in which some parties may be "taken advantage of, or forced to give in to claims which they do not view as legitimate" (JF 59) by requiring that (1) all participants must consent to a principle before it can be accepted and (2) all accepted principles must apply to all persons in precisely the same way.

As in Rawls's later account of the original position, the circumstances of choice are designed to be fair and, in particular, to eliminate bargaining advantage from the factors affecting the choice of principles. It is important, however, to note that Rawls's initial employment of the social contract notion does not lead him to suggest the idea of a hypothetical decision procedure similar to the categorical imperative procedure. Rather, Rawls develops the idea of social contract through an account of quasi-historical deliberation among members of a society "among whom a certain system of practices is *already* well established" (JF 52). Unlike choosers in the original position, participants retain full knowledge of their situated interests, such as social position and wealth. While the process is well designed to motivate choosers to avoid the choice of principles that *explicitly* discriminate against persons or groups, the process is not structured in a way that guards against the possible adoption of rules or principles with concealed differential impacts. Thus, Rawls's sketch of deliberations about justice in "Justice as Fairness" presents the notion of social contract as a regulative idea to guide the judgment of situated participants in the legislative process, but does not develop the idea as the basis for (1) a decision process that embodies the value of impartiality or (2) a hypothetical decision procedure.

In papers published between 1958 and 1967, Rawls relies upon this contractarian account of rational choice under fair circumstances as his model of just deliberation about principles of justice.[12] In "Distributive Justice," however, Rawls significantly extends his account of the theory of social contract, which he continues to describe as the "natural alternative to utilitarianism."[13] In particular, Rawls develops a precise account of the fair choice position under which acceptable principles of justice may be jointly chosen by free rational persons. This position, Rawls now states, is an "original position of equality" in which "no one knows his position in society, nor even his place in the distribution of natural talents and abilities."[14] In this choice position, "[a] veil of ignorance prevents anyone from being advantaged or disadvantaged by the contingencies of social class and fortune" (DJ 132). In "Distributive Justice," then, Rawls develops the procedural implications of his understanding of social contract doctrine. While Rawls's account of a fair choice position in this paper corresponds closely to his definitive view of the original position in *A Theory of Justice*, however, "Distributive Justice" still provides an account of the conditions under which the choice of principles of justice may be viewed as the product of a quasi-historical agreement, and not as the product of a purely hypothetical decision procedure.

Finally, in *A Theory of Justice*, Rawls further refines his account by eliminating the notion of a quasi-historical agreement. Rawls retains from "Distributive Justice" his account of the informational constraint imposed by the veil of ignorance, but describes the account of choice subject to that constraint as entirely hypothetical. Thus, Rawls's account of the original position emerges as an interpretation of Kant's idea of *social contract* and does not constitute an attempt to apply the categorical imperative to social problems.

Social Contract and Reflective Equilibrium

While the account of a fair choice position in "Distributive Justice" develops the Kantian contractarian strand in Rawls's argument, this account of a choice position grounded in an interpretation of the idea of social contract also provides a basis for the extension of the non-Kantian strand of Rawls's account of justification in ethics developed in "Outline of a Decision Procedure for Ethics." As noted above, that paper argues for a specific criterion for assessing the validity of moral judgments that is clearly related to Rawls's account of reflective equilibrium in *A Theory of Justice*. In both accounts, considered judgments constitute the raw material of valid moral judgments, and a valid judgment employs this raw material in a carefully specified process that is designed to eliminate – as far as possible – the usual sources of error and distortion in moral reasoning.

One essential element of Rawls's later approach is, however, not present in the earlier account of moral reflection. In the later approach, moral agents generate an account of the "significant bounds" that their considered judgments of justice, taken together, "impose...on acceptable principles of justice" (TJ 16), and these bounds are represented in the features of the original position. Once an acceptable account of the original position is specified, the parties (1) select acceptable principles of justice from that standpoint, (2) compare the judgments required by these principles in particular cases to those required by their more specific considered judgments, and (3) refine both their principles and their judgments until these produce the same results when applied. Rawls describes the point at which their principles and judgments coincide as *reflective equilibrium*.

The process of achieving reflective equilibrium imposes two conditions that refine both the set of considered judgments and principles: (1) the set of considered judgments must be consistent among themselves and (2) the set of considered judgments must be consistent with principles that "extend them in an acceptable way" (TJ 17). The second of these conditions imposes a significant constraint on the set of acceptable principles – such principles must specify grounds justifying the original set of considered judgments that are sufficiently general to support moral judgments that *extend* that original set of considered judgments. This condition is not imposed by the decision procedure of "Outline of a Decision Procedure for Ethics." The process of achieving reflective equilibrium thus provides Rawls's later account of justification in ethics with significant critical leverage that is lacking in his earlier account. It is the incorporation of the account of a choice position grounded in an interpretation of the idea of social contract, along with his account of the process through which the choice position is derived and justified, that provides Rawls's later approach to justification in ethics with this critical leverage. Rawls's interpretation of Kant's theory of social contract thus provides Rawls with one of the central features of his account of reflective equilibrium.

Social Contract and the Kantian Conception of the Person

The distinguishing feature of the fair choice position employed in Kantian constructivism, Rawls states, is its specification of "a particular conception of the person as an element of [the] reasonable procedure" that determines the choice of principles (KC 304). Thus, it is not the structure of the procedure itself, but rather the relation between that structure and a Kantian conception of the person, that is most fundamental to Kantian constructivism. While Rawls does not set out an explicit textual basis for this characterization of the Kantian conception of the person, Kant's political and moral theory provides support for Rawls's characterization.

Rawls's account of the Kantian conception of the person takes as its foundation the fundamental qualities attributed to the person as a citizen in Kant's political philosophy. In the "Theory and Practice" essay, Kant asserts that a state that is in conformity with right must be founded on a view of persons as free, equal, and independent (Kant 1996: 290–91 TP 290–91, see Kant, 1996, pp. 393–94; R 237). Persons are viewed as *free* in the sense that each may "seek his happiness in the way that seems good to him" (Kant, 1996, p. 291; TP 290), as *equal* in their authority to exercise coercive rights against one another, and as *independent* in their authority as co-legislators (Kant, 1996, pp. 294–96; TP 8.294–96). Rawls's view of the senses of *freedom* and *equality* that must be embodied in an acceptable decision procedure follows Kant fairly closely, while Rawls incorporates *independence* into his notion of freedom. Freedom, in Rawls's account, refers to the status of members of society as "self-originating sources of claims" (KC 334); equality refers to the fact that each member "has the same rights and powers"; and "freedom as independence" refers to the grounds that persons have to consent to legislation under the informational constraints of the original position (KC 335).

The third and fourth qualities that Rawls incorporates in the Kantian conception of the person – the abilities to act reasonably and rationally – Rawls draws from the *Groundwork*. Rawls employs the terms *reasonable* and *rational* to characterize the two forms of practical reason, pure and empirical. An employment of practical reason is *reasonable* if it reflects "willing[ness] to listen to and consider the reasons offered by others" and *rational* if it reflects the pursuit of rational advantage. The distinction, Rawls suggests, reflects Kant's distinction between pure and empirical reason as reflected in the distinction between categorical and hypothetical imperatives.[15] The terms reasonable and rational, Rawls suggests, reflect the most fundamental forms of the employment of practical reason and therefore reflect the two fundamental qualities that, in Kant's view, characterize persons as moral beings.

A Kantian conception of the person thus views the person as characterized by four qualities: (1) the rational, (2) the reasonable, (3) freedom, and (4) equality (KC 306). Each of these qualities is represented as a structural feature of the decision procedure. The *rational*, which "expresses a conception of each participant's rational advantage" (KC 316), is – Rawls claims – straightforward, and is represented simply by the motivations assigned to parties in the original position – their desire to advance their conception of the good and to develop and exercise their moral powers (KC 336). *The reasonable* is defined as the willingness to act from fair terms of cooperation and the ideal of reciprocity and mutuality implicit in those fair terms, and is represented by "the framework of constraints" within which the parties deliberate (KC 317). The *freedom* of moral persons is represented by several features of the decision procedure, the most significant of which is the fact that the choices of the deliberators are not restricted by any background view limiting permissible conceptions of the good (KC 331). The *equality* of moral persons is represented by two features of the original position: (1) all persons are situated symmetrically with respect to each other – none are assigned superior rights or powers (KC 336) – and (2) the veil of ignorance prevents any person from appealing to superiority in their share of natural or social endowments to justify proposed principles (KC 337–38).

Thus, in Kantian constructivism, the particular principles that give content to Kant's moral view are viewed as specified by a decision procedure that is designed to represent the four qualities that constitute the Kantian conception of the person. In modeling these four qualities, the decision procedure thus gives concrete expression to the Kantian intuition that reliable moral judgments are grounded neither in facts nor in independent and preexisting norms or principles, but rather in a process of reasoning, by establishing the relation that Rawls requires between a Kantian conception of the person and the procedure that defines the content of a Kantian moral view.

Constructivism, Facts, and Social Practices

In Rawls's account of ethical constructivism, then, the structure of the decision procedure is designed to represent structural features of a process of moral reasoning that is grounded, not in independently existing normative entities or facts, but rather in a process of reasoning. G. A. Cohen and Aaron James, however, argue that the structure represented in that procedure – as that procedure is described in *A Theory of Justice* – *does* assign authority in moral judgment to independently existing normative entities or facts. Both arguments, in fact, attempt to establish that Rawls's ethical constructivism is fact-sensitive *at the foundational level*; and both arguments necessarily fail because the structure of the original position ensures that Rawls's constructivist argument cannot be fact-sensitive at the foundational level. In this section, I (1) argue that both arguments offer confused readings of Rawls's account of ethical constructivism and (2) justify the claim that Rawls's ethical constructivism *cannot* be fact-sensitive at the foundational level.

Facts and Fact-Dependent Principles

Cohen argues that constructivist approaches in general derive principles of justice from "considerations of pure non-justice," considerations that include both "facts about human nature and society," and judgments "about the right procedure for generating principles of justice."[16] As a result, Cohen claims, constructivism deletes considerations of pure justice – the considerations that should be central to judgments of justice – from the set of factors relevant to the derivation of principles of social justice and, instead, attempts to derive those principles from "considerations that do not reflect the content of justice."[17]

Rawls's particular account of constructivism, Cohen claims, grounds its arguments in facts both directly and indirectly. That is, Rawls includes specific facts about human nature and society among the considerations that are considered relevant to the grounding of principles of justice and, in addition, Rawls's arguments appeal to the authority of fact-dependent principles (e.g., the Pareto Principle, the principle of publicity). Because of these aspects of his constructivist method, Cohen concludes, Rawls's account of justice does "not (really) investigat[e] the nature of justice as such"[18] and "systematically conflat[es] other questions with the question of justice."[19]

A number of commentators have accepted Cohen's claim that Rawls's constructivist approach grounds principles of justice in facts or fact-dependent principles, while disputing Cohen's claim that fundamental principles of justice *must* be derived considerations of pure justice.[20] Although many of these arguments are persuasive, these commentators nevertheless concede too much to Cohen's critique of Rawls. In fact, the *constructivist* strand of Rawls's argument does *not* ground its principles in facts or fact-dependent principles as Cohen suggests. To the extent that the facts and fact-dependent principles that Cohen cites are relevant to Rawls's justification of his theory, these considerations are employed only in Rawls's *intuitive* argument for the principles of justice, an argument that is separate and entirely distinct from his constructivist argument.[21]

Although Cohen mentions a number of specific facts that he claims ground judgments in Rawls's constructivist argument, he seems most concerned to criticize the role that he claims that *fact-dependent principles* play in Rawls's constructivist approach. Cohen discusses the role of three fact-dependent principles – the Pareto Principle, the principle of stability, and the principle of publicity – in Rawls's argument,[22] and focuses most particularly on the role of the Pareto Principle. In fact, Cohen's concerns regarding the role of the Pareto Principle emerge as a central theme of his final book, *Rescuing Justice & Equality*. Reliance upon arguments grounded in the Pareto Principle, Cohen claims, introduces both theoretical and practical problems into Rawls's argument. As a practical matter, endorsement of the Pareto Principle-based argument that inequalities are acceptable as part of a scheme that makes everyone better off (Cohen calls this argument the "Pareto argument"[23]) provides at least indirect support for regressive policies such as the tax cuts of the Thatcher, Reagan, and Bush administrations.[24] In addition, Cohen argues, Rawls's reliance upon the logic of the Pareto Principle generates serious theoretical problems. First, the Pareto argument introduces inconsistency into Rawls's theory, since the morally arbitrary inequality that is justifiable under the Pareto argument for the difference principle "contradicts the content of that very principle."[25] Second, reliance upon the Pareto argument renders the case for the difference principle "incoherent," as Brian Barry's defense of inequality under the difference principle as a "necessary *evil*" indicates.[26]

Remarkably, however, despite Cohen's strenuous criticism of Rawls's reliance upon the Pareto Principle in his constructivist argument, the Pareto Principle plays no role in that argument. In *A Theory of Justice*, Rawls develops two distinct arguments justifying his proposed principles of justice. In Chapter 2, Rawls develops an *intuitive* argument for the principles that makes no use of the idea of the original position and argues directly from substantive considered judgments of justice. It might be at least plausible to describe the justification of the difference principle developed in Chapter 2 as relying upon the Pareto Principle, but the argument developed in Chapter 2 is explicitly not a constructivist argument. In the *constructivist* case for the principles presented in Chapter 3, Rawls offers two arguments for the principles, neither of which relies upon the Pareto Principle. In the first argument, Rawls claims that rational choosers in the original position would select his proposed principles because those principles guarantee protections of fundamental liberties that are more satisfactory than those provided under any viable alternative theory (and therefore minimize the strains of commitment). In particular, the principles provide satisfactory protection of liberty interests by securing their *priority* over all other fundamental interests (TJ 154). Second, Rawls argues that the principles guarantee protections of the interest in a *fair* distribution of shares of social goods that are more satisfactory than under alternative theories by "manifest[ing] in the basic structure of society men's desire to treat one another...as ends in themselves" (TJ 156), thus securing for less-advantaged members of society a larger share of the primary good of self-respect than under alternate conceptions of justice (TJ 157–58). It is important to emphasize that neither of these arguments relies upon the Pareto argument. These arguments for the principles offer a *characterization* of the principles' adequacy in addressing fundamental interests and *not* a *description* of their sufficiency in making people better off. Cohen's argument that Rawls's constructivist argument relies upon the Pareto argument therefore fails.

In Chapter 2 of *Rescuing Justice & Equality*, Cohen himself appears to concede this point: "the Pareto argument...is not Rawls's official argument for the difference principle, since the Pareto argument *dispenses with the device of the original position.*"[27] Since Rawls's constructivist argument is *essentially* characterized by its employment of the original position, Cohen's concession that the Pareto argument and the original position are not employed in the same argument is equivalent to a concession that Rawls does not rely upon the Pareto argument in his constructivist argument. In Chapter 7, however, Cohen seems not to recall this insight. In that chapter, he simply – and without further argument – lists the Pareto Principle among the three fact-dependent principles that improperly affect Rawls's *constructivist* argument.

Cohen's arguments for the claims that Rawls's constructivist argument is dependent upon the fact-sensitive "principles" of *publicity* and *stability* are even less persuasive. Cohen's case that Rawls's argument is dependent upon a fact-sensitive principle of publicity fails both because Cohen describes the notion of publicity that is relevant to Rawls's argument incorrectly and because Cohen misunderstands that notion's status in Rawls's argument. Cohen describes the principle of publicity employed in Rawls's argument as requiring "that it should be possible to tell whether or not someone is observing a principle."[28] Rawls, however, presents the idea of publicity as a "formal constraint of the concept of right," not a principle, and he defines this constraint to require that (1) "everyone will know about [the proposed principles of justice] all that he would know if their acceptance were the result of agreement" and that (2) "the parties evaluate conceptions of justice as publicly acknowledged" (TJ 115). Once the relevant sense of publicity has been defined correctly, it is clear that publicity does not constitute a ground from which the principles of justice are derived, as Cohen claims. Rather, the formal constraint of publicity merely imposes a *condition* that the justification of the principles must satisfy. In particular, that justification must not rely on "secret reservation[s]" (TJ 115n8) or deceptions and must present reasons that all reasonable persons could acknowledge and accept. The constraint of publicity thus (1) imposes a merely formal condition on an acceptable justification for a principle of justice and (2) is not fact-sensitive.[29] Cohen's claim that a fact-dependent principle of publicity improperly grounds Rawls's argument for the principles thus fails.

Cohen defines the fact-sensitive *principle of stability* to require that "principles governing society should be self-reproducing."[30] Although Rawls does not refer to a *principle* of stability, he does argue that stability is an important consideration in reflection about the basic requirements of justice. In arguing that a conception of justice must be stable, Rawls means that the principles of justice "should be such that when they are embodied in the basic structure of society men...develop a desire to act in accordance with its principles" (TJ 119). Rawls does not, however, argue that principles should be designed to secure citizens' *unreflective* acceptance as Cohen seems to suggest. Rather, Rawls's concern once again relates to the kinds of reasons that may ground acceptance of principles of justice. The concern with stability is simply the concern that an acceptable conception of justice must be justified on the basis of reasons that can be accepted by all reasonable persons as reasonable. Once again, the "principle" that Cohen discusses is merely a formal constraint on the nature of an acceptable justification for an account of justice, and not a substantive and fact-sensitive ground from which the principles are derived. Cohen's argument regarding the principle of stability therefore fails.

What about the specific facts that Cohen argues count among the grounds of Rawls's constructivist argument? Cohen seems most concerned to emphasize the influence of two factual claims on Rawls's argument: (1) well-regulated market economies can function without generating too much inequality and (2) people require certain essential goods in order to pursue their life plans.[31] Once again, however, Cohen grounds his criticisms in considerations that may plausibly be viewed as relevant to Rawls's intuitive argument, but not to his constructivist argument. As noted above, in the arguments that constitute the "main grounds" of the *constructivist* case for the two principles, Rawls asserts that the principles (1) provide protections for liberty interests that are more satisfactory than those provided by any viable alternative principles of justice (by assigning absolute priority to the protection of fundamental liberty interests) and (2) provide protections for the interest in a *fair* distribution of shares of social goods that are more satisfactory than those provided by any viable alternative principles of justice (by ensuring that society's basic structure "manifests...men's desire to treat one another...as ends in themselves"; TJ 156). Neither of these arguments depends upon assumptions regarding the functioning of well-regulated market economies or the notion that people require certain essential goods to pursue their life plans effectively.

Rawls's constructivist argument is grounded neither in facts nor in fact-dependent principles. Rather, that argument focuses narrowly on the question of what principles free and equal rational persons, choosing from a fair standpoint, would view as providing satisfactory protections for their fundamental interests. This specific focus reflects the influence on Rawls of the Kantian intuition that the substance of morality is best understood as constructed by free and equal people under fair conditions. Cohen's confusion regarding the character of Rawls's argument thus reflects a failure to recognize the central role of this Kantian intuition in Rawls's theory.

Existing Social Practices

Like Cohen, James argues that Rawls's account of constructivism does not succeed in providing an account of moral and political judgment that is grounded in *a process of reasoning* rather than in facts or in fact-dependent premises. James argues that Rawls's account of constructivism in fact grounds the authority of moral reasoning in independent judgments about the nature and point of existing social practices. The authority of judgments regarding the purposes of distinct social practices in Rawls's account of moral reasoning, James argues, helps to explain why Rawls's account of domestic justice focuses on what is owed to *persons* while his account of justice in the global setting focuses on what is owed to *peoples*. In each setting, James argues, Rawls grounds his reasoning in judgments about the nature of existing practices and the agents who participate in them.

Rawls's constructivist method, James suggests, has been fundamentally misunderstood. Rather than working from freestanding considered judgments of justice to the description of a standpoint from which moral reasoning has independent and absolute authority, Rawls has instead "been following a single, abstract 'constructive' method, which begins from existing social practices."[32] Rawls's method has involved identifying social practices and their participants, specifying the practice's point or goal, representing participants as appropriately motivated by "an interest in the goods that the practice is designed to create," and designing a veil of ignorance that provides *all* parties with the same information but *no* parties with information that could undermine the fairness of any agreements reached.[33] Once we recognize that this description fits Rawls's approach, James notes, it will be clear that "original position reasoning has no authority as such; it must be grounded in independent judgments about what practices exist and what kinds of agents participate in them."[34] Moreover, since Rawls – in James's view – offers his theory as "an interpretive characterization of our basic structures," his arguments cannot properly make "any direct appeal to moral considerations."[35]

While James's account of constructivism as the constructive interpretation of social practices is of some interest on its own merits, that account cannot plausibly be described as an interpretation of Rawls's constructivism. Three claims are central to James's interpretation of Rawls's approach: (1) Rawls's constructivism limits the grounds of moral and political reflection to independent judgments about existing social practices, (2) Rawls's approach can make no direct appeals to moral considerations, and (3) original position reasoning possesses no authority independent of judgments about existing practices and participants in those practices. None of these claims, I argue, is consistent with Rawls's account of his approach to constructivism.

Arguments from Existing Practices

James is correct to note that persons engaged in reflection regarding moral and political questions will, in Rawls's account, include among the considerations most fundamental to their deliberations considered judgments regarding the nature and internal logic of their social practices. While reflection does *begin* with a set of ideas that focuses on such practices, however, Rawls does not argue that reflection should be limited to arguments grounded in this set, nor is reflection limited to appeals to *any* set of judgments relating to the background political culture.[36] Persons reflecting on moral and political questions, Rawls argues, properly *assess and revise* any and all notions received from their tradition.[37] Each person "look[s] to the public culture as the shared fund of implicitly recognized basic ideas and principles"; *but* in order "to be acceptable," our judgments of justice must accord, not with some description or sympathetic reconstruction of the nature and goals of shared practices, but "with our considered convictions, at all levels of generality, on due reflection...[in] 'reflective equilibrium'" (PL 8). And in due reflection, Rawls argues that the person must consider "*all possible descriptions* to which one might plausibly conform one's judgments" (TJ 43, my emphasis), and should take note of "alternate conceptions of justice and the force of various arguments for them" (PL 384n6). Rawls thus explicitly rejects the claim that the grounds of moral and political reasoning are limited to information regarding existing practices and their participants.

Appeals to Moral Considerations

James claims that Rawls's constructivism precludes direct appeals to moral considerations in grounding moral or political judgments. This claim, however, confuses the terms of debate in the original position with the standards of justification in Rawls's constructivism. It is certainly true that Rawls rules out moral considerations as grounds for judgments *by the choosers in the original position*. The choosers "decide solely on the basis of what seems best calculated to further their interests" (TJ 512). But this limitation on grounds for judgment merely reflects a division of labor designed to clarify the functions of various elements of Rawls's decision procedure: "[i]t is...to preserve [clarity between the differing ethical considerations relevant to choice] that I have avoided attributing to the parties [in the original position] any ethical motivation" (TJ 512).

The original position *itself* is in fact designed to represent fundamental *moral* considered judgments regarding the conditions under which judgments about fundamental questions of justice should be formed. The veil of ignorance represents the considered judgments that (1) considerations that are "irrelevant from the standpoint of justice" (TJ 17) should not determine the distribution of social goods and that (2) "it should be impossible to tailor principles of justice to the circumstances of one's own case" (TJ 16); the veto that each chooser possesses over any proposed principle represents the considered judgment that justice must respect the inviolability of the person (TJ 3); and the symmetrical situation of the choosers represents the considered judgment that the substance of morality is best understood as constructed by free and equal people under fair conditions. As Rawls notes, the design of the original position "includes moral features and must do so" (TJ 512). While the judgments of the choosers in the original position do not appeal to moral considerations, then, the judgments that ground acceptance of the original position as the preferred standpoint from which to judge questions of justice appeal directly to moral considerations, and judgments that are the product of original position reasoning are therefore grounded directly in moral propositions that are embodied in the original position's structure and not merely in norms associated

94   *Rawls and Ethical Constructivism*

with existing practices. James's argument that Rawls's constructivism precludes direct appeals to moral considerations therefore fails.

Authority Independent of Judgments about Existing Practices

James argues that original position reasoning possesses no authority independent of judgments about existing practices and participants in those practices. This claim, however, assumes the correctness of James's argument that Rawls's constructivism limits the grounds of moral and political reflection to independent judgments about existing social practices. If, as I have argued above, the grounds of moral judgment in Rawls cannot plausibly be viewed as limited to independent judgments about existing social practices, then the grounds of moral judgment constitute the entire set of considered judgments relevant to justice, and the authority of many judgments formed in the original position derive from their grounding in relevant considerations contained in this set that are not judgments about social practices. Note, moreover, that Rawls's argument for the authority of the Law of Peoples demonstrates that Rawls must reject James's claim about the limited authority of original position reasoning, since (a) Rawls argues that judgments formed in a suitably tailored original position should be viewed as authoritative transculturally by all reasonable or decent peoples and (2) Rawls assumes that the members of the set of reasonable or decent peoples do not share common practices. If the authority of original position reasoning were limited as James suggests, the Law of Peoples could not exercise authority for more than a single people. Thus, James's argument regarding the authority of original position reasoning is clearly inconsistent with Rawls's understanding of the scope of the authority of original position reasoning.

Conclusion

I want to conclude this section by justifying the claim that the arguments offered by Cohen and James *must* fail, because justifications generated from the standpoint of the original position cannot be dependent on facts or fact-sensitive principles at the foundational level. As discussed above, the structure of the original position is designed to embody four foundational considered judgments: (1) "it should be impossible to tailor principles of justice to the circumstances of one's own case" (TJ 16); (2) principles of justice may not be justified on the basis of considerations that are "irrelevant from the standpoint of justice" (TJ 17) or "arbitrary from the moral point of view" (TJ 63); (3) each person possesses an inviolability founded on justice (TJ 3); and (4) the substance of morality is best understood as constructed by free and equal people under fair conditions. Four *fact-insensitive* principles associated with these considered judgments – (1) justice must be impartial, (2) justice must not be arbitrary, (3) justice must respect the inviolability of the person, and (4) principles of justice should correspond to the principles that would be chosen by reasonable and rational persons under conditions that characterize them as free and equal – are embodied in structural features of the original position (e.g., the veil of ignorance, the symmetrical positions of the choosers, the veto that each chooser may exercise over proposed principles) and ground every argument made from that standpoint. If a judgment can be reached in the original position, it is because that judgment constitutes a practical implication or extension of one or more of these foundational and *fact-independent* principles.

Cohen argues that a principle of justice can respond to a fact only because it is also a response to a principle that is not a fact or a fact-sensitive principle. But this is precisely the case in the original position – any consideration that is relevant to the justification of principles of justice in the original position is relevant precisely because at least one of the four foundational fact-independent principles embodied in its structure justifies the view that that consideration is relevant; and if the principles of justice respond to any facts in the original position, that response is also a response to one of the fact-independent principles embodied in the structure of the original position.

Facts, fact-sensitive principles, and practices may be centrally relevant to the *intuitive* argument for the principles of justice, but the structure of the original position ensures that the justification of the constructivist argument cannot be dependent upon such facts, fact-sensitive principles, or practices at the foundational level. Since both Cohen and James offer interpretations of the *constructivist* argument, their claims that Rawls's argument is dependent at the foundational level on facts, fact-sensitive principles, and/or practices therefore *necessarily* fail.

Kantian Objections

While Rawls argues that the central role that his account of constructivism assigns to a decision procedure constitutes a procedural interpretation of Kant's ideas regarding moral reasoning and autonomy, a number of commentators – in particular, Larry Krasnoff[38] and Onora O'Neill[39] – have raised important objections to this claim. In particular, these commentators argue, Kant's account of moral reasoning employing the categorical imperative fails to "fit well"[40] with the central features of Rawls's account of constructivism. First, the categorical imperative does not enable moral reasoners to generate moral principles; rather, it serves as a "negative check" on the maxims of action that individuals assess in moral deliberation. Second, Rawls's decision procedure imposes more stringent restrictions on the scope of ethical concern than Kant's procedure requires. Finally, the categorical imperative does not model hypothetical choice; rather, it tests whether all persons could *possibly* choose to act from a particular maxim or principle of volition.

These objections, I will argue, fail. While Rawls's critics in fact exaggerate the distinctions between the two decision procedures, these objections are unpersuasive primarily because they argue from the incorrect assumption that Rawls presents his decision procedure as equivalent to the categorical imperative procedure. Rawls makes no such claim – his account of constructivism is Kantian, he argues, because it develops Kant's view that the substance of morality is best understood as constructed by free and equal people under fair conditions.

The Choice of Principles?

While the categorical imperative serves merely as a negative check on the person's specific maxims or principles of volition, Krasnoff[41] and O'Neill[42] argue, the original position is designed to enable the parties to generate new and general moral principles.[43] Rawls's decision procedure thus performs a task that is both more ambitious and less specifically practical than that performed by the categorical imperative. The output of Rawls's procedure is, these critics conclude, distinguishable from that of the categorical imperative procedure in two important respects. Principles generated in the original position (1) apply to a broader range of problems than maxims endorsed through the categorical imperative procedure and (2) are newly constructed, rather than merely endorsed from a rational standpoint.

First, it is important to note that this objection exaggerates the distinctions between the two procedures. While the categorical imperative procedure generally focuses on specific practical maxims that require specific acts or omissions, its proper employment is not limited to such maxims. The most common instances analyzed under Kant's procedure involve maxims connected with specific moral choices, but Kant also discusses cases in which application of the categorical imperative procedure requires that the person adopt wide duties (duties to adopt an end). Thus, for example, Kant discusses applications of the categorical imperative requiring that the moral person must recognize wide duties to develop her talents and to adopt the happiness of others as her own end (Kant, 1996, p. 81, G 4.430; Kant, 1996, p. 518, DV 6.387). These wide duties cannot, by definition, be satisfied by specific acts; rather, they require that the agent adopt general policies designed to further the respective ends of one's own perfection and the happiness of others. Rawls's decision procedure, then, does not necessarily focus on problems that are different in character from those examined by moral reasoners employing the categorical imperative procedure.

In addition, deliberations in the original position do not – as this objection suggests – generate fresh and newly minted moral principles. Rather, just as individuals applying the categorical imperative procedure consider and assess candidate maxims and principles of volition, parties in the original position consider and assess candidate principles. Rawls discusses "the presentation of alternatives" explicitly in Chapter 3 of *A Theory of Justice* (TJ 105–9). Ideally, Rawls states, "one would like to say that [the parties] are to choose among all possible conceptions of justice" (TJ 105). For the purposes of the exposition of his argument, however, Rawls "resort[s] to the ... device" (TJ 105) of listing the leading traditional views for consideration by the parties. While not exhaustive of all theoretical possibilities, the list includes utilitarian, perfectionist, intuitionist, egoist, and mixed (utilitarian and liberal), conceptions, as well as justice as fairness. The parties choose from among the sets of principles that define these conceptions. An argument for any candidate set of principles, Rawls argues, "is always relative to some list of alternatives" (TJ 109), and the best way to identify alternatives that are of "philosophical interest" is to examine traditional conceptions.

Most significantly, however, Rawls does not claim that the original position is formally or substantively equivalent to the categorical imperative procedure. Rather, Rawls argues that his procedure represents the "clearly discernible" *character* of Kant's moral theory by "enabl[ing] us to explain the sense in which acting from principles expresses our nature as free and equal rational persons" (TJ 226–27). As discussed in the second section, Rawls argues that it is not the structure of the procedure itself, but rather the relation between that structure and a Kantian conception of the person, that is most fundamental to Kantian constructivism. A Kantian conception of the person views the person as characterized by four qualities (the rational, the reasonable; freedom, equality), and each of these qualities is represented as a structural feature of the decision procedure.

Rawls, moreover, explicitly contrasts the distinctly social focus of his employment of Kantian constructivism in *A Theory of Justice* with the ethical focus of the categorical imperative. Kant, Rawls notes, "proceeds from the particular, even personal, case of everyday life; he assumed that this process carried out correctly would eventually yield a coherent and sufficiently complete system of principles." Rawls's employment of Kantian constructivism in *A Theory of Justice*, he concedes, "moves in quite the reverse pattern," aiming directly to identify acceptable principles to regulate the basic structure of a just society (KC 339). By modeling a Kantian conception of the person while reversing the direction of Kant's analysis, Rawls hopes to avoid the notorious difficulties associated with Kant's attempts to specify principles of social justice and an ideal of social life.[44]

The Scope of Ethical Concern

O'Neill, however, objects that it is precisely the social focus of Rawls's theory that distinguishes his approach to moral reasoning from Kant's moral thought. While Kant's constructivism conceives of human beings as merely "a plurality of agents lacking antecedent principles of coordination," Rawls's Kantian constructivism presents moral reasoners as citizens embedded within a particular political culture. The narrower focus of Rawls's constructivism restricts "the scope of ethical concern" to "a bounded liberal society." Thus while Kant's moral theory is cosmopolitan, Rawls's theory is "implicitly statist."[45]

It is important, however, to distinguish Rawls's argument for his conception of political justice from his account of Kantian constructivism. Kantian constructivism constitutes an approach to moral reasoning that defines a standard of justification that Rawls's theory of justice must itself satisfy. As Rawls emphasizes, his employment of Kantian constructivism in *A Theory of Justice* constitutes merely "one...variant" (KC 303) of that approach, a variant designed to focus moral judgment on questions of justice. Similarly, political liberalism constitutes merely a possible output of his constructivist approach to moral reasoning. It is in Rawls's arguments for political liberalism, and not in his general account of Kantian constructivism, that citizens are presented as embedded within a particular political culture. Political liberalism's narrower focus on the ethical concerns of "a bounded liberal society," then, does not represent a feature of Kantian constructivism as a method.

Moreover, in assuming that a form of decision procedure specifically designed to address social questions may be appropriate for examining the subset of moral issues relating to matters of social justice, Rawls follows Kant's approach to moral reasoning as O'Neill herself understands it. As O'Neill points out in *Acting on Principle*, Kant requires different forms of decision procedure to address different kinds of ethical problems, requiring different forms of the categorical imperative procedure, for example, to determine an act's moral and legal status.[46] O'Neill is at least potentially inconsistent, then, in arguing that Rawls's account of Kantian constructivism is unfaithful to Kant simply because Rawls's decision procedure is tailored to apply specifically to a distinctly social subset of moral issues.

Finally, it is important to note again that Rawls presents his decision procedure as a faithful interpretation of Kant's ethical thought, not because that decision procedure is equivalent to the categorical imperative procedure, but rather because it develops faithfully Kant's notion that the substance of morality is best understood as constructed by free and equal persons under fair conditions. Thus, O'Neill's objection, like the arguments of Cohen and James discussed in the third section, reflects a failure to appreciate the central significance in Rawls's argument of this Kantian intuition. Rawls's procedure constitutes an interpretation of this view because (1) the principles chosen are those that would be chosen by reasonable and rational persons under conditions that characterize them as free and equal, (2) the description of procedure "enables us to explain the sense in which acting from these principles expresses our nature as free and equal" (TJ 226), and (3) the employment of the procedure connects Kant's basic ideas concretely with human conduct.[47] The Kantian character of Rawls's constructivist procedure, as Rawls emphasizes, thus derives from its representation of "a certain conception of the person as free and equal [and] as capable of acting both reasonably and rationally" (KC 306), and not from the superficial similarity of the original position and the categorical imperative procedure.

Hypothetical or Possible Choice?

While Rawls's decision procedure asks what principles of justice could secure the hypothetical consent of rational and independent choosers, O'Neill argues, Kant's procedure asks whether all persons *could possibly* consent to proposed principles.[48] Krasnoff, who discusses and develops O'Neill's objection, therefore argues that a fundamental asymmetry exists between the original position and the categorical imperative procedure.[49] Rawls's procedure aims to identify a unique set of principles that would be the hypothetical choice of a designated set of deliberators, while Kant's procedure asks whether a particular principle could possibly be accepted by all persons who are actually to be subject to the authority of those principles.

This distinction is significant, O'Neill argues, because a theory employing a standard of hypothetical choice seems designed to identify principles that represent an equilibrium among the competing subjective interests of the choosing parties. A hypothetical agreement among the parties securing such an equilibrium, O'Neill claims, would simply represent the judgment that the principles chosen secured a balance of interests among the parties more effectively than the alternate candidates considered. O'Neill is particularly concerned that a theory employing a hypothetical consent standard would (1) justify the coercive enforcement of principles against people who do not *actually* consent and (2) allow the preferences and desires of the parties to play an inappropriate role in determining the content of a theory of justice.[50] A theory employing a standard of possible choice, in contrast, aims merely to avoid the adoption of principles or maxims that could not be accepted by persons who will be affected by the adoption of the principle or maxim. As O'Neill notes, Kant's argument against deceit, in the *Groundwork*, provides a paradigmatic example of a maxim to which an affected person could not consent.[51] If I act on a maxim of misleading a person in order to use her for my purposes, the person "cannot possibly agree with my way of behaving to him" (Kant 1996: 80; G 4.429–30). Under such a possible consent approach, both of O'Neill's concerns are addressed. First, principles to which others do not actually consent will not be adopted under a possible consent standard; and second, fundamental interests, rather than preferences and tastes, will determine the principles adopted under such an approach.

Once again, however, Rawls's critics exaggerate the significance of the distinction between these two standards. Persons deliberating about justice who adopt the perspective of the original position in order to focus their reflections are not aiming to secure equilibrium among competing subjective interests. Rather, such persons – in reflecting subject to the formal and substantive constraints that are imposed upon original position deliberations – are most accurately described as assessing the *possible* choice of the principles under consideration. The original position constraints – including the symmetrical position of the parties, the impossibility of appealing to the person's own situated interests, and the lack of information about the deliberator's own conception of the good – represent an undertaking to choose principles in the spirit of mutual respect and reciprocity. In choosing principles subject to these constraints, then, each deliberator may be viewed as asking herself: could the other members of society who will be affected by the principles under consideration *possibly* consent to their adoption? Thus, it is plausible to characterize deliberations in the original position, as well as deliberations employing the categorical imperative procedure, as testing proposed principles against a *possible consent* standard.

In fact, an argument of Thomas Hill's suggests that this conclusion should not surprise us because the distinction between possible and hypothetical consent "is not in itself deeply significant."[52] The standard of rationality that guides judgments regarding hypothetical consent, Hill argues, can be reformulated in terms of what rational agents could possibly consent to.

The rational standards on which the "could will" test relies can...be expressed in terms of what rational agents necessarily "would will if rational." Moreover...the prohibitions that hypothetical rational agents would will are just those that are rationally necessary for them to will, given their situation. Both formulas, then, presuppose as background some general standards of rational willing.[53]

Rawls's standard of hypothetical consent does not, Hill concludes, necessarily perform a role in moral reasoning materially different from or inconsistent with the role performed by Kant's standard of possible consent.

From Kantian Constructivism to Political Constructivism

In his later work on political liberalism, Rawls modifies his account of the form of constructivism that reasonable and rational persons would accept in reflective equilibrium. Rawls concludes that such persons would judge that *political* constructivism, rather than Kantian constructivism, constitutes the most acceptable method to determine the choice of principles of justice to regulate their basic political institutions. Two concerns motivate Rawls's modification of his account of constructivism. First, Rawls concludes that members of a society characterized by reasonable pluralism would not generally accept the Kantian conception of the person as the foundation of their moral judgments. Political constructivism, rather, employs a decision procedure that models intuitive ideas and considered judgments that are shared by citizens of a democratic society. The second concern relates to the status of judgments grounded in a constructivist approach. While political constructivism asserts that principles of political justice may be *represented* as the product of a decision procedure, this approach emphatically avoids the claim that such principles simply are the product of such a procedure. This emphasis is designed to address the concern that various conceptions of the good may (1) hold that principles of justice and morality are true and (2) state explicit criteria to determine the truth of claims of justice and morality. While persons holding such views would necessarily reject a form of constructivism that claimed that moral and political principles can only be the product of a constructivist approach, such persons could, Rawls argues, accept a form of constructivism that claimed merely that moral and political principles *may be represented* as the product of such an approach.

In revising his account of ethical constructivism, Rawls thus removes two central Kantian elements from his account. The decision procedure is no longer viewed as modeling the Kantian conception of the person; and the account of constructivism is no longer grounded in the Kantian assumption that moral principles simply are the products of the operation of practical reason. In continuing to *present* principles of justice as the product of a collective decision procedure whose structure models the operations of practical reason, however, Rawls's approach continues to develop the view that Kantian social contract constitutes "an ethical idea applicable to social arrangements irrespective of the question of origins" (TJ 223). While Rawls carefully redesigns his account of constructivism to avoid reliance upon any elements of Kant's comprehensive view, he thus retains two Kantian intuitions, which he assumes that reasonable persons who disagree about the good could nevertheless affirm on due reflection. First, he argues from the assumption that principles of justice are best represented as those principles that free and equal persons could jointly affirm under suitable conditions. Second, he continues to assume that moral judgments are best represented as the output of a procedure that models the requirements of practical reason. While political constructivism thus sets aside the Kantian view that moral judgments simply are the product of a process of reasoning, it continues to present such judgments as best viewed as the output of such a process.

Ironically, the account of moral reasoning that Rawls develops from these Kantian intuitions possesses a number of virtues that may provide the basis for realizing consensus, or at least reducing moral conflict, in societies characterized by a pluralistic diversity of moral views. First, political constructivism aims to clarify the structure of moral argument in order to ensure that moral reasoning is accessible to all persons. Second, this account of constructivism aims to ground moral and political reasoning in considered judgments that are consistent with the background (liberal) political tradition, and that are therefore widely shared among members of the culture. In particular, political constructivism avoids dependence upon premises rooted in particular comprehensive conceptions of the good. Finally, political constructivism employs a decision procedure that is designed to be acceptable to all reasonable persons on due reflection.

These qualities of political constructivism provide support for Rawls's claim that the view "articulate[s] . . . shared notions and principles" in order "to discover and formulate the deeper bases of agreement which one hopes are embedded" in our sense of justice or in elements of the political tradition (KC 306). If political constructivism does succeed in identifying bases of agreement among citizens who affirm plural and conflicting comprehensive conceptions of the good, then, Rawls's constructivism generates from Kantian intuitions a shared public point of view from which members of a society characterized by reasonable pluralism may evaluate and resolve basic questions of justice.

Conclusion: Constructivism and Justification

Rawls's account of Kantian constructivism develops and extends the implications of Kant's view that moral judgments are grounded neither in an independently existing order of values nor in special features of human psychology, but rather in a process of reasoning. Kantian intuitions thus lead Rawls to focus his moral analysis around the notion of a theory of social contract designed to secure reasonable and mutually justifiable social relations, and Rawls's development of the doctrine of social contract grounds his accounts of Kantian constructivism, reflective equilibrium, and justice as fairness.

Rawls's later work on political liberalism detaches his account of constructivism from Kant's conception of the person and develops the notion that a procedure that represents intuitive ideas and considered judgments that are shared by citizens of a democratic society can generate principles of justice that can constitute the focus of an overlapping consensus of reasonable views. Political constructivism nevertheless remains grounded in the Kantian intuitions – which Rawls assumes that reasonable persons who disagree regarding the good could nevertheless affirm on due reflection – that (1) principles of justice are best represented as those principles that free and equal persons could jointly affirm under fair choice conditions and that (2) moral judgments are best represented as the output of a procedure that models the requirements of practical reason. Rawls's work on constructivism thus reflects his continuing conviction that an approach based upon Kantian intuitions offers the most promising foundation for a theory that aims to provide the basis for realizing consensus, or at least reducing moral conflict, in societies characterized by a pluralistic diversity of moral views.

Notes

1 See Krasnoff (1999), p. 85.
2 See Cohen (2008), pp. 278–86.
3 Cohen (2008), p. 287.

4 Cohen (2008), p. 280.
5 James (2005), p. 282
6 Korsgaard (2008), p. 309.
7 Use of the term "intuition" here might seem inappropriate, since Rawls rejects intuitionism as a plausible approach to theorizing justice. While Rawls argues against intuitionism as an approach to political reasoning; however, he does not completely reject reliance upon intuition in moral or political judgment. Rather, he takes the position that "any conception of justice will have to rely on intuition to some degree" (TJ 36). In rejecting intuitionism, Rawls rejects only the view that "there exist no higher-order constructive criteria for determining the proper emphasis for the competing principles of justice" (TJ 30). Rawls explicitly states that his aim, in responding to intuitionist concerns, "is that of *reducing and not eliminating* entirely the reliance on intuitive judgments" (TJ 39, my emphasis).
8 Samuel Freeman provides a helpful discussion of intellectual influences on Rawls's account of justification. Freeman (2007), pp. 23–25.
9 This view of ethics, Rawls claims, is "perfectly clear in its Kantian formulation" (DJ 132).
10 "Kant's idea of autonomy requires that there exists no [independent] order of objects determining the moral duties among free and equal persons. Rawls (n.d.-b), p. 24. "Kant insists that a good will is not good because of . . . its fitness to some independently specified . . . end." Rawls (n.d.-b), p. 7.
11 References to and citations of Kant's work are given parenthetically in the text using the following abbreviations and citing the page numbers of the relevant volume of *Kants gesammelte Schriften* (published by the *Preussische Akademie der Wissenschaften*, Berlin). *Grounding of the Metaphysics of Morals* (G) (1785); *The Doctrine of Virtue (Tugendlehre)* (DV) (1797); *Rechtslehre* (R) (1797); "On the Common Saying: 'This May Be True in Theory, but it does not Apply in Practice'" (TP) (1793). I have used the translations of these works contained Mary J. Gregor (trans.), *The Cambridge Edition of the Works of Immanuel Kant: Practical Philosophy* (Cambridge: Cambridge University Press, 1996) (Kant, 1996). Citations in the text will set out (1) the page number in the *Cambridge Edition* (e.g., Kant, 1996, 55) followed by (2) the proper citation to the *Prussian Academy* edition (e.g., G 4.400).
12 See Rawls (1963a); Rawls (1963b); Rawls (1964), p. 123.
13 Rawls (1967), p. 131.
14 Rawls (1967), pp. 131–32.
15 Rawls (n.d.-b), p. 9.
16 Cohen (2008), p. 281.

17 Cohen (2008), p. 283.
18 Cohen (2008), p. 301.
19 Cohen (2008), p. 3.
20 See Barry (1989); Scheffler (2003).
21 Rawls's intuitive argument, presented in Chapter 2 of *A Theory of Justice*, develops a justification for the second principle of justice directly from substantive considered judgments of justice. This argument is not constructivist and makes no use of the original position.
22 Cohen (2008), pp. 285–86.
23 Cohen (2008), pp. 15–16.
24 Cohen (2008), pp. 27–30.
25 Cohen (2008), p. 156.
26 Cohen (2008), p. 113, my emphasis.
27 Cohen (2008), p. 88, my emphasis.
28 Cohen (2008), pp. 285–86.
29 Rawls, in fact, asserts that "[t]he publicity condition is clearly implicit in Kant's doctrine of the categorical imperative" (TJ 115).
30 Cohen (2008), p. 286.
31 Cohen (2008), p. 293.
32 James (2005), p. 282.
33 James (2005), p. 282.
34 James (2005), p. 282.
35 James (2005), p. 305.
36 "[T]here are no judgments on any level of generality that are in principle immune to revision." (Rawls 1975), p. 289.
37 "[W]e may [on reflection] reaffirm our particular judgments and decide instead to modify the proposed conception of justice with its principles and ideals...It is a mistake to think of abstract principles and general conceptions as always overriding our more particular judgments" (PL 45).
38 Krasnoff (1999).
39 O'Neill (1989).
40 Krasnoff (1999), p. 401.
41 Krasnoff (1999), p. 400.
42 O'Neill (1989).
43 "Kantian maxims do not entail...rules for all possible contexts." (O'Neill 1989), p. 117.
44 See Kaufman (1999) for an account of political judgment in Kant's later political writings.
45 O'Neill (2008), p. 362.
46 O'Neill (1975), pp. 74–75.

47 "No longer are these notions purely transcendent and lacking explicable connections with human conduct" (TJ 226).
48 O'Neill (1989), pp. 110–11, 216–17.
49 Krasnoff (1999), p. 401.
50 O'Neill (1989), p. 109.
51 O'Neill (1989), pp. 112–13.
52 Hill (2002), p. 65.
53 Hill (2002), p. 65.

4 | *A Satisfactory Minimum Conception of Justice*
Reconsidering Rawls's Maximin Argument

In *A Theory of Justice*, John Rawls argues that it is possible to describe an appropriate initial situation from which to form reliable judgments about questions of justice.[1] This initial situation, which Rawls calls the "original position," models the practical implications of fundamental and shared intuitions regarding justice, in particular intuitions concerning the role that considerations regarding fairness, impartiality, and the avoidance of arbitrariness should play in grounding judgments of justice. Once these intuitions are modeled faithfully, Rawls argues, the structure of the resulting choice problem dictates that rational persons occupying the original position should apply a maximin rule of choice in choosing principles of justice to regulate their joint social relations. As a result, the structure of the choice problem narrows the set of acceptable choices sufficiently to require the choice of a unique pair of principles. According to this argument (the "maximin" argument), then, the constitution of an account of justice may accurately be represented as a problem of rational choice under uncertainty. The maximin argument plays a central role in Rawls's justification of his account of justice in *A Theory of Justice*, and Rawls continued to emphasize the centrality of this argument to the justification of his theory throughout his discussions of the original position procedure, from the 1970s through his last published works.[2]

It is a striking irony that while *A Theory of Justice* is widely regarded as the most influential work of political philosophy of the last century, the maximin argument – which constitutes Rawls's most salient justification for the acceptance of his two principles of justice – has widely been dismissed as unpersuasive. This argument is often described, even by sympathetic interpreters, as "perhaps the single worst argument in *Theory*."[3] Indeed, as Rex Martin suggests, the credibility of Rawls's entire theoretical project has been undermined by his reliance upon the apparently unpersuasive logic of the maximin argument.[4]

The current unsympathetic view of the maximin argument is the product of a number of apparently devastating critiques published during the decade after the initial publication of *A Theory of Justice*. Rawls's argument, it was argued, relies upon an imprecise account of the satisfactory minimum to be secured under the maximin rule. In the absence of specific information regarding the minimum share of goods that the choosers may secure for themselves, Brian Barry argues, it is impossible to determine "whether ... maximizing the minimum is a good idea or not."[5] Moreover, critics claimed, the maximin rule is not the only or even the most attractive decision rule that is available to rational persons facing choice under extreme uncertainty. In particular, John Harsanyi argues that the appropriate decision rule for choice in the original position is the Bayesian expected-utility maximization rule.[6] The objections thus criticized both Rawls's analysis of the choice under uncertainty problem facing choosers in the original position and his choice of a decision rule to regulate that choice. As will be discussed below, these objections have strongly influenced the interpretations of Rawls offered by Ken Binmore, Daniel Hausman, Michael McPherson, John Roemer, Robert Taylor, and Philippe van Parijs, among others.[7] These objections have been particularly influential both because they were offered by leading rational choice theorists and because they appealed to assumptions widely shared among such theorists, such as the view that one decision rule – the Bayesian criterion – is uniquely appropriate to govern rational choice under uncertainty. While Rawls could respond persuasively that the particular nature of choice in the original position – involving both extreme uncertainty and a choice problem involving the selection of principles rather than goods – differed from the conditions that characterize standard problems in rational choice, criticism of the maximin argument on grounds persuasive to rational choice theorists seriously undermined its credibility.

These objections were formulated more than thirty years ago and have been more or less taken for granted since that time. I will argue, however, that the maximin argument is more robust than has generally been recognized and that this argument performs a number of important functions in clarifying the nature and implications of Rawls's argument for justice as fairness. First, Rawls's employment of the maximin rule as a central element of his argument for the two principles underlines the fact that justice as fairness is not an allocative theory designed to regulate the division of a collection of goods among definite individuals.[8] Rather than providing support for an account of justice that focuses on (1) securing an optimal distribution of expected utility or (2) maximizing the share of the least advantaged, the maximin argument "forc[es] us to consider what our fundamental interests really are" (JAF 99). Second, the maximin rule guides reflections in the original position regarding the choice of (1) standards to determine the acceptability of basic social institutions, *not* (2) guaranteed shares of objects or goods. Rawls's maximin justification of the principles of justice therefore develops, not an account of the *value* of goods or social surplus to be realized through application of the principles, but rather an account of the *reasons* that require the adoption of standards to regulate basic social institutions. Third, a conception of justice capable of satisfying the maximin rule must establish conditions that – taken as a whole – provide satisfactory protections for each person's fundamental interests. This focus on the realization of social conditions that secure protections for fundamental interests establishes a clear contrast between justice as fairness and consequentialist theories of justice that aim primarily to compensate persons for deficits in well-being. Finally, the maximin argument illustrates the potential of Rawls's ethical constructivism to identify structural features of moral questions that are not obvious from a merely discursive presentation of those questions. Once it is accepted that the original position constitutes the uniquely appropriate standpoint from which to form judgments of justice, Rawls argues, a careful consideration of the structure of the particular conditions of choice in the original position identifies the maximin rule as the uniquely appropriate decision rule to govern those judgments.

In order to develop my argument, I will first sketch Rawls's account of choice under uncertainty, emphasizing the structure of the choice problem that faces Rawls's hypothetical choosers. I will then examine the objection, developed by Brian Barry and Allen Buchanan, to Rawls's claim that a rational chooser in the original position will feel no need to secure advantages above a guaranteed satisfactory minimum. The objections presented by Barry and Buchanan that are discussed in this section constitute the most influential examples of the argument that the maximin argument relies upon an imprecise account of the satisfactory minimum to be secured under the maximin rule. I will reject the assumption – central to this objection – that the satisfactory minimum that persons employing the maximin rule seek to achieve is a minimum level of *primary goods*. Next, I will examine John Harsanyi's criticisms of the maximin choice criterion – the most influential example of the objection that the maximin rule is not the only or even the most attractive decision rule that is available to rational persons facing choice under extreme uncertainty. In response, I will argue that Rawls provides persuasive arguments for rejecting the view that the Bayesian criterion could be an acceptable criterion to guide choices of fundamental importance under conditions of complete uncertainty. Finally, I will argue that the application of the maximin rule under the specialized social contract conditions of the original position performs an important function in focusing deliberations on identifying the central concerns that an acceptable conception must address. Both this final argument and the discussion of Harsanyi's argument respond to the objection that the maximin rule is not the most attractive decision rule that is available to rational persons facing choice under extreme uncertainty.

The Maximin Argument

If we accept the claim that a just distribution of social goods should not be determined by "factors [that are] arbitrary from a moral point of view" (TJ 63), Rawls argues, then we will agree that deliberations regarding the nature and requirements of justice should be conducted from the standpoint of an original position in which information is not available regarding a society's (1) endowments of resources, (2) current level of wealth and economic development, and (3) distribution of wealth, income, and power. If, in addition, we accept the claim that persons should not be able to "tailor principles [of justice] to the circumstances of [their] own case" (TJ 16), Rawls argues, then we will agree that information regarding one's own situated interests should not be available. Rawls represents these informational constraints through the imposition of a veil of ignorance that deprives deliberators of information regarding (1) their society's wealth and level of development and (2) their situated interests – in particular, information regarding both *social* endowments, which include inherited wealth, social position and class advantages; and *natural* endowments, which include talents, abilities, intelligence, ambition, and other physical and psychological traits. In depriving the choosers of information regarding their endowments, the original position represents concretely the intuition that an appeal to the mere possession of an inherited trait or status does not provide a satisfactory justification for a claim to goods: justice should not, for example, reward people simply for being intelligent or talented, although it may reward the employment of those qualities (TJ 87–89).

In order to prevent all appeals to arbitrary factors in deliberations about justice in the original position, Rawls argues, the veil of ignorance must deprive persons not merely of knowledge regarding their specific endowments, but also of knowledge regarding the nature of the society they will occupy when they emerge from behind the veil. Otherwise, arbitrary particular facts regarding a society's level of development and wealth at a particular point in history might determine the parties' general judgments regarding the requirements of justice; and rational choosers pursuing their own interests would be likely to base their choice of principles on probabilistic assessments of the likely effects of the principles chosen on relative advantage.

Rawls argues that it is rational for persons facing such a constrained choice problem under uncertainty to employ a maximin rule of choice – a rule that instructs the chooser to select that option that secures the most "satisfactory minimum" state of affairs (TJ 133–35). While the maximin rule is not appropriate for all, or even most, choices under uncertainty (TJ 133), Rawls argues that it is the appropriate rule to regulate judgments behind the veil of ignorance because of three features of that choice position.[9] First, choosers in the original position would know nothing about the probabilities of possible outcomes. Second, Rawls argues that rational choosers in such a position will be more concerned to secure a satisfactory minimum than to secure the possibility of receiving greater advantages. If potential losses and gains are both unlimited, Rawls asserts, it is rational to be more concerned to avoid the worst possible outcomes than to insist upon preserving the possibility of the greatest possible gains. In particular, if the choosers are able to ensure that the minimum guarantee is an attractive one, they may feel little need to ensure the possibility of securing significantly greater advantages (TJ 135). Third, the choosers in such a position will insist upon ruling out completely certain unacceptable outcomes. If, for example, slavery is a real possibility – as it must be for persons behind a veil of ignorance – and if a person can eliminate that possibility *simply* by choosing a principle forbidding slavery; then, Rawls argues, any rational person would insist upon the choice of that principle.

It is important to emphasize that Rawls does not claim that choosers in the original position will seek to achieve the guarantee of a minimum income or bundle of primary goods. Rather, Rawls argues that the "satisfactory minimum" that choosers will attempt to secure constitutes "an adequate minimum conception of justice" – that is, the conception that provides the most satisfactory minimum guarantee of protections of their fundamental interests (TJ 153). In particular, Rawls argues, the choosers will choose a theory that (1) minimizes invasions of fundamental rights, (2) promotes equal opportunity to develop and exploit their talents, and (3) mitigates the inequalities that continue to exist in a social order that ensures equal opportunity.

The Nature of a Satisfactory Minimum

Brian Barry offers an influential objection to this argument that was later elaborated by Allen Buchanan. Barry and Buchanan object to the claim that a rational chooser in the original position will feel no need to secure advantages above a guaranteed satisfactory minimum. In the absence of information about the precise minimum share of goods that may be secured by the maximin criterion, Barry argues, "we cannot say...whether in any particular situation maximizing the minimum will be a good idea or not."[10] In addition, Buchanan argues, in making such a claim, Rawls relies upon unrealistic assumptions about diminishing marginal value. Both of these objections, however, focus on the size and value of a share of goods to be assured under the maximin rule. As a result, I will argue, both objections reflect a confusion regarding *the character of the satisfactory minimum* that Rawls argues that rational choosers will seek to secure through their choice of principles. In particular, as I discuss below, both objections falsely assume that the satisfactory minimum sought under the maximin rule is a share of primary goods assured under the difference principle.

A Minimum Threshold and Diminishing Marginal Value

Barry argues that choosers in the original position will only view the maximin rule as an attractive criterion if they can be sure that the minimum share of primary goods attainable under the rule will be at least equal in value to the threshold amount above which they care little for any gains. Unless they can be certain that the attainable minimum falls at or above this amount, Barry argues, the choosers cannot be certain whether they prefer to maximize the minimum or to adopt some other principle.[11] In particular, if the guaranteed minimum falls below the minimum threshold amount, the choosers will assign positive value to gains above that minimum. Moreover, Buchanan asserts, Rawls's claim that a chooser cares little for any gain above a minimum stipend requires an implausibly strong assumption about the diminishing marginal value of goods.[12] It may be plausible, Buchanan concedes, to claim that there exists some minimum threshold amount above which gains are of negligible value compared with the disutility of falling below that minimum;[13] but it does not follow that parties who are assured of this minimum will care very little for gains above it. Moreover, Buchanan asserts, Rawls cannot consistently assume such a level of diminishing marginal value because Rawls, himself, attacks utilitarians for making similarly extreme assumptions regarding diminishing marginal value.

Defenders of Rawls's theory have responded to these objections by arguing that choosers in the original position would focus on the minimum guarantees secured by the principles because securing such minimum protections will (1) strengthen the bases of self-respect and secure social stability,[14] (2) elicit cooperation from all members of society,[15] or (3) vindicate intuitions reflected in the structure of the original position.[16] Such responses, however, fail to identify the most serious shortcoming of the objections offered by Barry and Buchanan.

These objections are unsound because they are based upon the assumption that the satisfactory minimum that the choosers seek to achieve is a minimum level *of primary goods*.[17] Such a view conflates the idea of a *satisfactory minimum* with the idea of a *guaranteed minimum level of primary goods*, because such a view assumes that it is the difference principle that secures the satisfactory minimum sought under the maximin rule by guaranteeing a minimum bundle of primary goods to the least advantaged members of society. This view, however, is contradicted by Rawls's explicit account of the character of the satisfactory minimum sought under the maximin rule.

A Satisfactory Minimum

The view that the satisfactory minimum sought by the choosers in the original position is simply a share of primary goods – in particular, the share of income or primary goods to be allocated to the least advantaged – is so widely shared[18] that it is remarkable to consider how completely such a view is contradicted by Rawls's account of the deliberations in the original position. Rather than a share of primary goods, the satisfactory minimum sought by the parties is "a satisfactory *conception* [of justice]" that is "assured by the two principles in lexical order" (TJ 135). A conception of justice is defined as (1) "a set of related principles for identifying the relevant considerations which determine... a proper balance between competing claims" (TJ 9) and (2) associated priority rules (TJ 37–38, 266). During deliberations in the original position, the parties focus on the task of ranking conceptions of justice by their acceptability.[19] In order to select the most acceptable conception, the parties assess "a definite list of traditional conceptions" (TJ 102) and choose from that list the conception that constitutes the most satisfactory "minimum conception" (TJ 153) of justice. The task of the choosers is therefore to assess the *acceptability* of conceptions of justice. The most acceptable conception must (1) provide the most adequate protections for citizens' fundamental interests and (2) establish the right kind of priority between claims grounded in competing fundamental interests. Thus, the parties in the original position focus, *not* on choosing an allocation of primary goods to be assigned to the least advantaged, but rather on assessing the character of different conceptions of justice – the kinds of interests that they protect, the kinds of balance that they establish between fundamental interests, and the kind of political and social world that would result from the adoption of each conception.

The choosers thus apply the maximin rule to a very specific task – they assess the substance and practical implications of a wide range of proposed conceptions (e.g., justice as fairness, classical utility theory, perfectionism, intuitionism, mixed conceptions), and they aim to choose a conception that is satisfactory in the sense that it provides the most satisfactory protections for the fundamental interests of citizens corresponding to the "two coordinate roles" (JAF 48) of the basic structure of society: (1) securing equal basic liberties and (2) providing background institutions that secure social and economic justice (TJ 53, see JAF 48).[20] In addition, and crucially, the choosers consider the priority ranking that each proposed conception establishes between conflicting claims grounded in these interests. Rawls emphasizes that a conception of justice is defined not merely by the principles it contains, but by the priority rules that determine the relative weight to be assigned to the requirements of each principle.[21] The priority that his conception establishes among citizens' fundamental interests is central to Rawls's argument that choosers in the original position would prefer that conception to utilitarianism.[22] Thus, a satisfactory minimum conception is satisfactory because of the relation that it establishes between content and structure.[23]

Rawls develops a number of arguments to support his claim that a conception of justice consisting of his two proposed principles and the associated priority rules constitutes a satisfactory minimum conception. Justice as fairness provides the most satisfactory minimum protection of *liberty interests*, Rawls argues, because it secures their *priority* over all other fundamental interests. Rawls develops this argument by noting that the acceptance of any conception of justice will generate "strains of commitment" – strains generated by the justified reservations of persons subject to principles of justice regarding the effects of those principles (TJ 153–54). The most severe strain on commitment, Rawls suggests, occurs in cases in which some must "acquiesce in a loss of freedom ... for the sake of a greater good enjoyed by others" (TJ 154). A conception of justice that parties to the choice "can rely on one another to adhere to" (TJ 157) must therefore provide the most complete protection possible against this kind of injustice; and Rawls's first principle, with its foundational commitment to the inviolability of the person, responds to the strains of commitment more effectively than any other viable alternative principle because it insures completely "against the worst eventualities" involving losses of liberties (TJ 154). Thus, justice as fairness will minimize the strains of commitment, Rawls argues, precisely because it guarantees the most acceptable minimum protection of liberty interests.

Justice as fairness provides the most satisfactory protection of the interest in *the fairness in the distribution of social burdens and benefits* because, in addition to ensuring equal opportunity and fair compensation, it provides the most satisfactory minimum guarantee regarding the social bases of self-respect – and, Rawls argues, self-respect is an essential primary good required for the successful pursuit of the individual's conception of the good.[24] General affirmation of the second principle – and thus shared agreement to an arrangement that secures basic liberties and aims to mitigate the influence on life chances of factors that are arbitrary from the moral point of view (see TJ 156) – publicly expresses the respect of each member of a well-ordered society for every other member.²⁵ This public expression of respect, Rawls notes, provides support to the self-respect of members of society that would not be provided under even a generous utilitarian conception that accepted the liberty principle if that conception did not aim to mitigate arbitrary influences on life chances.²⁶ Thus, in choosing the principles of justice as fairness, the choosers "insure their self-respect as it is rational for them to do" (TJ 156).²⁷

It is the conception *taken as a whole* that constitutes the satisfactory minimum: the requirements of the chosen principles "are tied together as one conception of justice which applies to the basic structure of society as a whole" (TJ 136; see JAF 99), and the fact that this conception secures a "satisfactory political and social world" – not merely a bundle of goods, resources, and protections – "is crucial for the argument" (JAF 100). The choosers have a rational interest in ensuring that each member of society is guaranteed both the liberty and the effective capacity to pursue his or her conception of the good.²⁸ Justice as fairness provides the most satisfactory protection of this interest because of the combined effect of its basic guarantees, which unite the assurances that (1) liberty interests will be assigned priority over all other social claims, (2) arbitrary factors will not justify inequalities of opportunity or social status, and (3) society will honor legitimate expectations of fair compensation (TJ 273–77). Rawls refers to *this combination of guarantees*, and not to a minimum guaranteed income or bundle of primary goods, when he argues that a chooser in the original position would "care very little, if anything, for what he might gain above the minimum" guaranteeable level (TJ 134).²⁹

It could be argued, however, that Barry's and Buchanan's objections can be reformulated in a manner that avoids conflating of the idea of a satisfactory minimum with a guaranteed level of primary goods supplied under the difference principle. According to this view, both the first objection – that the maximin rule will only be attractive if the attainable minimum exceeds some threshold level of value – and the second objection – that the maximin argument is grounded in an implausible assumption about the diminishing marginal value of wealth and other primary goods – could be reformulated to refer to the value of the protections of fundamental interests provided by the two principles rather than to the value of a bundle of primary goods.

A reformulation of the Barry and Buchanan objections, however, would require a precise estimate of the value of the interests protected by the two principles – and no such precise estimate is available, because the two principles do not guarantee the provision of any particular social goods, resources, or level of welfare. The claim that the two principles secure the most satisfactory minimum protection of citizens' fundamental interests, in fact, involves a *characterization* of the principles' adequacy in addressing fundamental interests and *not* a *description* of its sufficiency in guaranteeing resources or welfare.

Both the Barry and the Buchanan objections, however, *depend upon* the idea of a minimum guarantee of a bundle of objects with specifiable and determinate values. Thus, in order to illustrate his claim that the maximin rule is attractive only if a threshold level of value can be achieved, Barry offers an example in which the maximin rule is unattractive because only ten apples can be provided to each person, while the threshold level with respect to apples is twelve.[30] Since the guaranteeable minimum is below the threshold level, Barry argues, the maximin rule would be less attractive than a rule requiring that we give twelve apples to as many people as possible while allowing a few people to receive fewer than ten apples.

The fundamental interests protected by a satisfactory minimum conception of justice, however, are unlike apples or other material goods because those interests are not objects or goods with a definitive form and specifiable value. Nor is it plausible to suggest that some unique threshold exists below which the protection of these interests would become so much less desirable that members of society would necessarily judge that the decision rule requiring the protection of fundamental interests should be replaced by some other rule (e.g., a rule requiring maximizing expected utility). To see why this is true, consider the following example. A stable and homogeneous society initially guarantees a satisfactory system of equal basic liberties. This commitment to the protection of liberties reflects the generally shared judgment among members of the society on due reflection (on the basis of arguments similar to those that Rawls presents) that a just society should ensure the most satisfactory feasible minimum protection of fundamental interests. After the society has been destabilized by violent conflict resulting from religious discord, however, the level of liberty protections that can be sustained is more limited than the original system of protected liberties – people must submit to metal detector tests, invasive searches, curfews, and other restrictions on liberty. The level of protection for liberties, in fact, falls below the threshold of acceptability for many members – perhaps a majority – of the society. Would such circumstances justify abandonment of the *decision rule* that required selecting principles that protect fundamental interests? The short answer would appear to be *no*. Due reflection – a careful consideration of all relevant considerations under conditions conducive to sound reflection subject to none of the usual errors in reasoning – justified the adoption of the maximin decision rule. Members of society might be justified in abandoning this decision rule on the basis of considerations relevant to the grounds for the choice of that rule – for example, if Buchanan could justify his claim that the reasoning supporting the argument for the maximin rule relied upon an implausible assumption about diminishing marginal utility. The fact that social conditions prevent the optimal protection of one of the set of fundamental interests whose protection is required by the decision rule, however, is not a consideration relevant to the reasoning that justified the adoption of the decision rule.

Even a reformulated version of Barry's example fails to ground a relevant objection to the maximin argument because a choice problem involving the selection of principles differs in character from a choice problem involving the selection of a minimum guaranteed supply of goods. In Barry's example involving a minimum supply of apples, apples are determinate goods with identifiable value, and the value of the bundle of apples that can be supplied under the decision rule is a consideration directly relevant to the justification of the decision rule itself. If the value of that bundle falls below a certain threshold, that fact could – as Barry notes – justify the employment of a different decision rule. The decision facing persons in the original position, however, involves the choice of principles of justice. A principle of justice is not an object or good, but rather a standard that can be employed to assess the acceptability of institutions, legislation, and policy. The choice of such a standard reflects an underlying judgment regarding the kinds of reasons that can justify an institution, legislation, or policy. The choice of a principle requiring the protection of liberty interests, for example, reflects the judgment that the fact that a policy or piece of legislation promotes or protects liberty constitutes a sufficient reason to support or adopt that policy or legislation. Such a choice is justified, then, not by consideration of the value of the objects supplied to persons under the principle, but rather by consideration of the *reasons* that justify affirmation of the principle. The value realized or lost as a consequence of adopting the principle may be relevant – for example, if adopting a principle would destroy all social value – but the mere fact that persons would assign a lesser value to a form of implementation of a principle that they still endorse on due reflection would not count as a consideration justifying the abandonment of the decision rule that led to the choice of the principle. Since Barry's argument necessarily assumes that the objects chosen in the decision procedure have a specific form and a specifiable value, his objections cannot readily be reformulated to apply to a choice problem in which the choice focuses on principles rather than goods.

The objections raised by Barry and elaborated by Buchanan nevertheless continue to influence many leading interpretations of Rawls's work. Many leading scholars have been influenced to identify the maximin rule with the difference principle and to view the choice in the original position as concerned solely with the distribution of goods over persons. John Roemer, for example, claims that the task of choosers in the original position is "the choice of [a] distribution [of goods] from behind a veil of ignorance."[31] Ken Binmore[32] and Philippe van Parijs[33] conflate the idea of a satisfactory minimum under the maximin rule with a guaranteed level of primary goods under the difference principle. Daniel Hausman and Michael McPherson claim that the choosers *in the original position* would design social and political institutions "to advance maximally the interests of the worst-off group."[34] And Robert Taylor, in his recent book on Rawls, claims that the reasoning of the choosers in the original position can be summarized as follows: (1) the difference principle is the maximin rule among distributive principles; (2) the maximin rule is rational under three conditions; (3) these conditions hold in the original position; therefore (4) the parties in the original position should choose the maximin rule among distributive principles.[35] The analyses of Rawls's arguments presented by these leading scholars – all of whom cite Barry's *The Liberal Theory of Justice* as a leading interpretation of Rawls's arguments – are thus distorted by fundamental confusions regarding the substance and role of the maximin argument deriving from Barry's critique.

Maximin and Choice under Uncertainty

Harsanyi's objection focuses on the plausibility of the maximin rule as a decision criterion for choice under uncertainty. While the maximin rule was viewed as an optimal decision rule when the issue of rational choice under uncertainty first attracted attention, Harsanyi claims, the limitations of that approach quickly became apparent.[36] Consider, he suggests, a choice between option A, in which a New York City resident interviews only for mediocre jobs in New York, and option B, which involves the opportunity to interview for a superior job in Chicago. The worst outcome that could result from choosing option A is mediocre employment; but the worst outcome that could result from choosing option B is death in a plane crash. A maximin rule would therefore require that a rational person must always select option A. Since the maximin decision rule produces such implausible results, Harsanyi concludes, it cannot provide an appropriate decision criterion for choice under uncertainty.[37] Rather, the appropriate decision rule is the Bayesian expected-utility maximization rule.

Note, however, that this objection is not responsive to Rawls's argument that maximin is an appropriate decision rule *only* under the carefully defined conditions of uncertainty that hold in the original position – extreme conditions of uncertainty in which the choosers possess no information at all about probabilities. Harsanyi's example merely demonstrates that maximin is an inappropriate decision rule for choices under conditions in which choosers have a great deal of information about probabilities, although the precise probability of each outcome is not known. Harsanyi's objection, then, does not address, much less refute, Rawls's arguments that the maximin rule is the appropriate criterion for rational choice under the conditions of extreme uncertainty that exist in the original position.

Harsanyi's objection, however, is motivated by the view that the criterion for rational choice does not and should not vary under differing choice conditions.[38] According to such a view, an argument demonstrating that maximin is an inappropriate decision rule for any particular category of choices necessarily establishes that maximin is an inappropriate decision rule for all categories of choices. If this view is accepted, Harsanyi's example counts decisively (1) against Rawls's maximin argument and (2) in favor of the claim that the Bayesian expected-utility maximization rule is the uniquely appropriate decision rule for choice under uncertainty. This strand of Harsanyi's argument has been influential, particularly among rational choice theorists.[39] Harsanyi's argument is, however, vulnerable to a number of serious objections.

It is important to note, first, that the claim that expected-utility maximization is the uniquely appropriate decision rule for choice under uncertainty is "highly controversial"[40] among rational choice theorists.[41] As Daniel Hausman and Michael McPherson note, talk of maximizing expected utility "is obscure when probabilities and even the range of possible outcomes are not known."[42] Decision theorists such as Isaac Levi argue instead that it would be rational for a person choosing under conditions of uncertainty to follow a rule requiring the choice of only those options that would produce the highest security level when combined with at least one hypothesis that is true if that option is chosen.[43] According to this view, when expected-utility considerations fail to require the choice of any particular option, reliance upon a secondary decision criterion is rational. Indeed, as Erik Angner notes, the information available to the parties in the original position underdetermines rational choice in precisely the manner described in Levi's argument.[44] The parties know nothing about (1) the distribution of wealth and other resources or (2) their own conceptions of the good. They therefore lack sufficient information to assign utilities to outcomes, much less to maximize expected utility, so that reliance upon a secondary decision criterion is rational.

A number of leading defenses of the maximin argument, including those presented by Gail Corrado[45] and Binod Agarwala,[46] have offered similar responses to the objections raised by Harsanyi – they have argued, that is, that the information available to the choosers is inadequate to ground calculations of expected utility, and that under such conditions maximin reasoning is a rational alternative. While these theorists argue that the Bayesian criterion may be supplemented or replaced in conditions in which that criterion cannot be applied or its meaning is obscure, Rawls presents arguments in Sections 27 and 28 of *A Theory of Justice* that provide a persuasive basis for rejecting altogether the view that the Bayesian criterion could be an acceptable criterion to guide choices of fundamental importance under conditions of complete uncertainty.

First, the Bayesian criterion is objectionable as a criterion to guide significant social choices under conditions of complete uncertainty because choosers under such conditions have no basis for estimating the subjective probabilities necessary in order to calculate expected utility, while assessments of probability that are to serve as the basis for rational decision "must have an objective basis" (TJ 149). The necessity of such an objective basis becomes more urgent as the importance of the judgment increases. A decision involving the choice of principles which will determine the extent to which the most fundamental of human interests receive protection would clearly involve the highest degree of urgency. This urgent need cannot be met in conditions of complete uncertainty. Even if it were possible to assign an equal probability to an unknown number of outcomes, the choosers would have no objective basis for that probability assignment. As Samuel Freeman notes, if the choosers lack sufficient information to assign any set of probabilities to outcomes, they also lack sufficient information to assign equal probabilities.[47] Parties forming judgments regarding fundamental questions of justice under conditions of complete uncertainty would therefore lack a sufficient informational basis to apply the principle of maximizing expected utility.

In addition, an individual who employs an expected-utility criterion in conditions of complete uncertainty cannot base her judgments upon a unified system of preferences. While expected-utility calculations are usually derived from the perspective of an individual with a single unified system of preferences, a chooser in the original position does not have "aims which he counts as his own" (TJ 150). Any calculation of expected utility from this perspective must therefore incorporate the hypothetical utility functions of many individuals. An argument for the employment of the Bayesian criterion, then, would have to assume that reliable interpersonal comparisons of utility can be made – a highly controversial view.[48] Even putting that problem aside, however, Rawls argues persuasively that expected-utility calculations based upon the assumption that one may turn out to be any one of a number of persons are of doubtful validity (TJ 150). In particular, it is not clear what scale of value one should employ in evaluating the worth of another person's way of life and system of ends – should one apply one's own scale of values or the scale of values favored by that person? Conflicting claims of justice arise not merely because people want similar sorts of things but because their conceptions of the good life differ. Even the choosers in the original position are aware that their final ends differ and are subject to no commonly acceptable criterion of value. Thus, no plausible criterion of value is available to provide a basis for attempts to calculate expected utility from a standpoint of complete uncertainty.

This problem is particularly acute for an argument in favor of the Bayesian criterion of choice, Rawls notes, because such an argument *requires a unified account* of the chooser's expectations. Such an argument must therefore, it would seem, assume that everyone thinks of themselves as having the same utility function. The argument for the Bayesian criterion is thus based upon a conception of the person as having no determinate independent character of will. If we judge that it is more plausible to view persons as having higher-order interests and preferred ends, then we must reject the argument for the Bayesian criterion (TJ 151–52).

In the absence of further argument, then, the balance of reasons would appear to weigh against the conclusion that the Bayesian criterion is the appropriate criterion to guide choice under the extreme uncertainty of the original position. Rather, it seems more plausible to argue with Rawls that rational choosers under conditions of extreme uncertainty who (1) are more concerned to secure a satisfactory minimum than to secure the possibility of receiving greater advantages and (2) insist upon ruling out completely certain unacceptable outcomes (3) should therefore be guided in their choices by the maximin rule.

Conclusion

In interpreting Rawls's arguments for the principles of justice, it is essential to keep in mind the limited role of the maximin rule in Rawls's formal argument. In developing this argument, Rawls represents – in the form of his decision procedure – "weak and widely shared" considered judgments regarding the qualities that should characterize fair conditions for resolving questions of justice. The character of the model generated through this constructivist process, Rawls argues, reveals important qualities of the process of judgment in questions of justice. The decision problem of moral deliberators faced with such questions, Rawls concludes, has the formal structure of a problem of choice under uncertainty, and the specific character of this particular choice problem justifies the judgment that a particular decision rule – the maximin rule – is uniquely appropriate to regulate the judgments of the choosers. The maximin rule recommends the choice of the most satisfactory minimum alternative and – since the task of the choosers is to select a set of principles of justice that constitute an acceptable conception of justice – the maximin rule in this case recommends the selection of those principles that, taken together, constitute the most satisfactory minimum conception of justice.

Conclusion

This sketch of the choice process in the original position describes the *full* extent of the operation of the maximin rule in Rawls's argument. The maximin rule neither justifies nor describes the operations of the difference principle, nor does it apply directly to any substantive questions of justice or morality. It *certainly* does not require that a just society must maximize the well-being or share of goods of the least advantaged. Rather, the maximin rule is simply a rule for choice that is appropriate, Rawls argues, to guide reflections regarding the choice of principles of justice under the particular conditions that characterize the original position.

While the role of the maximin rule in Rawls's argument is thus more limited than has often been appreciated, the rule – as the choosers apply it under the special circumstances of the original position – nevertheless performs a number of important functions in Rawls's argument. In particular, Rawls argues, the process of judgment involved in applying the rule under the specialized social contract conditions of the original position is well designed to focus the choosers on identifying and protecting their real interests. In addition, the choosers' complete lack of information regarding the social position that any one of them may occupy after the veil is lifted justifies the choosers' rational judgment that satisfactory protections of fundamental interests must be provided to *all* members of society. Application of the maximin rule under conditions of uncertainty, Rawls argues, ensures that even mutually disinterested rational choosers must select principles that require that social institutions are to be constituted in a manner than abstains "from the exploitation of the contingencies of nature and social circumstance" (TJ 156). Thus, application of the maximin rule leads to the adoption of principles that can be seen as "a fair undertaking between the citizens as free and equal with respect to these inevitable contingencies" (JAF 124).

If it is assumed that (1) Rawls's theory is designed simply to translate the requirements of maximizing rationality into moral principles and that (2) the central guarantee of Rawls's theory is the difference principle, then the theory will appear to focus primarily on the redistribution of income according to a rigid formula. Once these confusions have been corrected, the theory can be brought into sharper focus. In protecting basic liberties, guaranteeing equal opportunity and a fair distribution of social goods, and establishing the proper priority relation between these interests, Rawls argues, the theory ensures the realization of a "satisfactory political and social world" (JAF 100) – a world in which basic liberties are respected, all persons are guaranteed the opportunity to succeed to the extent permitted by their talents, and the society's public conception of justice affirms the value of each person as a moral being and not merely as a productive factor in the market. The fact that the satisfactory minimum constitutes a satisfactory form of social life, and not merely a bundle of goods, Rawls asserts, "is crucial for the argument" (JAF 100). It is this satisfactory form of social life to which Rawls refers when he suggests that it will not be worthwhile to jeopardize the minimum guarantee for the possibility of further gains.

The principal critiques that I have assessed and rejected have played an important role in shifting attention away from some of Rawls's central arguments in *A Theory of Justice* and have obscured the function and significance of the maximin argument in Rawls's justification of the two principles of justice. Addressing the confusions in the interpretation of Rawls's maximin argument, then, should make possible a more balanced appraisal of Rawls's overall argument.

Notes

1 Rawls defines the original position as an "initial status quo which insures that the fundamental agreements reached in it are fair" (TJ 15).
2 In his final statement of the argument for the principles of justice in *Justice as Fairness:*, Rawls continues to emphasize the central role of the maximin rule in his argument. See JAF 96–110.
3 Wolf (2000), pp. 103–4.
4 Martin (1985), p. 102.
5 Barry (1973), p. 98; see Buchanan (1980).
6 Harsanyi (1976), pp. 37–63.
7 See Binmore (1994), p. 146; Hausman and McPherson (1996), p. 155; Roemer (1996), pp. 172–76; van Parijs (2003), pp. 200–240; Taylor (2011), p. 194.
8 Justice as fairness "does *not* interpret the primary problem of distributive justice as one of allocative justice.... [In allocative justice]," "a given collection of goods is to be divided among definite individuals with known desires and needs" (TJ 77, my emphasis). The justice of a distribution is determined by assessing the justice of the system as a whole and examining "what individuals have done in good faith in light of established expectations" (TJ 76).

9 Rawls presents this argument in a series of sections in which he develops the argument for the two principles in a pairwise comparison with the principle of average utility. The claim that choosers in the original position would recognize the maximin rule as the appropriate decision criterion to govern their choices, however, appears to be perfectly general and not limited to comparisons between the two principles and the principle of average utility. Rawls states explicitly in Section 26 of *Theory* that the maximin rule should be employed to govern the reasoning in *all* pairwise comparisons between the two principles and other alternatives: "if the list of traditional views (Section 21) represents the possible decisions, these principles would be selected [from pairwise comparisons among principles on the list] by the [maximin] rule" (TJ 135).
10 Barry (1973), p. 98.
11 Barry (1973), pp. 97–98.
12 Buchanan (1980), p. 27.
13 Buchanan (1980), p. 27.
14 J. Cohen (1989), pp. 736–50.
15 Pogge (1989), p. 264.
16 Kymlicka (1990), p. 70: The justifications for the choice of the principles of justice "are mutually supported by reflecting on the intuitions we appeal to in our everyday practices.... Because Rawls is seeking such a reflective equilibrium, criticisms like those of Barry and Hare are overstated."
17 See Buchanan (1980), p. 27. The satisfactory minimum sought by the choosers under the maximin rule, Buchanan claims, is simply a level of "primary goods covered by the Difference Principle." Buchanan (1980), p. 27. Similarly, Barry claims that the satisfactory minimum is simply a bundle of primary goods including a set of liberties plus "a set minimum amount of wealth and power." Barry (1973), p. 102. Barry therefore concludes that the formal argument for the difference principle is simply "the result of applying the maximin criterion" from the standpoint of the original position. Barry (1989), p. 226.
18 See, e.g., Arrow (1973), p. 251; Barry (1989), pp. 213–17, 226–41; Binmore (1994), p. 146; Roemer (1996), pp. 172–76; van Parijs (2003), pp. 200–240; Taylor (2011), p. 194.
19 "Conceptions of justice are to be ranked by their acceptability" (TJ 16).
20 Rawls provides the clearest statement of this point in *Justice as Fairness: A Restatement*, when he writes that the parties in the original position act to secure the "fundamental interests [of the persons that they represent] in their freedom and equality – in the conditions adequate for the development and exercise of their moral powers and effective pursuit

their pursuit of their conception of the good on fair terms with others" (JAF 85).

21 "The assignment of weights is an essential and not a minor part of a conception of justice" (TJ 37).

22 The assignment of priority "beyond the calculus of social interests" to the first principle, Rawls argues, supplies the quality of justice as fairness that ensures that the choosers will recognize that that conception is "more effective than the principle of (average) utility in guaranteeing the equal basic liberties." See JAF 115.

23 Rawls emphasizes that "justification rests upon the entire conception," justification is a matter "of everything fitting together into one coherent view" (TJ 507). Justice as fairness constitutes the most satisfactory conception of justice because it "combine[s] into one conception the totality of conditions that we are ready upon due reflection to recognize as reasonable in our conduct with regard to one another" (TJ 514).

24 "Unless we feel that our endeavors are respected by [others], it is difficult if not impossible for us to maintain the conviction that our ends are worth advancing" (TJ 155–56, see 386). "[P]erhaps the most important primary good is that of self-respect.... Without it nothing may seem worth doing, or if some things have little value for us, we lack the will to strive for them. All desire and activity becomes empty and vain, and we sink into apathy and cynicism. Therefore the parties in the original position would wish to avoid at any cost the social conditions that undermine self-respect. The fact that justice as fairness gives more support to self-esteem than other principles is a strong reason for them to adopt it" (TJ 386).

25 Under the publicity condition, members of a well-ordered society fully understand and accept "the complete justification of justice as fairness in its own terms" (JAF 121). "[I]n a society well ordered by the principles of justice as fairness,....[e]quality is present at the highest level in that citizens recognize and view one another as equals" (JAF 132).

26 "In a public utilitarian society men, particularly the least advantaged, will find it more difficult to be confident of their own worth" (TJ 158).

27 In *Justice as Fairness*, Rawls reformulates this argument to justify the choice of the two principles in preference to a mixed conception that Rawls refers to as *the principle of restricted utility*. Under that principle, the basic structure is "to be arranged so as to maximize average utility consistent, first, with guaranteeing the equal basic liberties (including their fair value) and fair equality of opportunity, and second, with maintaining a suitable social minimum" (JAF 120). In the reformulated argument, Rawls argues that satisfactory minimum protection of the interest in fairness in the distribution of goods requires the maintenance of a

social minimum protections "derive[d] from an idea of reciprocity appropriate to political society so conceived" (JAF 130). While the substance of the argument is somewhat altered in this reformulation, its form remains unchanged – Rawls, that is, continues to argue that rational choosers in the original position would choose his two principles over the alternative by determining which principle(s) secured the most satisfactory minimum protections of fundamental interests as required by the maximin rule: to justify the claim that the choosers would prefer Rawls's two principles to the principle of restricted utility, "we argue that the second condition of the maximin rule is fully satisfied, or nearly enough so to provide an independent argument for the principles" (JAF 120).

28 "[T]he parties regard themselves as having certain fundamental interests that they must protect.... They must try to secure favorable conditions for advancing these [interests]" (TJ 160).

29 Rawls concedes that "[t]his important point about the guaranteeable level.... is never expressly stated in *Theory*," and that the failure of *A Theory of Justice* to make this point explicit "led some to think of the guaranteeable level as a natural, nonsocial, level below which individual utility drops to negative infinity." "[A]s the text shows," Rawls emphasizes, "this was not the intention" (JAF 100). The principles "are to guarantee equally for all citizens the social conditions necessary for the adequate development and full and informed exercise" of both their conceptions of the good and the sense of justice (JAF 112).

30 Barry (1973), p. 98.

31 Roemer (1996), p. 177.

32 Binmore asserts that "[the] 'difference principle' is little more than a direct application of the maximin criterion" and refers to "the maximin criterion that Rawls calls the difference principle." Binmore (1994), p. 176.

33 Van Parijs conflates the requirements of the difference principle with the maximin rule, stating that the difference principle "amounts to asking that the minimum of some index of advantage should be maximized." van Parijs (2003), p. 200.

34 Hausman and McPherson (1996), p. 155.

35 Taylor (2011), p. 194.

36 Harsanyi (1976), pp. 38–39.

37 Harsanyi (1976), pp. 39–43.

38 "I cannot see how anyone can propose the strange doctrine that scale is a fundamental variable in moral philosophy." Harsanyi (1976), p. 60.

39 See Goldman (1980), pp. 346–94; Hardin (1988), p. 135; Barry (1989), p. 215; Hare (1989), p. 107.

40 Hausman and McPherson (1996), p. 31.

41 See McClennen (1990); Levi (1986); Sen (1985); Ellsberg (1961); Allais (1979).
42 Hausman and McPherson (1996), p. 31.
43 Levi (1984), p. 132; see Levi (1980); Levi (1974); Levi (1967).
44 See Angner (2004), p. 16: "Since expected utility considerations fail, agents may perfectly rationally resort to maximin reasoning when choosing between [options]."
45 Corrado (1980), pp. 160–64.
46 Agarwala (1986), pp. 250–54.
47 See Freeman (2003), pp. 15–18.
48 See Hausman and McPherson (1996), pp. 67–116, for a helpful discussion of some of the problematics of interpersonal comparisons of utility.

PART II

Democratic Equality

5 The Difference Principle

Cohen's Ambiguities

Rational choosers in the original position, Rawls argues, would choose the principles of justice as fairness to constitute their public conception of justice. Among those principles, the difference principle has generated the greatest interest and has received the most focused scrutiny. Although it is widely assumed that the difference principle derives its justification directly from the maximin argument, Rawls justifies the difference principle through an argument that develops the practical implications of the considered judgment that a just distribution of goods should not be determined by factors that are arbitrary from a moral point of view (see TJ 57–73). In particular, Rawls argues, it is essential to ensure that the distribution of natural and social endowments does not determine the distribution of goods. Principles of justice are thus required to regulate the basic structure of society in order to regulate the influence of these two forms of endowments on life chances. The principles of fair equality of opportunity and the difference principle perform this function in justice as fairness.

The difference principle is thus justified by a strand of the informal argument developed in Chapter 2 of *A Theory of Justice*, and not by the maximin argument that is employed in the formal argument developed in Chapter 3. Rawls's reliance upon the informal argument – rather than the choice under uncertainty argument of Chapter 3 – to determine the structure and substance of the second principle thus illustrates the interplay of different levels of Rawls's complex approach to theory construction in ensuring that Rawls's two principles correspond to the considered judgments of a reasonable and rational person in reflective equilibrium.

The central focus of much of the secondary literature on the difference principle might seem surprising, since that principle is lexically subordinate to both the liberty principle and the principle of fair equality of opportunity. Disproportionate attention to the difference principle in the literature of distributive justice, however, is perhaps best explained as reflecting the response of commentators to the apparent strength of the principle's requirement that inequalities in income or holdings enjoyed by the more fortunate are just only to the extent that they are to the advantage of the worst off.

While some commentators[1] have criticized Rawls's view that a theory of justice should assign special priority to the claims of the worst off, however, G. A. Cohen argues that Rawls's approach is fatally flawed by its deference to the selfish maximizing preferences of the more fortunate members of society. Cohen's later work criticizes the difference principle for tolerating "deep inequalities" in income in cases in which permitting such inequalities generates at least some benefits for the least advantaged members of society. Principles that permit such inequalities, Cohen argues, may constitute a sound basis for policy in a world in which justice can be realized only in a compromised form, but such principles tell us little about the substance of justice itself.

Rawls's accommodationist approach to inequality in incomes, Cohen asserts, introduces both theoretical and practical problems into his theory. As a practical matter, Rawls's arguments licensing selfish maximizing behavior provide unwarranted support for conservative policies such as the regressive Lawson and Bush tax cuts. As a theoretical matter, Cohen argues, Rawls's arguments involve two ambiguities relating to (1) the degree to which permissible inequalities must be *necessary* in order to benefit the least advantaged and (2) the proper definition of the basic structure of society. The resolution of these ambiguities, in Cohen's view, produces a dilemma for Rawls's view of justice.

First, Cohen argues, Rawls provides an ambiguous account of the sense in which inequalities must – under the difference principle – be *necessary* to improve the position of the worst off, so that two inconsistent readings of this requirement can be defended on the basis of Rawls's argument. It is important to note that Cohen, in construing this requirement, assumes that the test of necessity is applied directly to the earnings or holdings of individuals or small groups of similarly situated or endowed individuals.[2] Cohen thus grounds his objections to Rawls in the assumption that, in order to satisfy the difference principle's necessity requirement, *each* more fortunate individual who receives unequal compensation must be able to justify that inequality as necessary to benefit the worst off. The necessity requirement – as Cohen understands it – is thus satisfied only when each more fortunate person can justify her holdings in this way.

Second, Cohen argues that there is a "fatal ambiguity" in Rawls's specification of the basic structure of society. The basic structure – the primary subject of Rawls's account of justice – may consist solely of institutions that are legally coercive, or it may consist of both legally coercive institutions and practices and conventions that are entrenched but not legally coercive. If the basic structure consists solely of legally coercive institutions, then the principles that regulate the basic structure – including the difference principle – do not apply directly to the choices of individuals in the market.

Once the ambiguities in Rawls's argument are resolved, Cohen argues, it is clear that (1) an acceptable interpretation of the difference principle permits only inequalities that are strictly necessary in order to benefit the least advantaged and that (2) the requirements of the difference principle apply squarely to the choices of individuals in the market. It is also clear, Cohen concludes, that the difference principle justifies little or no inequality in incomes. The preferences of the talented to demand high levels of compensation for the value of their services are, according to Cohen's reading of Rawls, clearly inconsistent with the Rawls's own account of the requirements of justice. Thus, the account of the difference principle that Rawls presents in *A Theory of Justice* appears to license *unjust* choices to demand high levels of compensation.

While much of the secondary literature discussing Cohen's critique has accepted Cohen's claims that Rawls's accounts of the difference principle and of the basic structure of society suffer from ambiguity,[3] I will argue that both claims fail and that Cohen's critique is therefore not persuasive. First, I will argue that Cohen's claim that the difference principle licenses unjust choices is grounded in a confused reading of that principle. On one hand, the difference principle does not – as Cohen claims – require that inequalities must be "necessary" in order to benefit the least advantaged; on the other hand, the difference principle does not license unrestrained selfish maximizing behavior. As a result, Rawls and his defenders have no need to argue that (1) the basic structure consists solely of coercive institutions or that (2) the requirements of the difference principle do not apply to the selfish maximizing behavior of individuals.

Cohen's First Ambiguity: The Difference Principle

When Rawls states that "inequalities are just [under the difference principle] if they are *necessary* to improve the position of the worst off,"[4] Cohen argues, Rawls does not provide a clear account of the relevant sense of necessity. As a result, Cohen claims, two incompatible readings are consistent with Rawls's account of the requirements of the difference principle "so that he has in effect two positions on the matter."[5] On a lax reading, inequalities are consistent with justice even if the inequalities are only made necessary because the more talented employ their advantageous bargaining position to demand unjustly unequal compensation. On a strict reading, inequalities are consistent with justice only if they are necessary independent of the intentions or bargaining strategies of the persons subject to the principle.

Although elements of Rawls's argument provide some support for both the strict and the lax reading of the difference principle, Cohen argues, Rawls's "unqualified endorsement of unequalizing incentives"[6] commits him to the lax reading as his official view. Yet, Cohen insists, only the strict reading can be justified according to Rawls's own standards of justification – the strict interpretation is in fact "mandatory" if we accept Rawls's own description of the nature of his theoretical project – and the strict interpretation would view incentive payments to the more talented as inconsistent with the requirements of justice.

Rawls, Cohen notes, describes his project in *A Theory of Justice* as an exercise in ideal theory. His argument is designed to identify those principles of justice that should regulate the basic structure of a well-ordered society of persons who are fully motivated by the sense of justice. Since concerns of justice constitute the entire motivational set for these persons, they will necessarily consult their principles of justice (in particular, the difference principle) when determining the level of compensation that they are willing to accept for the employment of their talents. And if the difference principle holds that inequalities are consistent with justice only when they are necessary to benefit the least advantaged, then members of a well-ordered society will neither request nor accept compensation above median wage unless that excess compensation is literally necessary to benefit the least advantaged. They will therefore affirm the version of the difference principle that rules out the selfish maximizing behavior that Rawls's version of the difference principle allegedly licenses. Thus, Cohen concludes, the strict reading of the difference principle is mandatory for Rawls's theory.

In claiming that the strict reading of the difference principle is mandatory, Cohen intends to underline what he believes to be a deep tension in Rawls's argument. Rawls's argument, Cohen assumes, works from the assumption that considerations that are arbitrary from the moral point of view should not determine the shares of goods that members of society enjoy. Since the considered judgment that differences in shares of endowments (such as talent) cannot justify differences in shares of social goods is a foundational assumption of Rawls's argument, that argument cannot, therefore, justify a principle (such as the difference principle, in its lax reading) that permits members of society to exploit their unequal shares of talent to generate unequal compensation. Only a principle that rejects such unequal compensation as unjust (that is, the difference principle in its strict reading) can be justified through that argument. The strict reading of the difference principle is thus – Cohen concludes – mandatory.

If Cohen's assumptions regarding Rawls's argument were correct, then, Cohen could argue persuasively that the strict reading of the difference principle is mandatory. I will argue, however, that Cohen's central assumption regarding Rawls's argument is false. The difference principle does not require that permissible inequalities must be *necessary* to improve the position of the least advantaged. In particular, Rawls neither requires nor suggests – as Cohen assumes – that each more fortunate individual who receives unequal compensation or possesses unequal holdings must be able to justify that inequality as necessary to benefit the worst off.

Necessary to Improve the Position of the Least Advantaged

The assumption that the inequalities permitted by the difference principle must be *necessary* to benefit the least advantaged is crucial for Cohen's critique of Rawls. Without this assumption, Cohen cannot argue that Rawls's employment of the notion of necessity is ambiguous; and if Rawls does not, as Cohen claims, exploit the ambiguity of his employment of the notion of necessity to exclude the private choices of talented wage earners from the coverage of the difference principle, then Rawls and his defenders need not argue, as Cohen claims that they do, that the exclusion of such private choices from the jurisdiction of the difference principle is justified because those choices occur within, and do not determine, the basic structure of society.[7] Cohen's critiques of *the incentives argument* and *the basic structure objection* both, therefore, depend critically upon the claim that Rawls argues that just inequalities in holdings must be *necessary* to benefit the least advantaged.

Remarkably, however, Rawls makes no such an argument. Rawls states the requirements of the difference principle twice in *A Theory of Justice*, and the two statements are not entirely equivalent. In neither statement, however, does Rawls argue that just inequalities must be *necessary* to benefit the least advantaged. Rawls first states the requirements of the difference principle at the beginning of Section 13 of *Theory*. Rawls introduces the principle as an interpretation of the more general requirement of justice that permissible inequalities must be "to everyone's advantage." The difference principle, Rawls states, requires that "the higher expectations of those better situated are just if and only if they work as part of a scheme which improves the expectations of the least advantaged members of society" (TJ 65). Rawls describes the requirements of the principle differently at the end of the same section where he restates the second principle of justice to incorporate the principles of fair equality of opportunity and the difference principle. In this second statement, the difference principle requires that "[s]ocial and economic inequalities are to be arranged so that they are ... to the greatest expected benefit of the least advantaged" (TJ 72). Both of the passages from Section 13 establish a relationship between permissible inequalities and benefit to the least advantaged, but that relationship is *not* necessity.

The first passage, requiring that permissible inequalities must "work as part of a scheme that benefits the least advantaged," does not appear to require the demonstration of *any* precise connection between particular inequalities and benefit to the least advantaged. Just inequalities must work as part of a scheme, and that scheme must benefit the least advantaged, but Rawls's first statement of the difference principle's requirements does not indicate that it must be possible to demonstrate anything more than a loose connection between the inequalities and the benefit. In order to illustrate the kind of inequalities that are permissible under this description of the difference principle's requirements, Rawls offers the example of members of the entrepreneurial class in a property-owning democracy. Members of this class, Rawls notes, enjoy significantly better initial prospects than unskilled laborers, and this inequality derives directly from an inequality in social endowments such as inherited wealth. This initial inequality in life prospects, which clearly derives from the influence of factors that are arbitrary from the moral point of view, is nevertheless justifiable if the greater expectations allowed to the entrepreneurial class "encourages them to do things which raise the prospects of [members of the] laboring class" (TJ 68). An arrangement of the basic structure that permits this form of inequality, the example suggests, is just if the inequalities permitted function as part of a scheme that, taken as a whole, benefits the disadvantaged laborers. There is, however, no requirement that it must be possible to demonstrate that all instances of unequal expectations permitted to members of the entrepreneurial class were *necessary* to produce benefits for the laborers. Rawls's example does not rule out inequalities that are part of the scheme that benefits the laborers but that do not, themselves, actually have the effect of producing any such benefits. The requirement is much looser – as long as permitting a range of benefits to the entrepreneurs encourages them to do things that can be seen to operate as part of a scheme that functions to raise the prospects of the least advantaged to some reasonable degree, the difference principle is satisfied.

The second passage in Section 13 describing the requirements of the difference principle states that inequalities "must be arranged to the greatest advantage of the least advantaged." Note that the passage refers to the *arrangement* of inequalities, not the creation, licensing, or generation of permissible inequalities. The passage, then, refers to the arrangement within basic social institutions of practices that permit or encourage inequalities that are potentially consistent with justice. "Potentially consistent with justice" under what standard, one might wonder, since the difference principle is supposed to provide the ultimate standard of justice for inequalities. But Section 13 provides a ready response to this query – "potentially consistent with justice" under the standard requiring that inequalities in expectations must work as part of a scheme that improves the expectations of the least advantaged.

In *Justice as Fairness: A Restatement*, Rawls confirms that this reading of the passage is correct: "[t]o say that inequalities are to be arranged for the greatest benefit of the least advantaged simply means that we are to compare schemes of cooperation by seeing how well off the least advantaged are under each scheme, and then to select the scheme under which the least advantaged are better off than they are under any other scheme" (JAF 59–60). Cohen's understanding of the requirements of the difference principle – in particular, his assumption that the principle requires that each fortunate individual who receives unequal compensation or possesses unequal holdings must be able to justify that inequality as necessary to benefit the worst off – thus goes far beyond Rawls's understanding of the principle's requirements. While Rawls's account of the difference principle favors schemes that produce the greatest advantage for the least advantaged, there is no requirement, explicit or implicit, that each more fortunate person enjoying unequal holdings or earnings under the scheme must be able to show that their unequal holdings or earnings are necessary to benefit the least advantaged. The justice of an arrangement is judged on the basis of an assessment of the impact of the scheme *as a whole*, and not on the basis of an assessment of the impact of particular inequalities permitted under the scheme (see JAF 62–63). Thus, when Rawls states that the difference principle requires that "if the legitimate expectations of the more advantaged were less, those of the less advantaged would also be less" (JAF 64), he refers to the collective expectations of the more advantaged, not to the expectations of particular individuals – as Rawls glosses this passage, "[s]*ociety* [should] always be on the upward-rising part or at the top of the OP curve" (JAF 64, my emphasis). Inequalities that are an element of a scheme that improves the expectations of the least advantaged but that are not themselves necessary to improve those expectations remain just under such a standard.

In discussing the nature of a scheme that is "just throughout," Rawls does – in one passage – state that in such cases, "the expectations of *all those* better off at least contribute to the welfare of the more unfortunate" (TJ 68, my emphasis). However, if – as Rawls states – the effect of inequalities on the least advantaged is judged on the basis of an assessment of the impact of the scheme as a whole, then any inequality that works as part of a scheme that benefits the least advantaged is to be viewed as contributing to the welfare of the more unfortunate, simply by virtue of constituting a part of that scheme. In *Justice as Fairness*, Rawls states the same idea in a manner that more clearly applies the requirement to the more advantaged collectively, rather than individually: "the difference principle directs society to aim at the highest point on the OP curve [which plots collective benefits to the most advantaged against collective benefits to the least advantaged] of the most effectively designed scheme of cooperation" (JAF 63).

The language in the second passage in Section 13, then, provides no support for the claim that inequalities permissible under the difference principle must be *necessary* to benefit the least advantaged. To the requirement from the first passage – that inequalities must work as part of a scheme which improves the expectations of the least advantaged – the second passage adds the requirement that a just arrangement will select the particular scheme that provides the greatest benefit to the least advantaged. But since the first passage contained no requirement that particular inequalities occurring *within* the schemes must be necessary to benefit the least advantaged, and since the second passage simply orders the schemes licensed as just by the first passage, the second passage carries over the first passage's *indifference* to the question of whether particular inequalities occurring within the operations of a permissible scheme are necessary to benefit the least advantaged. Thus, Rawls's text provides no support for Cohen's claim that the difference requires that particular inequalities must be necessary to generate benefits for the least advantaged.

Since the difference principle does not state that inequalities are consistent with justice only when they are necessary to benefit the least advantaged, members of a well-ordered society will not, as Cohen claims, necessarily affirm a version of the difference principle that rules out unequal and higher compensation to talented members of society who employ their talents to contribute to the public good. Nothing in Rawls's argument, in fact, justifies the view that rewarding the productive employment of talent with large salaries is inconsistent with justice.

Arbitrariness and Returns to Talent

But, Cohen might respond, what about Rawls's underlying commitment to the view that factors that are arbitrary from the moral point of view – such as endowments of talent – should not determine the distribution of goods? If Rawls's theory is fundamentally concerned with neutralizing the influence of arbitrary factors on life chances, then – Cohen could assert – a reading of the difference principle that licenses significant rewards for the productive employment of talents, thus allowing natural endowments of talent to significantly influence life chances, necessarily introduces serious inconsistency into Rawls's theory.

Such an objection, however, fundamentally misunderstands the status within Rawls's argument of the concern regarding the influence of natural endowments on life chances. Unlike theories of luck equality, Rawls's account of justice as fairness does not take as foundational the principle that arbitrary influences on life chances must be neutralized. Rawls, it is important to remember, insists that the arbitrary distribution of natural endowments is "neither just nor unjust" (TJ 87), and Rawls explicitly rejects the view that natural endowments should not affect the distribution of goods.[8] Injustice, in Rawls's theory, occurs only when social institutions reinforce or exacerbate the natural inequality of endowments by making the possession of certain endowments or sets of endowments a necessary condition of access to valued social positions and opportunities (TJ 87–88). A reading of the difference principle that licenses significant rewards for the productive employment of natural endowments of talent thus introduces no inconsistency at all into Rawls's argument.

Rawls, in fact, emphasizes that fair compensation for contributions to the public good – compensation that involves significant rewards for the productive employment of talents – is a *fundamental concern of justice*. Rawls provides the clearest statement of this view in his early paper, "Justice as Fairness." In that paper, Rawls asserts that acceptable principles of justice must express three basic ideas: liberty, equality, and "reward for services contributing to the common good" (JF 48). Fair compensation for such services, this passage emphasizes, constitutes a fundamental concern of justice. While Rawls later modified some of the views expressed in "Justice as Fairness," he maintained and defended this claim regarding the justice of unequal compensation for unequal contribution in his later work. In "The Independence of Moral Theory" – published in 1975, four years after the publication of *A Theory of Justice* – for example, Rawls emphasizes that a just distribution of goods must provide unequal rewards for unequal contributions: "the links of responsibility and contribution have to be traced through and distribution suitably related to them."[9] Rawls makes a similar point in *Theory* in arguing that the principal evil of exploitation is that "the precept of contribution is violated" (TJ 272).

Rawls's concern with fair compensation may explain the significant role that he assigns to price system mechanisms in a well-ordered society. Rawls seems to assume, in fact, that a just distribution of goods is appropriately generated, for the most part, by the price system (regulated by the second principle of justice). Once a suitable social minimum is ensured, Rawls argues, "it may be perfectly fair that the rest of total income be settled by the price system" (TJ 245).[10] In a system in which markets encourage marginal cost pricing and therefore efficient levels of production and market-clearing wages and prices, Rawls suggests, the claims to differential compensation that are generated may be viewed as just, not because they are to the benefit of the least advantaged, but because they are the product of free exchanges in the context of fair economic arrangements – that is, in the context of economic arrangements regulated, first, by fair equality of opportunity and, second, by the difference principle.

Neither the difference principle nor the fair equality principle, it is important to emphasize, directly grounds claims to goods. Rather, both principles state *conditions* whose satisfaction establishes conditions within which claims to goods may be justified. Economic arrangements that satisfy *both* of these principles, Rawls argues, constitute an instance of pure procedural justice, and the distribution of shares of goods generated in an economic context that satisfies both principles is therefore "just whatever it happens to be" (TJ 74). The two principles regulate the kinds of returns that just economic arrangements provide to effort and human capital (see TJ 270), but claims to compensation generated within a just economic arrangement derive their fundamental justification from the fact that individuals have employed their abilities in a manner that society has announced it will reward.

Consider, then, the claim to goods of a talented person who has employed her talents in a way that society has announced it will reward with unequal income and within conditions that satisfy the requirements of fair equality of opportunity and the difference principle. While the claim is thus permissible under the combined requirements of the second principle of justice, the decisive support for recognition of the claim comes from the fact that the individual has employed her abilities to perform tasks that society has announced it will reward with unequal compensation. The resulting and justified expectation of *unequal* compensation thus derives significant foundational support from considerations of justice independent of the difference principle. The claims of the talented to receive unequal compensation for the employment of their talents – under conditions consistent with the second principle of justice – are thus *claims grounded in considerations of justice*.

Far from representing a compromise between concerns of justice (the aim of neutralizing arbitrary influences on life chances) and concerns of policy (providing incentives to motivate the talented to contribute optimally), then, the difference principle *balances concerns of justice*. Rawls, in fact, explicitly notes that the requirements of distributive justice require such a balance among concerns of justice: "[i]t is widely agreed... that the distribution of income should depend upon the claims of entitlement... weighed against the claims of need and security."[11] Cohen's claim that the difference principle constitutes merely "a principle of public policy"[12] rather than a principle of justice therefore fails.

Selfish Maximizing Behavior

Cohen fails to grasp precisely this point when he suggests that Rawls might be tempted to defend the "lax" reading of the difference principle as reflecting "an understandable compromise between justice and self-interest."[13] Such a defense would necessarily fail, Cohen argues, because the assistance to the least advantaged required by this compromise version of the difference principle would differ from the amount of assistance required by pure considerations of justice. The lax (compromise) reading of the difference principle is thus "not, what it is supposed to be, a fundamental principle of justice." The lax reading cannot, therefore, be "what agents committed to difference principle justice affirm."[14]

If Cohen were correct in arguing that permissible inequalities under Rawls's official view of the difference principle are designed to reflect a pragmatic compromise between justice and self-interest, his criticism of Rawls's official view of the difference principle as an unacceptable compromise would be persuasive. As discussed above, however, the difference principle is not designed to reflect a compromise between considerations of justice and pragmatic considerations. Far from licensing selfish maximizing behavior, the difference principle merely defines the conditions that just claims to unequal compensation must satisfy in order to remain consistent with justice. The difference principle, in fact, offers a *restrictive* reading of the conditions under which expectations of unequal compensation may constitute *legitimate* expectations – such expectations are legitimate only if permitting the resulting unequal distribution of goods works as part of a scheme that benefits the least advantaged.

While Cohen insists that Rawls – in order to remain faithful to his fundamental commitments – must characterize the pursuit of significant rewards for the productive employment of talent as selfish maximizing behavior by the talented, such a view is warranted only on a narrow and reductive reading of Rawls's project. Rawls, in fact, insists that the fundamental concerns of his theory could and should not be reduced to a small set of "self-evident principles from which a sufficient body of standards and precepts can be derived to account for our considered judgments" (TJ 506). Rather, Rawls argues, the justification of an account of justice "is a matter of the mutual support of many considerations, of everything fitting together into one coherent view" (TJ 507). Since Rawls's argument is not grounded in a single-minded concern to neutralize arbitrary influences on life chances, Rawls's view that natural endowments may play a role in affecting life chances does not constitute a deep tension in his theory. Cohen's claim that the "lax" reading of the difference principle permits "selfish maximizing" by the talented does not, therefore, identify a fatal ambiguity in Rawls's theory – it merely constitutes a verbal flourish on Cohen's part.

Cohen's Second Ambiguity: The Basic Structure of Society

Rawls's specification of the basic structure of society, Cohen argues, suffers from a "fatal ambiguity." The basic structure may consist solely of institutions that are legally coercive, or it may consist of both legally coercive institutions and practices and conventions that are entrenched but not legally coercive. Rawls favors a specification that limits the basic structure to institutions that are legally coercive, Cohen argues, because Rawls intends that the principles that regulate the basic structure should not apply to the practices, conventions, and usages that order social behavior *within* coercive social institutions. Although Rawls favors such a narrow specification, Cohen argues, he cannot justify limiting the specification of the basic structure in this way because Rawls's justification for designating the basic structure as the primary subject of justice – the fact that its effects on life chances are so profound from the start – applies not merely to coercive institutions, but also and equally to practices, conventions, and usages.

It is important to note the motivation of this argument. Cohen has argued that the difference principle, properly construed, must proscribe (as unjust) the selfish maximizing behavior that Cohen claims Rawls intends to license under the lax reading of the difference principle. Cohen expects defenders of Rawls's view to offer a particular objection to this argument. Cohen calls the argument that he expects Rawls's advocates to advance *the basic structure objection*. According to this objection, even if Cohen's argument in favor of the strict reading of the difference principle were decisive, the argument would still not establish that the selfish maximizing behavior of the talented is unjust under the difference principle. Rather, according to the basic structure objection, the requirements of the difference principle do not apply to such behavior because Rawls's principles of justice regulate social institutions but not the behavior that occurs within those institutions. Cohen's argument is designed to show that defenders of Rawls's theory cannot consistently assert the basic structure objection. If Rawls cannot plausibly limit the specification of the basic structure to coercive institutions, then the application of the principles that regulate the basic structure must extend beyond the coercive institutions themselves to the behavior that occurs within those institutions. And if those principles – in particular the difference principle – necessarily apply to the behavior that occurs within the institutions that make up the basic structure, then the basic structure objection fails.

As discussed above, however, Rawls does not argue that the difference principle licenses selfish maximizing behavior. Rawls therefore has no need to insulate individual choices from the requirements of justice by arguing that the range of application of the principles of justice does not extend to choices made within the institutions of the basic structure. Cohen's argument, nevertheless, raises an important issue: does the most plausible specification of the basic structure of society include merely coercive institutions, or does it include the practices, conventions, and usages – in particular private choices – that occur within those institutions?

Specification of the Basic Structure

The answer to this question, I suggest, is both more subtle and less ambiguous than Cohen recognizes. Rawls's specification of the basic structure does limit the direct operations of the principles of justice to regulation of the basic structure, so that most private behavior is not directly subject to the principles. Nevertheless, the principles do effectively regulate practices, conventions, and usages, including the effects of private choices, when those practices produce departures from background justice. Thus, it is not possible to determine whether an institution is part of the basic structure simply by describing its structure and general function. Institutions may be considered to be part of the basic structure to the extent that they have a profound effect upon the system of social cooperation (e.g., by enhancing or reducing equal opportunity) and may not be considered to be part of the basic structure to the extent that they fulfill other functions.

How does Rawls restrict the scope of the principles, and what is the significance of that restriction? It is important to emphasize first that Rawls does not simply exempt private behavior from the requirements of justice. Rather, to explain the degree to which individual behavior remains subject to regulation by the principles of justice, Rawls distinguishes between the perspectives of individuals as citizens and individuals as members of private associations (JAF 165). As citizens, he notes, we have reasons to impose the constraints of justice on private associations, but as members of those associations, we have reasons to limit those constraints. For example, as members of families, we have good reason to insist that the internal life of families not be regulated by political principles; but as citizens we have reasons to insist that members of families must not be permitted to behave in ways that invade or restrict the rights, liberties, or opportunities of other family members (JAF 166).

Rawls's account therefore requires that when private behavior within the basic structure erodes or violates rights, liberties, or fair opportunities, justice requires adjustment and/or compensation to repair the departure from justice.[15] Even if the private behavior that produces the departures from background justice is not itself unjust, the basic structure remains just only if institutions within the basic structure continually and effectively repair the "inevitable tendencies away from background fairness" (PL 268) that result from the collective effects of individually blameless behavior. Thus, wage agreements might appear to constitute merely the product of individual choices within the basic structure; but if, as a result of "underlying social conditions," "excess market power," or the absence of "fair opportunity" (PL 266–67), wage agreements fail to maintain background justice, then justice requires the employment of special mechanisms within the basic structure to restore background justice. A just basic structure, in fact, must include "operations that continually adjust and compensate for the inevitable tendencies away from background fairness" (PL 268). If, for example, private choices erode fairness in the distribution of property, the required special mechanisms will take the form of "income and inheritance taxation designed to even out the ownership of property" PL 268). Far from viewing private choices that erode fairness in the distribution of goods as private behavior that is beyond the jurisdiction of justice, Rawls emphasizes that (1) such private behavior is inconsistent with justice, (2) the basic structure of a just society must include special mechanisms to correct for the effects of that behavior, and (3) a failure to maintain such mechanisms constitutes a failure of justice under the two principles of justice.

Cohen points to what he describes as "Rawls's wobble on the matter of whether or not the family belongs to the basic structure of society"[16] as a particularly dramatic example of ambiguity in the specification of the basic structure. Cohen assumes that Rawls can only accept the family as an element of the basic structure if he recognizes that the principles of justice must apply squarely to *individual choices* within the family that undermine the fairness of social arrangements. Feminists such as Susan Okin who argue that Rawls's theory could "readily admit the family into the basic structure"[17] fail, in Cohen's view, to recognize the structural significance of the question for Rawls's theory:

> Rawls cannot admit the family into the basic structure without abandoning his insistence that it is to the basic structure only that principles of justice apply. In supposing that he could include family relations, Okin showed failure to grasp the *form* of the feminist critique of Rawls.[18]

If Rawls maintains that the basic structure is exclusively a set of institutions, so that "the principles of justice do not judge the actions of people within" institutions,[19] Cohen argues, Rawls cannot condemn the behavior of males within the family who pressure females to conform to repressive stereotypes.[20]

Cohen's argument, however, fails to take note of Rawls's view – discussed above – that when private choices erode the justice of basic social arrangements, the overall effect of these choices becomes an appropriate subject for regulation under the principles of justice. In *Justice as Fairness*, Rawls applies the logic of this argument directly to private choices within the family: the principles of justice, Rawls argues, "impose essential constraints on the family as an institution and guarantee the basic rights and liberties and fair opportunities of all its members."[21] These requirements of justice, in fact, apply with full force to guarantee the opportunities, equality, and independence of females within the family. John Stuart Mill, Rawls notes, argued that the family of his day "was a school for male despotism"; if so, Rawls argues, then the requirements of justice "can plainly be invoked to reform it" (JAF 166).

But this description of Rawls's specification of the basic structure might seem to confirm a significant part of Cohen's argument. While the specification of the basic structure may be less ambiguous than Cohen suggests, it could be argued on Cohen's behalf that it is precisely Rawls's willingness to describe as blameless the private behavior that produces departures from background justice that accounts for his willingness to license selfish maximizing behavior by the talented. In fact, this argument might continue, Rawls's distinction between *blameless private behavior* that leads to departures from justice and *operations of the basic structure* that correct and adjust to restore background justice seems consistent with Cohen's description of the operations of the difference principle which – in Cohen's view – permits maximizing behavior inconsistent with the ethos of Rawlsian justice and then requires compensation to restore background justice.

Note, however, that the operation of the difference principle does not correspond to the process of adjustment that Rawls describes as appropriate in cases in which *blameless* private behavior leads to a departure from background justice. Rawls's example of injustice in the family illustrates the difference. In that example, private behavior produce's *injustice as defined by the terms of the principles of justice* – private behavior invades interests that are explicitly protected by the two principles (rights, liberties, opportunities). The operations of the difference principle, however, do *not* permit injustice as defined by the principles. Rather, under the difference principle, the talented generate expectations that are *consistent* with the requirements of justice. They simply employ their asymmetric talents in a manner encouraged by the principle of fair equality of opportunity to generate claims of justice to unequal compensation. The claims generated are grounded entirely in considerations of justice. The operations of the difference principle, then, do not correspond to the operation of mechanisms of the basic structure that compensate for departures from background justice. Cohen cannot, therefore, argue persuasively that Rawls's justification of the difference principle depends critically upon the notion that individual choices necessarily fall outside of the jurisdiction of the principles of justice.

Note the manner in which these conclusions respond to Cohen's criticisms of Rawls. Cohen argues that Rawls develops the "basic structure objection" – the argument that the requirements of justice apply to institutions, not to the behavior of individuals – in order to justify licensing the maximizing behavior of the talented. Cohen then responds to the basic structure objection by asserting that Rawls's specification of the basic structure is ambiguous, and that the proper resolution of that ambiguity requires that individual behavior must be directly subject to the requirements of justice. In response, I have argued that Rawls's specification of the basic structure is not ambiguous. Rather, Rawls's specification is sufficiently clear to establish an unambiguous relation between the principles of justice and private behavior that produces injustice; and Rawls's account of the relation of the principles to background injustice within the basic structure does not account for his willingness to license selfish maximizing behavior by the talented, since Rawls does not license such behavior.

Conclusion

Cohen claims that Rawls requires the basic structure objection to defend a claim about the requirements of distributive justice – that acceptable principles of justice license selfish maximizing behavior by the talented – that Rawls would have rejected. Cohen then proceeds to criticize the basic structure objection by offering an unpersuasive case for an ambiguity in Rawls's specification of the basic structure. Cohen's arguments cannot, therefore support a successful internal critique of Rawls's position.

It is unfortunate that Cohen presents his argument regarding the degree to which it can be just to permit arbitrary influences to affect life chances as an internal critique of Rawls, because the argument could be developed more persuasively as an external critique. While Rawls argues persuasively for the liberal view that that just arrangements must allow individuals to employ their natural endowments to generate unequal earnings even as they aim to reduce the influence

Conclusion

of arbitrary considerations on life chances, Cohen offers a plausible counterargument for the more thoroughly egalitarian view that just arrangements must assign priority to the concern to counter arbitrary influences on the distribution of goods.

In support of this argument, Cohen cites John Stuart Mill's view that the principle of remuneration that rewards greater productivity with greater compensation "is in itself a principle of injustice...when [the difference in productivity] depends on natural difference of strength or capacity."[22] Such a principle, Mill argues, "is giving the most to those who have; assigning most to those who are most favored by nature."[23] Such a principle may be expedient, Mill argues, but it is not just. Rawls, then, is consistent in arguing that justice requires the acceptance of institutions that allow the talented to employ their talents to generate unequal earnings, but Cohen can respond compellingly that such an approach tolerates too much arbitrary inequality to be just.

While Cohen's development of these Millian insights is of significant independent interest, he is unable to develop them into a compelling internal critique of Rawls because he fails to recognize that Rawls's concerns regarding the influence of arbitrary factors on life chances are qualified in a manner that Mill's concerns are not. Cohen thus fails to establish that the difference principle contains an important ambiguity that can only be resolved by adopting a reading that forbids unequal compensation to the more talented.

Cohen's critique of Rawls, however, is perhaps best understood as motivated less by concerns regarding theoretical consistency and rigor than by concerns regarding Rawls's substantive conclusions and their practical implications. In particular, Cohen is concerned that in allowing respect for entitlements to dilute his commitment to the goal of neutralizing arbitrary influences on life chances, Rawls constructed a political theory that tolerated unacceptably high levels of inequality. The true ground of Cohen's disagreement with Rawls is therefore a disagreement regarding the status of entitlements in an acceptable account of distributive justice.

In allowing considered judgments regarding entitlements and legitimate expectations to weaken his theory's commitment to fairness in distribution and to determine the character and content of the difference principle, Cohen worried, Rawls gave aid and comfort to the regressive policies of the Reagan, Bush, and Thatcher administrations – in particular, the regressive Lawson, Reagan, and Bush tax cuts. Any account of distributive justice that provided intellectual support for injustice on such a massive scale, Cohen argued plausibly, must provide an unsatisfactory account of distributive justice.

If Cohen could demonstrate that his characterization of Rawls's theory and its practical implications was correct, such a demonstration would, in fact, raise considerable doubts about the plausibility of Rawls's approach to theorizing distributive justice. How close has Cohen come to making such a case? As discussed in this paper, Cohen fails to establish that Rawls's theory (1) licenses selfish maximizing or (2) exempts individual choices to pursue selfish advantage from the requirements of justice. But are Cohen's practical claims – that Rawls's theory provides intellectual support for regressive policy on a massive scale – more persuasive? If so, Cohen's critique would still justify significant doubts regarding Rawlsian justice.

Conservative advocates of tax cuts for the better situated often claim that their policies satisfy a criterion that is roughly equivalent to the difference principle – that is, they argue that such tax cuts work as part of a scheme that benefits the least advantaged. Are these claims justified?

Consider the Bush tax cuts. These tax cuts cost $2.5 trillion over a period of eight years. A total of $1.13 billion of these cuts went to earners in the top 1 percent of the distribution whose median annual income was $1.1 million. Another $400 billion went to the remaining earners in the top quintile. In contrast, the earners in the bottom 60 percent of the distribution, taken as a group, received a total of $325 billion (12.7 percent of the total cost of the tax cut). The immense cost of the tax cut forced drastic reductions in almost all forms of assistance to the least advantaged.

This information is sufficient to establish the regressiveness of the policy. Defenders of the policy, however, argued that the tax cuts were designed to work as part of a scheme that benefited the least advantaged. Under this scheme, tax cuts to the wealthy would stimulate national and private savings, and the increase in the rate of savings would stimulate the economy, creating new job opportunities and other benefits to the least advantaged. The application of a criterion roughly equivalent to the difference principle, it was argued, would thus vindicate the justice of the tax cuts.

The Bush tax cuts, of course, failed to produce the promised growth, but that failure might be the consequence of the recent collapse of the

Conclusion

US economy rather than the consequence of a defect in the rationale underlying the tax cuts. Were the Bush tax cuts well designed to produce benefits to the least advantaged under more favorable economic conditions? The experience of the Reagan tax cuts of the 1980s provides evidence that is directly relevant. Like the Bush tax cuts, the Reagan tax cuts expended trillions of dollars on tax cuts that benefited primarily the rich on the theory that (1) tax cuts to the rich would stimulate a sharp rise in national and personal savings and that (2) the increase in the level of savings would stimulate economic growth that would generate benefits for the least advantaged. The plan to subsidize national and personal savings therefore constituted the "scheme" that was to "improve the expectations of the least advantaged." Unless the subsidy worked as described, however, no argument could be made that the tax cuts were consistent with the difference principle.

And the subsidy did not work as described. Not only did levels of savings not increase as a result of the tax cuts, but also the rates of both national and personal savings fell significantly. The rate of personal savings fell from 7.1 percent of disposable income in 1980 to 3.8 percent in 1986. The rate of national savings fell from 16.2 percent of gross national product in 1980 to 12.8 percent in 1986.[24] Defenders of the tax cuts might argue that the policy, while not producing the predicted increase in the rate of savings, nevertheless triggered an economic recovery. In fact, real GNP growth between 1980 and 1986 averaged an anemic 2.4 percent, well below the average rate of growth in the 1970s.[25] And while it is possible that the Reagan tax cuts did provide a traditional demand-side stimulus that encouraged *some* economic growth in the mid-1980s, the effect of these tax cuts certainly would not have satisfied the second half of Rawls's criterion – that inequalities must be arranged to the greatest advantage of the least advantaged. Between 1979 and 1989, the income share of the lowest quintile of earners fell by 11 percent; the income share of the second lowest quintile of earners fell by 8.6 percent; and the income share of the middle quintile of earners fell by 5.7 percent.[26] Moreover, Reagan's tax cuts were financed in part by severe cuts in programs designed to assist the least advantaged. Between 1982 and 1986, funding for employment and training for the disadvantaged was cut by more than 52 percent; funding for education was cut by more than 28 percent; and low-income assistance was cut by more than 12.3 percent.[27] The

Reagan and Bush tax cuts were not, therefore, justifiable as consistent with the difference principle either in conception or in execution.

Cohen's concerns, then, are not justified. Rawls's incorporation in his theory of considered judgments regarding entitlements did not lead to the generation of a theory that provides intellectual support for regressive policies such as the Lawson, Reagan, or Bush tax cuts. Rawls, in fact demonstrated that a theory of distributive justice can give full weight to the claims of entitlements without sacrificing its commitment to fairness in the distribution of social goods.

Notes

1 See Gauthier (1974), Nozick (1974).
2 "On my view of what it means for a society to institute the principle, people would mention the norms of equality when asked to explain why they and those like them are willing to work for the pay they get." Cohen (2008), p. 74.
3 See Julius (2003), Pogge (2000), Murphy (1999), Williams (1998). Samuel Scheffler, for example, writes that "Cohen's masterful arguments expose two highly significant areas of unclarity in Rawls's theory." Scheffler (2006), p. 112.
4 Cohen (2008), p. 68, my emphasis.
5 Cohen (2008), p. 69.
6 Cohen (2008), p. 74.
7 Cohen (2008), p. 124.
8 Rawls ([1975] 1999), p. 299; TJ 272.
9 Rawls ([1975] 1999), p. 299.
10 The price system, Rawls makes clear, may operate within a capitalist market or within some form of socialist regime: "But it is clear that, in theory anyway, a liberal socialist regime can also answer to the two principles of justice" (TJ 247). He notes that in a just socialist society there is something akin to the price system at work as well.
11 Rawls ([1967] 1999), p. 152.
12 Cohen (2008), p. 85.
13 Cohen (2008), p. 71.
14 Cohen (2008), p. 72.
15 "When separate and independent transactions" by private individuals erode the justice of basic social arrangements, "we require special institutions to preserve background justice" (PL 267).
16 Cohen (2008), p. 117.
17 Cohen (2008), p. 117.

18 Cohen (2008), pp. 117–18.
19 Cohen (2008), p. 132.
20 Cohen (2008), p. 135.
21 "[P]olitical principles do not apply directly to [the family's] internal life, *but they do impose essential constraints on the family as an institution and guarantee the basic rights and liberties of all its members*" (JAF 164, my emphasis).
22 Cohen (2008), p. 85.
23 Cohen (2008), p. 85.
24 Blinder (1987), p. 99.
25 Blinder (1987), p. 99.
26 US Census Bureau (2000), Table No. 745, p. 471.
27 Palmer and Mills (1982), p. 82.

6 | *Justice as Fairness and Fair Equality of Opportunity*

In its most general form, Rawls's second principle of justice sets out two distinct requirements. Basic social institutions must ensure both that (1) all members of society enjoy real equal opportunity to achieve economic success and participate in political life and that (2) inequalities are to everyone's advantage. These separate requirements address concerns regarding the distinct effects of different categories of endowments. The guarantee of equal opportunity addresses the concern that social endowments (e.g., inherited wealth, class position) might determine a person's prospects of success or failure. The requirement that inequalities must be to everyone's advantage addresses the concern that even after opportunity is equalized, diversity in natural endowments (e.g., talents, interests) will lead persons to engage in diverse occupations that generate unequal levels of compensation. If the resulting inequality is too great, then natural endowments will have generated an unjustifiable inequality in shares of social goods.

The second of these two concerns, and in particular the role of this concern in the argument justifying the difference principle, has received by far the greater share of attention in the secondary literature. Early commentators on Rawls's work, in fact, often treated the difference principle as the sole requirement of Rawls's account of distributive justice. The first concern – addressed by the principle of fair equality of opportunity – however, constitutes the more fundamental issue in justice as fairness. Rawls specifies that fair equality of opportunity is lexically prior to the difference principle in the same way that the first principle is lexically prior to the second (TJ 77–78, 265–67). If concerns regarding opportunity conflict with concerns regarding the fairness of the distribution, concerns regarding equal opportunity are to be assigned absolute priority. The secondary literature that presents the difference principle as the dominant or sole requirement of justice as fairness thus seriously distorts Rawls's account of distributive justice.

Such an understanding of justice as fairness is particularly misleading because of the character that it assigns to Rawls's theory. If justice as fairness requires nothing more than satisfaction of the difference principle, the policies required to secure distributive justice will focus primarily on the redistribution of income through tax and transfer programs. Since the principle of fair equality of opportunity is the more fundamental requirement of Rawls's theory, however, the policies required to secure distributive justice will primarily emphasize education, training, and manpower policy. Policies to redistribute income will play at most a secondary role.

The distinct character of fair equality of opportunity as a principle of justice can be illustrated by examining the division of labor between fair equality of opportunity and the difference principle in regulating questions of policy. Suppose, for example, that a policy-maker wishes to determine whether justice as fairness justifies support for legislation requiring a minimum wage. According to a conventional understanding of Rawls's argument, the legislator need only consider the effect of adopting such legislation on the least advantaged representative person. According to this view, the difference principle requires the adoption of any policies required to maximize the expectations of the persons who occupy the least advantaged social position. If minimum wage legislation best serves the realization of this goal, according to the conventional view, then the difference principle requires the adoption of such legislation.

This view has the advantage of being consistent with conventional understandings of Rawls but the disadvantage of misrepresenting Rawls's actual argument. The most important flaw in this reading is the assumption that the difference principle justifies the adoption of any policy required to maximize the expectations of the least advantaged. As discussed in Chapter 5, the difference principle simply regulates the relation between the earnings of the more fortunate and the earnings of other members of society – in particular, the principle requires that the greater advantages enjoyed by the more fortunate must be "to everyone's advantage" in the sense that they must work as part of a scheme that benefits other members of society, in particular the persons who occupy the least advantaged social position. In the case of minimum wage legislation, however, the issue considered does not involve the permissibility of higher earnings or benefits for the more fortunate. If the legislation is adopted, the minimum wage will be a requirement of law, whether or not the more fortunate enjoy greater earnings. The difference principle, then, has *no bearing* on the minimum wage issue. The minimum wage example therefore constitutes a counterexample to the assumption that grounds the second error in the conventional understanding of Rawls's argument – the assumption that any question relating to the distribution of goods, particularly a question relating to the well-being of the disadvantaged, is properly resolved through an application of the difference principle. Whether the minimum wage is a requirement of justice must be determined under Rawls's other principle of distributive justice, the principle of fair equality of opportunity. In order to resolve this question, we require a developed account of the meaning and implications of this principle.

This chapter will present such an account. In the first section, I sketch the general requirements of this principle. The next section presents a more developed account of the principle's substantive requirements. The final section discusses the implications of this account for Rawls's account of responsibility for disadvantage.

Fair Equality of Opportunity

The principle of fair equality of opportunity requires that persons "with similar abilities and skills should have similar life chances" (TJ 63). The principle requires not merely the enforcement of legal protections of formal equal opportunity, but "that all should have a fair chance" to attain success. Persons "similarly motivated and endowed" should have "equal prospects of culture and achievement" regardless of their initial social position.[1] The principle is thus designed to implement the considered judgment that factors that are arbitrary from the moral point of view – in particular, social endowments – should not determine life chances. In order to implement this considered judgment, the principle aims to neutralize the influence of social endowments on the opportunities available to each individual through the policies implemented by "a certain set of institutions that assures similar chances of education and culture for persons similarly motivated" (TJ 245, see JAF 44).

The principle is designed to ensure both that (1) social and economic positions remain effectively open to all and that (2) each member of society enjoys the same opportunity to develop the capacities necessary to compete for these positions. Fair equality of opportunity addresses the first concern by preventing the kind of "excessive accumulations of property" (TJ 63) that allow privileged groups to monopolize social advantages. In justification of this requirement, Rawls cites R. H. Tawney's argument that the concentration of property leads directly to social stratification and the monopolization of opportunity (TJ 63n11).[2] Such stratification, Tawney argues, does not merely lead to "different levels of pecuniary income... [and] different opportunities for mental development and civilization."[3] In addition, the concentration of wealth and property in the possession of a tiny minority produces a system that "vest[s] in particular classes a special degree of public influence and an exceptional measure of economic opportunity."[4] Differences of wealth of this sort, Tawney asserts, accounted for the hierarchical quality of the social system in nineteenth-century England.[5] Tawney's argument thus provides significant support for Rawls's view that the guarantee that opportunities remain open to all "on the basis of qualities and efforts reasonably related to the relevant duties and tasks... [is] put in jeopardy when inequalities of wealth exceed a certain limit" (TJ 245–46).

The government in a well-ordered society is to guard against accumulation of advantage and thus underwrite equal economic opportunity "by policing the conduct of firms and private associations and preventing the establishment of monopolistic restrictions and barriers to the more desirable positions" (TJ 243). In order to implement this requirement, the distribution branch is "to correct the distribution of wealth" in order "to prevent concentrations of power detrimental to...fair equality of opportunity" (TJ 245). The distribution branch performs this task by enforcing "laws regulating bequest and inheritance of property, and other devices such as taxes, to prevent excessive concentrations of power" (JAF 51).

The principle addresses the second concern – that each member of society must enjoy the same effective opportunity to compete for advantageous positions – by ensuring access to services such as education, training, and health care that are necessary to ensure that each individual "acquire[s] the cultural knowledge and skills" (TJ 63) necessary to ensure equal opportunity to compete for advantageous positions. The life chances "of those with the same abilities and aspirations" (TJ 63), Rawls argues, should not be determined by their starting position and initial set of social endowments. Rather, in order to realize fair equal opportunity, a just society must guarantee fully equal access to services including (1) education (TJ 63, 243), (2) skill training (TJ 270), and (3) health care (JAF 174). In addition, the government must aim to ensure full employment and free choice of profession (TJ 244).

Among the interventions designed to secure equal opportunity, Rawls assigns the highest priority to "maintaining equal opportunities of education for all" (TJ 63). A just society must ensure "equal chances of education and culture for persons similarly endowed and motivated" (TJ 243, 245, see JAF 44). Initially, in fact, Rawls's discussion of the principle of fair equality of opportunity might seem to suggest that access to education constitutes the sole substantive guarantee required to assure equal opportunity. The discussion of means to realize the principle in Section 12 of *A Theory of Justice*, for example, discusses only education as a policy tool. As Rawls develops his account of the practical implications of the equal opportunity principle, however, he clearly establishes that the guarantees under the principle are far more extensive than a guarantee of equal access to education. First, the principle requires the guarantee of access to the training necessary so that persons from less-advantaged backgrounds may develop the skills necessary to compete effectively for advantageous positions (TJ 270). Fair equality of opportunity ensures that "many more people receiv[e] the benefits of education and training" (TJ 270) in order to secure "open competition between...greater numbers of the well-trained and better educated" (JAF 67). In addition, equal opportunity requires equal access to medical care: "provision for medical care...to meet the needs of citizens as free and equal...falls under the general means necessary to underwrite fair equality of opportunity" (JAF 174). Moreover, Rawls argues, special provisions of family law are necessary in order to ensure that "the burden of bearing, raising, and educating children does not fall more heavily on women, thereby undermining their fair equality of opportunity" (JAF 11). In order to ensure that the recipients of education, training, and other services have the effective opportunity to employ their skills, the stabilization branch must aim to ensure "reasonably full employment in the sense that those who want work can find it and the free choice of occupation" (TJ 244).

Most significantly, however, Rawls makes clear that the scope of guarantees under fair equality of opportunity extends far beyond that of the limited set of guarantees that he discusses explicitly. Rawls provides only a sketchy explicit account of the principle and its

Fair Equality of Opportunity

requirements, he notes, because he assumes that "the elements of this framework are familiar enough" (TJ 63). The principle, he assumes, embodies liberal notions of egalitarian justice discussed in the work of nineteenth and early twentieth-century liberal philosophers and theorists such as Henry Sidgwick and R. H. Tawney. For a more thorough account of the nature and necessary conditions of equal opportunity, he refers the reader to specific passages in Sidgwick, Tawney, and Bernard Williams (TJ 63n11). An adequate understanding of the character, scope, and substance of the guarantees required under the principle therefore requires an examination of these passages, which Rawls incorporates by reference.

Sidgwick, Education, and Ideal Justice

Rawls cites most particularly a passage from Sidgwick's *The Method of Ethics* in which Sidgwick argues that "ideal justice" would require the removal of "the inequalities that are attributable to circumstances *by bringing the best education within the reach of all classes*, so that all children might have an equal opportunity of being selected for any functions for which they seem to be fit."[6] Inequality deriving from unequal access to education, Sidgwick asserts, is "arbitrary"[7] and therefore unjust. Ideal justice does not, then, require *merely* policies to improve the quality of public schools or to provide access to private schools. Equal opportunity, according to Sidgwick's argument – incorporated by reference into justice as fairness – is not realized while the less advantaged are denied the equivalent of the "best education" that is available to the more privileged. Any set of institutions that fails to meet this standard allows arbitrary inequality of opportunity to determine the distribution of social goods and opportunities.

Tawney and Environmental Influences on Prospects

While unequal educational opportunity may be the single most significant factor generating social stratification, Tawney argues – in the passage that Rawls cites – that the effects of unequal education are powerfully reinforced by unequal access to other essential goods and services that affect life chances profoundly and to which a just society must therefore provide equal access. Tawney cites, for example, reports that a significantly larger percentage of the children of working-class families than of the children of privileged families suffer from serious health problems.[8] In addition, he notes, only a small minority of these children are adequately nourished.[9] Finally, these working-class children are "exposed to [environmental] conditions in which health, if not impossible, is necessarily precarious."[10] Such disparities in access to health care, adequate nourishment, and safe environments, Tawney argues, "are more powerful as instrument[s] of social stratification even than the difference of income of which they are the consequence."[11]

Moreover, Tawney emphasizes, such disparities in health care, nutrition, and environment reinforce the enormous disparity in educational opportunity that exists between children of the working class and children of the privileged classes. Working-class children are educated in environments "which would not be tolerated for an instant in the schools attended by the well-to-do."[12] The defective quality of the early years of education provided to this class is reinforced by their lack of access to higher education: "the proportion of children leaving the elementary schools who enter ... secondary schools is, in England and Wales as a whole, less than one-seventh, and in some areas less than one-tenth."[13] Thus, working-class children "end their education just at the age when their powers are beginning to develop."[14]

Bernard Williams and the Scope of Equal Opportunity

Finally, the passage that Rawls cites from Williams's paper "The Idea of Equality" provides the clearest account of the full scope of the requirements of the principle of fair equality of opportunity. Equal opportunity, Williams argues, is best understood as requiring "that a limited good shall in fact be allocated on grounds which do not *a priori* exclude any section of those that desire it."[15] A proper understanding of equal opportunity therefore requires that "people from all sections of society have an equal chance of satisfying" the necessary conditions for the acquisition of any particular social good.[16] If education at an expensive elite school is a necessary condition of entry into certain careers (e.g., medicine, law, investment banking), Williams argues, a society that allows elite schools to allocate positions in their classes on the basis of ability to pay fails the test of fair equality of opportunity. Under such an arrangement, children who are not born into wealthy families will clearly not "have an equal chance of satisfying" the necessary conditions of achieving a particular social good – the opportunity to compete for advantageous positions.

More generally, Williams argues that if social arrangements are such that children from privileged homes have greater opportunity to succeed than children from less-advantaged homes because of qualities specifically associated with privileged homes (e.g., greater access to elite schools, greater access to adequate nutrition and health care, a healthier and safer living environment), then the society fails to satisfy the requirements of equal opportunity. The difference in opportunity to succeed is simply the product of "environmental factors" whose effects could be eliminated or reduced by "imaginative social reform."[17] To give two persons equality of opportunity of opportunity, then, "involves *regarding their conditions, where curable, as themselves part of what is done*" to the persons:[18] "Their identity, for these purposes, does not include their curable environment, which is itself unequal and a contributor of inequality."[19] A social system, then, fails to secure equal opportunity if the distribution of a social good is unequal and those who receive less advantageous shares "are under a disadvantage which could be removed by further reform or social action."[20] For example, Williams argues, " "[w]e have every reason to suppose that" the inferior educational performance of children from working-class homes, relative to children from professional homes, is "the product, in good part, of environmental factors."[21] Moreover, we also know that "imaginative social reform . . . would favorably [a]ffect those environmental factors."[22] A society that fails to undertake the necessary reforms, Williams argues, "falls short of equality of opportunity."[23] In incorporating Williams's account of equal opportunity by reference as an account of the concept of equal opportunity that is "familiar enough," Rawls thus indicates that fair equality of opportunity, if fully implemented, would require "imaginative social reform" to address *any* deficits of education or training and any inequalities of access to health care or advantageous environmental factors that might result in unequal ability to compete for advantageous positions.

Rawls's understanding of the requirements of equal opportunity, then, is far from limited to the requirement that the government must attempt to eliminate overt discrimination and reduce disparities between the quality of education available to the privileged and the less advantaged. Rather, a society fails to achieve fair equality of opportunity *if any person or group suffers from a deficit in skills, education, or other capacity required to compete effectively for a desirable position, and that deficit (1) is the product of environmental factors and (2) could be removed by social policy.* Under this standard, more effective and extensive versions of the Head Start program, manpower training programs such as those authorized under the CETA program, manpower policies of the sort pursued by Sweden and Denmark, housing subsidies, and universal health insurance – as well as any other programs required in order to compensate for deficits in education, skill, or capacity to compete – are all potential elements of a set of requirements of equal opportunity that must be implemented *before* distributional issues under the difference principle are to be considered.

The passages from Sidgwick, Tawney, and Williams provide information that is essential to an adequate understanding of the requirements of fair equality of opportunity. These passages establish that the requirements of the principle are both substantial and wide-ranging. The passage from Sidgwick establishes that fair equality of opportunity imposes a demanding standard of equality of educational opportunity. The passage from Tawney suggests the wide range of environmental factors to which the principle applies. And the passage from Williams establishes the full scope of the obligation to equalize opportunity under the principle – if a deficit in capacity to compete is the product of an environmental factor, a *just* government *must* employ imaginative social policy to anticipate and address that environmental impediment to equal opportunity.

Just Institutions

Once the character and requirements of the principle of fair equality of opportunity are understood, the conclusion becomes unavoidable that the conventional understanding of the requirements of justice as fairness represents an unacceptable distortion of Rawls's theory. According to the conventional view, a well-ordered society must (1) secure basic liberties, (2) prevent overt discrimination, (3) ensure that the school system is designed "to even out class barriers" (TJ 63), and then (4) realize a distribution that maximizes the position of the least advantaged through tax and transfer policy. This view thus presents Rawls's theory as requiring that – once a just constitution has secured basic liberties and protections against discrimination in schools and the workplace – officers of the state must determine in advance the distribution of social goods required by justice and must secure that distribution primarily through tax and transfer policy. Thus, the conventional view presents Rawls's account of distributive justice as a theory designed primarily to allocate "a given collection of goods...among definite individuals" (TJ 77). This picture bears very little resemblance to the requirements of justice as fairness.

In Chapter 5 of *A Theory of Justice*, Rawls presents a very different account of the nature of basic social institutions that satisfy the requirements of his account of distributive justice (TJ 243). Just institutions must assign the highest priority to protection of the basic liberties and to securing the fair value of liberty, but the guarantee of fair equality of opportunity is second only to liberty in priority. As a minimum requirement, just institutions must guarantee "equal chances of education and culture for persons similarly endowed and motivated" and equal opportunity "in economic activities and in the free choice of occupation" (TJ 243). Once these minimum guarantees have been secured, various branches of government are to implement additional policies to equalize opportunity. The stabilization branch is to strive "to bring about reasonably full employment...and the free choice of occupation" (TJ 244). The distribution branch is to secure funds for "public goods,...[including] fair equality in education, and the like" through proportional expenditure or income taxes (TJ 247). The allocation branch is to prevent the formation of the kind of "unreasonable market power" (TJ 244) that could allow classes or groups to dominate opportunities to achieve advantageous social positions. Rawls emphasizes the importance of these institutions because it is "the set of institutions that assures similar chances of education and culture for persons similarly motivated...that are put in jeopardy when inequalities of wealth exceed a certain limit" (TJ 245–46).

To what extent additional adjustments of the distribution are necessary under the difference principle to secure justice can be determined only after fair equality of opportunity is assured. Once equal opportunity has been secured within economic institutions, the distribution of income will remain to some degree unequal because "the price system" will inevitably provide different levels of compensation to persons with differing skills. The price system – even properly regulated – will predictably provide higher levels of compensation to investment bankers that to physicists, composers, or carpenters. This inequality is not entirely consistent with justice since it results in significant part from the influence of natural endowments that are distributed through an arbitrary natural lottery. The difference principle is necessary to address this inequality by designating as *most thoroughly just* that arrangement that, through a combination of compensation in the market, stimulative fiscal policy, wage subsidies, policies designed to provide primary goods, training, increased opportunities for the disadvantaged, and – if necessary – transfers, ensures that permissible inequalities benefit the least advantaged. The difference principle, then, merely applies final modifications to a distribution that is determined primarily by individual efforts within a set of institutional arrangements that guarantee freedom and equal opportunity to pursue a rational life plan.

Far from advocating social arrangements in which a centralized decision process determines the shares of goods that individuals receive, then, Rawls argues for a conception of justice under which the justice of a distribution "cannot be judged at all apart from the claims (entitlements) of individuals earned by their efforts within the fair system of cooperation" (JAF 50, see TJ 76) so that "what a person is entitled to depends on what he does" (TJ 74). A just distribution cannot be identified until persons have actually participated in the market and have generated their legitimate claims. Once economic markets are "properly regulated" (TJ 244) and a social minimum that secures the worth of liberty is guaranteed, in fact, "it may be perfectly fair that [the distribution of] the rest of total income be settled by the price system" (TJ 245).

Just institutions are thus designed primarily to provide individuals with the equal liberty and equal opportunity to achieve advantageous social positions through the provision of education, training, health care, nutrition, and any other services required by "imaginative social reform" in order to address the disadvantageous effects of environmental factors. The specific policies required to realize equal opportunity must be chosen by the legislature, but if the legislature fails to adopt adequate policies, the society will be – to that extent – unjust. The principle of fair equality of opportunity is designed to secure the opportunity to "achieve the widest regulative excellences of which each is capable" (TJ 463) in order to participate effectively in the economy. The justice of a distribution is thus determined in significant part by what people have actually done within their economic institutions.

The conventional view that justice as fairness requires that social institutions secure a just distribution primarily through tax and transfer policy thus misrepresents Rawls's theory precisely because the conventional view describes justice as fairness as an *allocative* conception of justice – a conception that aims simply to divide a given collection of goods "among definite individuals with known desires and needs" (TJ 77). Rawls explicitly *rejects* allocative approaches to theorizing justice "as incompatible with the fundamental idea by which justice as fairness is organized: the idea of society as a fair system of cooperation organized over time" (JAF 50). Allocative justice applies, Rawls asserts, in conditions in which (1) the goods to be allocated are not the product of the individuals who are to receive the goods and (2) "there are no prior claims on the things to be distributed ... [since] [t]he collection is not the product of these individuals" (TJ 77). In contrast, justice as fairness does not assess the justice of a distribution by attempting to distribute "a stock of benefits available ... [among individuals] with given desires and needs" (TJ 76). Rather, Rawls's theory requires that "[a] distribution cannot be judged in isolation from ... [consideration of] what individuals have done in good faith in light of established expectations" (TJ 76). To paraphrase Robert Nozick, the conventional view of Rawls's view presents justice as fairness as a theory constituted by end-state principles – principles that consider only the distribution of goods when assessing the justice of a situation.[24] In fact, however, justice as fairness assigns central significance to historical information: determination of the justice of present claims must – in Rawls's account of distributive justice – assign decisive importance to claims of entitlement that have been generated in the past. Like Nozick's theory, as Rawls notes, justice as fairness "give[s] a fundamental role to ... pure adjusted procedural justice. It follows that neither of these doctrines are end-state views."[25]

Democratic Equality and Luck Equality

Finally, it is important to emphasize the distinction that this contrast establishes between justice as fairness and the account of distributive egalitarianism offered by philosophers who favor theories of luck equality – a view that some of its advocates have argued provides an extension of some of Rawls's argument that is "truer than Rawls's own conception of justice to some of his fundamental insights."[26] Luck egalitarians such as Richard Arneson, G. A. Cohen, Ronald Dworkin argue that egalitarian justice must focus on the relation between choice and consequences at the individual level and must aim to compensate persons for – and only for – well-being deficits for which it is not reasonable to hold the person responsible.

While luck egalitarians share Rawls's concern that arbitrary factors should not determine life chances, then, luck equality interprets this concern to require a conception of distributive justice that (1) focuses precisely on the needs and claims of individuals and (2) aims to compensate those individuals for well-being deficits for which they cannot reasonably be held responsible. In thus aiming to allocate a given stock of goods over a given set of persons, luck equality constitutes precisely the kind of allocative conception of justice that Rawls explicitly rejects. In fact, Rawls specifically criticizes two qualities typical of allocative conceptions of justice that are central features of luck equality. First, he argues against a particularistic focus on the situations of individuals: "It is a mistake to focus attention on the varying relative positions of individuals and to require that every change, considered as a single transaction viewed in isolation, be in itself just" (TJ 76). The acceptance of the two principles, Rawls notes, "constitutes an understanding to discard as irrelevant ... much of the information and many of the complications of everyday life" (TJ 76). Allocative approaches that focus on the relative positions of individuals, Rawls notes, have the practical disadvantage that they make it necessary to "keep track of the endless variety of circumstances and the changing relative positions of particular persons" (TJ 76). Second, he criticizes the notion that a conception of distributive justice should aim to compensate persons for deficits in well-being. Rather, Rawls argues, it is the arrangement of the basic structure that must be judged. Unlike luck egalitarians, then, Rawls argues for a conception of justice that requires that the distribution of goods is to be secured primarily by the employment of human capital in the context of economic institutions that ensure pure procedural justice.

Fair Equality of Opportunity and Responsibility for Disadvantage

The central role that Rawls assigns to the principle of fair equality of opportunity in determining the nature of a just distribution ensures that justice as fairness is a theory of pure procedural justice and therefore cannot be plausibly described as an end-state theory. Nevertheless, a number of influential early commentators on *A Theory of Justice* – Robert Nozick in particular – insist, to the contrary, that Rawls offers an essentially end-state theory of justice in distribution. The view that Rawls's theory aims primarily to secure a precise desired distribution of a fixed stock of goods, moreover, continues to exercise a significant influence on the literature of distributive justice. Even philosophers generally sympathetic to Rawls's approach are often influenced by this view regarding the fundamental character of justice as fairness and, as a result, conclude that Rawls's account of distributive justice is insufficiently sensitive to entitlements and to the issue of responsibility for disadvantage.

Nozick – who provides the definitive account of justice as fairness as an end-state theory – argues that Rawls theory aims to impose "an external patterned criterion"[27] specified by the difference principle on economic practices in order to produce a unique desired distribution of goods. This argument, however, is grounded in a number of false assumptions. First, Nozick assumes that the difference principle constitutes the sole substantive requirement of Rawls's account of distributive justice. Second, he assumes that the difference principle aims to produce a particular and specific distribution of goods. Finally, he assumes that the difference principle requires maximization of the share received by the least advantaged. Arguing from these assumptions, Nozick claims that Rawls's theory is insensitive to claims of entitlement and is more generally insensitive to historical information that is essentially relevant to the determination of just shares of goods. Nozick's argument thus defines the view that constitutes the foundation of more recent arguments that Rawls is insensitive to the particular claims of individuals and is more generally insensitive to a particular kind of historical information that is centrally relevant to justice – information regarding individual responsibility for disadvantage.

If Nozick's assumptions were correct, his conclusions might be plausible. As we have seen, however, his three central assumptions are false. First, the difference principle does not constitute the only – or even the principal – requirement of distributive justice in justice as fairness. The principle of fair equality of opportunity constitutes the fundamental requirement of Rawls's account of distributive justice, and that principle is designed to ensure that "what a person is entitled to depends on what he does" (TJ 74). Fair equality of opportunity thus ensures that the kind of historical information that Nozick views as essentially relevant to justice in fact plays the central role in determining the nature of a just distribution of goods in justice as fairness. The difference principle operates merely to reduce the degree of inequality in holdings deriving from the influence of natural endowments that persists after equal opportunity is ensured. Second, the difference principle aims for no particular distribution of goods. Rather, the difference principle requires merely the maintenance of a particular relation between unequal positions and sets of expectations and holdings – the superior expectations and holdings of the more fortunate must work as part of a scheme that benefits the least advantaged. Finally, the difference principle does not require maximization of the share of the least advantaged. As a result, Nozick's argument seriously misrepresents the character and requirements of justice as fairness.

While Nozick is concerned primarily with what he perceives as the failure of justice as fairness to respect entitlements, more recent contributors to the egalitarian literature have argued from the assumption that justice as fairness is an end-state theory to the conclusion that Rawls's theory is insufficiently sensitive to the individual's responsibility for her own disadvantage. For example, Ronald Dworkin, arguing from the assumption that justice as fairness requires strict equality in shares of primary goods "save as works to the advantage of the least advantaged class,"[28] concludes that justice as fairness focuses on the interests of classes rather than individuals and cannot, therefore, provide an account of distributive justice "that is individualized for each and that therefore can be seen to set entitlements... from the point of view of each person."[29] While Dworkin does not directly accuse justice as fairness of being insensitive to responsibility for disadvantage, that charge is clearly implicit in his claim that the theory fails to take proper account of the individualized information necessary to justify holdings from the point of view of the person.

G. A. Cohen, similarly, argues that Rawls's view that "the idea of rewarding desert is impracticable" necessarily requires that, under justice as fairness, "effort deserves no reward at all."[30] Rawls's theory, Cohen thus claims, requires that we must ignore the efforts of individuals within economic arrangements in determining the nature of a just distribution. According to Cohen's interpretation of justice as fairness, an individual's productive efforts justify no claims to social goods, and an individual's failure to make any effort does not reduce or otherwise affect the size of his just share of social goods – Rawls's view, that is, takes no account of justified entitlements or responsibility for disadvantage. As discussed above, however, Cohen's view is clearly contradicted by Rawls's account of legitimate expectations which specifies that the nature of an individual's just share is determined primarily when "persons and groups take part in just arrangements" and, as a result, "acquire claims on one another defined by the publicly recognized rules" (TJ 273) so that, in justice as fairness, "what a person is entitled to depends on what he does" (TJ 74). While Rawls rejects the view that a notion of moral desert could be incorporated into a political conception of justice, then, he offers the notion of legitimate expectation as "a replacement [for the moral notion of desert] that belongs to a reasonable political conception" (JAF 73). While effort may not justify claims of *moral desert of a reward*, then, effort does ground legitimate expectations of reward. Cohen's view that, in Rawls, effort is irrelevant to distributive justice thus reflects an oversight – a failure to take note of the definitive component of Rawls's theory of distributive justice

Finally, John Roemer claims that the issue of responsibility "appears only embryonically in the work of Rawls and Sen."[31] Roemer bases this claim on the assumption that justice as fairness requires that "only an allocation of resources which maximizes the index of primary goods going to the worst-off group is fair."[32] If this view constituted a plausible interpretation of Rawls, it *would* seem to justify the claim that justice as fairness is insensitive to the issue of responsibility. According to this view, justice as fairness determines the nature of a fair or just distribution of goods through a method that takes no account at all of the actual behavior of members of society. Justice, according to this view, requires that a just society must maximize the share of the least advantaged no matter how responsible the members of this group are for their own disadvantage. As discussed above, however, justice as fairness does *not* require that a just society must maximize the share of the least advantaged; rather, it requires that the determination of a just distribution of goods must be sensitive to level of ambition as reflected in the efforts that individuals have made within just economic arrangements.

Responsibility and Pure Procedural Justice

Justice as fairness, then, takes serious account of the individual's responsibility for disadvantage. It does so, however, in a manner that contrasts sharply with the manner in which these concerns are incorporated in theories of luck equality. Rather than focusing on the behavior of each individual member of society and aiming to generate an account of justice in distribution that is "individualized for each,"[33] justice as fairness incorporates concerns regarding responsibility in its account of basic social institutions. Just as Rawls aims to represent the full set of considered judgments relevant to the resolution of basic issues of justice in the structure of the original position, Rawls aims to represent the set of considered judgments relevant to basic questions regarding the just distribution of social goods in the structure of basic institutions. In both cases, the aim is to ensure pure procedural justice. If the original position is properly designed, the principles chosen there will be just whatever they happen to be, while if the basic structure of society is properly designed, the distribution of income that is generated by individual efforts within social institutions will be just whatever it happens to be (see TJ 73–78).

Rawls specifies that the principle of fair equality of opportunity secures pure procedural justice in social institutions.[34] Thus, it is this principle that incorporates concerns regarding responsibility in Rawls's theory by determining the character and structure of social and economic institutions – in particular, by establishing that the basic commitment of just institutions is to secure opportunity, not to guarantee outcomes or to compensate for well-being deficits. In its central emphasis on the guarantee of equal opportunity to pursue a life plan, then, Rawls's theory offers an attractive interpretation of Dworkin's account of the aim of egalitarian justice: securing freedom to choose what form of life to lead.

Because justice as fairness – unlike luck equality – incorporates concerns regarding responsibility at the level of institutions, the structure and substance of Rawls's theory contrasts sharply with that of theories of luck equality, which generally attempt to incorporate concerns regarding responsibility by (1) assessing the relation of a person's choices to their condition and (2) limiting compensation for deficits of well-being to cases of disadvantage for which a person cannot reasonably be held responsible. Justice as fairness rejects three features of luck equality's approach: (1) the focus on the choices and circumstances of individuals, (2) the aim to assign individualized levels of responsibility for disadvantage, and (3) the notion that *compensation* for disadvantage constitutes the principal aim of distributive justice.

In contrast, Rawls's theory aims to ensure to individuals the opportunity to generate justified entitlements to shares of goods and to secure well-being through their own efforts. Since luck equality's aim of providing targeted compensation for disadvantage reflects a widely shared contemporary understanding of the aim of distributive justice, the distinctive character of Rawls's approach to responsibility can be best illustrated by contrasting the mechanisms employed by justice as fairness to incorporate concerns regarding responsibility in the theory with the mechanisms employed by theories of luck equality to achieve the same purpose.

Dworkin's theory of resource equality requires that the claims of distributive justice are satisfied if everyone is provided with a bundle of resources to which they assign a value at least equal to the value of every other person's bundle. The nature of this bundle is determined in a Walrasian auction in which each person's particular choices and preferences determine the trades s/he is willing to make in order to secure the bundle that most closely fits his or her needs and preferences. In addition to material resources, each person's bundle will include insurance against instances of bad brute luck such as disease and lack of skill. In practice, Dworkin's theory would estimate the amount that a reasonable person would spend on such insurance against disability, skill deficits, and other aspects of a person's circumstances that might influence the person's life chances and for which it is unreasonable to hold the person responsible. Resource equality would multiply that amount by the number of members of society, and employ funds equal to the aggregate sum to a policy or policies designed to compensate persons for their disadvantage. Dworkin also argues that equality of resources must compensate persons for disadvantage that is the product of historic injustice. Once a person has been assured equality of resources, Dworkin argues that the person is responsible for any disadvantage that he or she suffers – the person can assert no claim of justice for assistance addressing such disadvantage.

The structure of Dworkin's theory, then, is typical of the structure of theories of luck equality. First, in resource equality, a just share of goods is determined through an analysis that focuses on the circumstances experienced by individuals and the choices made in those circumstances. Second, the theory aims to identify a canonical moment at which responsibility for disadvantage attaches. Finally, resource equality aims to compensate persons for disadvantage for which the person is not responsible.

Arneson's account of equal opportunity for welfare has a similar structure. Under this theory, egalitarians should recognize a duty of justice to assist only persons who have not been assured *equal opportunity for welfare*. When, precisely, has the individual been assured equal opportunity for welfare? If we model a person's opportunity for welfare in terms of a decision tree that assigns value to payoffs based upon an individual's *ideally considered* preferences (defined as those preferences that are the product of the person's thorough-going deliberation about her preferences with full information, in a calm mood, and making no reasoning errors[35]) and weight the value of each branch of the decision tree according to the probability of success, equal opportunity for welfare has been realized if all individuals face decision trees upon which the expected value of comparable choices is effectively equivalent. A person who has not been provided with equal opportunity for welfare is not responsible for his or her disadvantage and may assert claims of justice for compensation. Once a person has been assured equal opportunity for welfare, however, s/he is considered fully responsible for any disadvantage s/he experiences and may assert no claim of justice for compensation to address that disadvantage.

Thus, equal opportunity for welfare also includes the three features that typify theories of luck equality. The theory focuses on the circumstances and choices of individuals, defines a canonical point at which responsibility attaches, and compensates for disadvantage for which the person is not responsible.

Cohen's theory of equal access to advantage contains similar features. Cohen's theory (1) requires that egalitarians should compensate persons only for disadvantage for which it is unreasonable to hold the person responsible and (2) would hold a person responsible for disadvantage generated by her free choices only if the resulting disadvantage is so intrinsically connected to constitutive commitments that the individual would not choose to be without it. Thus, Cohen's theory also (1) focuses on the circumstances and choices of the individual, (2) defines a canonical standard of responsibility for disadvantage, and (3) aims to compensate persons for disadvantage for which it is unreasonable to hold them responsible.

Each of these three leading theories of luck equality thus aims to determine the degree to which each individual is responsible for her level of well-being and to compensate her for – and only for – that degree of disadvantage for which it is not reasonable to hold her responsible. Justice as fairness, in contrast, aims to create fair economic institutions within which the individual is free to determine her own level of well-being. Acceptable institutions must satisfy demanding standards of fairness – within such institutions, all persons must enjoy real equal opportunity, and permissible inequalities must be to everyone's advantage. Once these guarantees secure fairness, however, the efforts of individuals determine the distribution of goods, which is "just whatever it happens to be."

In his discussion of allocative justice, Rawls criticizes precisely the features that distinguish luck equality from justice as fairness. Allocative justice, Rawls notes, aims simply to divide "a given collection of goods among definite individuals with known desires and needs" (TJ 77). As a result, allocative approaches are insufficiently sensitive to claims of entitlement, in particular because (1) the collection of goods to be allocated is not produced by the beneficiaries and (2) "there are no prior claims on the things to be distributed... [since] [t]he collection is not the product of these individuals" (TJ 77). Since luck equality is characterized by both of these qualities, Rawls's argument suggests that luck equality – like other allocative approaches – is insufficiently sensitive to claims of entitlement.

In addition, luck equality – like other allocative approaches – insists upon "individualized" treatment of each person's circumstances and choices, while Rawls – as noted above – argues explicitly against "focus[ing] attention on the varying relative position of individuals." It is the justice of "the arrangement of the basic structure" and not "every change, considered as a single transaction" that is relevant from the standpoint of justice (TJ 76). If we accept the idea that the two principles of justice are those principles that free and equal persons would choose for themselves, then that acceptance represents "an understanding to discard as irrelevant much of the information and many of the complications of everyday life" (TJ 76). Restriction of the focus of justice as fairness to the justice of institutions, moreover, constitutes a practical advantage because this narrowed focus limits the theory's attention to questions that are properly within the scope of distributive justice. Luck equality's broad focus on the quality of the individual's choices within his or her particular circumstances, in contrast, arguably raises questions that extend beyond justice's proper scope. Cohen, for example devotes significant attention to the question of whether a society "over-resources" a person if that person receives a share of goods equal to the median share when he could achieve a median level of utility with fewer resources (because of his "cheap tastes"). Rawls would, of course, object to Cohen's employment of a utility metric to measure well-being. But, more significantly, Rawls would argue that it is not the business of justice to fine-tune the distribution of goods to persons' desires and needs. A share of goods can only be *unjustly* large if it is not generated within institutions that guarantee equal liberty, equal opportunity, and fair compensation. If institutions satisfy these standards, Rawls would argue, then the question of whether the share that a person has generated within those institutions is too large – whether the person has been "overresourced" – cannot be a question of justice. Cohen's analysis of this example in fact reflects the aspect of allocative justice that Rawls finds most problematic. That is, Cohen's discussion of this example ignores the person's role as a producer of social goods and the justified claims of entitlement that the person may have generated in that role. Rather, as is typical in allocative approaches, Cohen's example treats distributive justice as simply the problem of allocating a stock of preexisting goods over a set of persons who have no entitlements except those determined with respect to their needs and preferences.

Finally, allocative theories in general and luck equality in particular embody an approach to reasoning about justice that Rawls rejects – an approach that aims to sets up in advance "an independent standard for deciding which outcome is just" (TJ 74) and to impose that standard on the distribution of goods. Luck equality thus seems to treat the substance of morality as fixed by an independently existing order of values, while Rawls argues from the assumption that justifiable moral judgments are best understood as grounded neither in an independently existing order of values nor in special features of human psychology, but rather in a process of reasoning that can be represented as a procedure that models the requirements of practical reason. As Cohen concedes, his disagreements with Rawls stem – to a great extent – from the fact that Oxford people of his vintage "do not think that philosophy can move as far away as Harvard people think from pertinent pre-philosophical judgment."[36] Rawls could respond, however, that his understanding of moral judgment as a process of reasoning, rather than a process that discovers preexisting truths, possesses a number of

Fair Equality of Opportunity and Responsibility for Disadvantage 177

attractive qualities. First, such an approach aims to clarify the structure of moral argument in order to ensure that moral reasoning is accessible to all persons. Second, this account of moral reasoning aims to ground moral and political reasoning in considered judgments that are consistent with the background (liberal) political tradition, and that are therefore widely shared among members of the culture. In particular, political constructivism avoids dependence upon premises rooted in particular comprehensive conceptions of the good. Finally, Rawls's approach employs a decision procedure that is designed to be acceptable to all reasonable persons on due reflection.

Responsibility and the Difference Principle

Even if the principle of fair equality of opportunity seems to take satisfactory account of concerns relating to responsibility when the principle is considered independently, it could be objected that the principles that constitute justice as fairness, viewed collectively, provide a less satisfactory treatment of those concerns. In particular, it has been objected that the difference principle requires redistribution of social goods in a manner that takes no account of what the individual has done to generate claims to goods, so that justice as fairness does in fact – as claimed in the conventional understanding of Rawls's theory – require that officers of the state must determine much of the distribution of social goods without taking responsibility for (dis)advantage into account and must secure that distribution primarily through tax and transfer policy.

Such a view, however, would only be persuasive if the difference principle in fact required redistribution in a manner that takes no account of what persons have done. The difference principle does not, however, redistribute income or goods in such a manner. That principle requires merely that (1) the superior expectations of the more fortunate must work as part of a scheme that benefits the least advantaged and (2) the arrangement of schemes incorporating such inequalities that produces the greatest advantage for the least advantaged is preferred as a matter of justice. To illustrate the nature of a scheme that satisfies the difference principle in this way, Rawls offers the example of entrepreneurs whose greater expectations provide them with incentives to innovate and increase the efficiency of their operations in ways that lead to more or better compensated employment for the least advantaged. The greater expectations of the least advantaged are thus to be secured primarily through the operations of economic institutions, and not by transfers organized by the state. Rawls designs the difference principle principally to ensure that, once equal liberty and fair equality of opportunity are ensured, persons whose skills are not assigned a high value by the price system receive a fair level of compensation for their efforts. Rawls makes the principle's focus on fair *compensation* explicit when he notes that, after equal liberty and fair equality of opportunity are assured, "the difference principle can be roughly satisfied by adjusting upward or downward the level of income exempt from the proportional income tax" (JAF 162). Like the principle of fair equality of opportunity, then, the difference principle implements the notion that "what a person is entitled to depends on what he does" (TJ 74).

Responsibility and the Social Minimum

It might be objected, however, that the difference principle requires the provision of a social minimum for the destitute, and that this minimum is financed through transfers and administered in a manner that takes no account of responsibility for disadvantage. In response to such an objection, it is important to note, first, that the social minimum does not constitute a requirement under the difference principle. Rather, the social minimum is a "constitutional essential" required to protect basic liberties under the first (liberty) principle (PL 228–29).

The social minimum *would* be provided unconditionally, however, and without regard for responsibility for disadvantage. While Rawls describes the minimum in the context of developing an account of ideal theory, in which all members (1) are motivated by the sense of justice and (2) will not therefore assert claims to the social minimum in a manner that unfairly exploits the earnings of others, it is important to demonstrate the strength of the considerations that support the unconditional provision of a social minimum even in a nonideal context. To illustrate these considerations, it is useful once again to contrast Rawls's view with the contrasting view of a luck egalitarian. Dworkin, in particular, insists that (1) concerns regarding responsibility for disadvantage must constitute a decisive consideration in all judgments of justice and that (2) otherwise unacceptable inequalities must be viewed as justified if they result from the person's choices

Fair Equality of Opportunity and Responsibility for Disadvantage 179

and not from his circumstances. Dworkin's account of luck equality, that is, would compensate persons for disadvantage that results from bad brute luck, but not for disadvantage – even severe destitution that would normally justify the provision of a social minimum – that is the product of option luck.

Dworkin's discussion of the role of insurance in transforming differences in fortune from bad brute luck to option luck illustrates Dworkin's understanding of the conditions under which concerns regarding responsibility justify the denial of claims to assistance to a person suffering from severe disadvantage. Assume, Dworkin suggests, that two victims of an accident had an equal chance of going blind and an equal opportunity to insure, but only one of them chose to insure. The uninsured victim could expect no compensation from the insured victim, even if the uninsured person were the only one blinded. The failure to insure would convert the difference in circumstances between the insured and uninsured victims from bad brute luck to option luck. By analogy, Dworkin argues, if everyone had the same risk of suffering such a catastrophe, knew the odds, and had adequate opportunity to insure, no victim could assert a legitimate claim to compensation against other members of society.[37]

Uninsured victims could assert no claim of justice against fellow citizens, under such circumstances, because the choice not to insure transforms the element of misfortune that distinguishes the victim's condition from his fellows into the product of his own choice. Luck equality respects this choice and assigns responsibility for his condition to the person, Dworkin tells us, because the choice reflects the victim's preference for a certain form of life–a life that "contains, as an element, the factor of risk."[38] To redistribute resources to the victim would therefore deprive him of the form of life that he prefers.[39]

But this claim is not obviously true. Dworkin's claim that persons may prefer to preserve the factor of risk in their lives is most persuasive if interpreted as a claim about risk relating to economic and social mobility. Most persons, it seems reasonable to assume, are willing to assume a significant risk of downward mobility in these dimensions in order to preserve the possibility of upward mobility. The risk of seriously disabling injury, however, is of quite a different order; and Rawls's contrasting approach to reasoning about justice provides the basis for an argument that a rational person, reflecting prospectively from the standpoint of a fair choice position on the form of life that she would like to lead – as Dworkin presents persons reflecting at the hypothetical auction at which resources are allocated in his theory – would prefer to rule out risk of this type.

Rawls argues that reasonable and rational persons reflecting from such a standpoint would choose to protect themselves against certain unacceptable possibilities (TJ 13, 130–39, 153–60). Since the structure of a fair choice position would deprive persons of information regarding their social position and prospects, persons occupying the choice position would be particularly concerned to preserve their ability to realize their conceptions of the good, and would therefore choose to rule out the possibility of serious losses of liberty (TJ 135). Examples of unacceptable losses of liberty include not merely slavery and serfdom, but also the inability to take advantage of one's rights and opportunities (TJ 179). Among the causes of such an inability, Rawls includes the lack of fundamental natural primary goods, including good health and basic physical powers.[40] Since the loss of basic physical powers would constitute an unacceptable loss of liberty, reasonable and rational persons would view outcomes involving physically disabling injuries as among the unacceptable possibilities to be ruled out. Such persons *would not*, therefore, view gambles involving the possible loss of such powers as an element of life that they wished to preserve. Rather, they would reject as unjust a form of social life that failed to provide adequate protections against such risks.

The Rawlsian argument is particularly relevant to an assessment of Dworkin's argument because Dworkin, like Rawls, offers a theory of distributive justice constructed from the standpoint of a fair choice position that is designed to neutralize the influence of arbitrary factors (such as bad brute luck) on life chances. The choice of persons occupying such a position not to insure is motivated, in *Dworkin's* account, by an unreflective and unchosen preference for risk.[41] In refusing to assist accident victims who made such a choice, however, Dworkin shows himself to be less consistent than Rawls in his treatment of brute luck. The choosers in Rawls's fair choice position are specifically denied information regarding their attitudes toward risk because such attitudes merely reflect the influence of genetic heredity or of environment, both of which are influences whose incidence is determined by morally arbitrary natural lotteries.[42] Since the distribution of such attitudes, and their influence on life chances, is the product of "risks...that are not...deliberate gambles,"[43] the distribution of attitude toward risk

Fair Equality of Opportunity and Responsibility for Disadvantage 181

constitutes an instance of brute luck whose influence Dworkin should also wish to neutralize. In refusing to assist accident victims whose choice not to insure was motivated by an unreflective preference, then, Dworkin's theory refuses to address an inequality that was generated by bad brute luck. In order to vindicate his constitutive commitment to neutralizing the influence of bad brute luck, Dworkin must therefore concede that uninsured accident victims *can* assert a legitimate claim to compensation against other members of society.

The idea of responsibility performs an important role in an account of distributive justice when it operates to check willful extravagance. Thus, considerations of justice should not (1) justify compensation for voluntarily acquired expensive tastes or (2) allow exploitation of the labor of the industrious by the willfully idle. The uninsured victim, however, is not willfully idle or extravagant. Dworkin's best explanation of the failure to insure describes the choice as determined merely by the victim's endowment of risk-seeking preferences. If the victim's choice not to insure is determined by such an endowment, however, the choice cannot be described accurately as *willful*; and if the choice does not reflect willful extravagance, it would be inappropriate to apply the notion of responsibility here to deny relief in the case of serious injury. More generally, Rawls's argument suggests that concerns regarding responsibility cannot justify rejecting claims for assistance in cases of severe destitution. The provision of an unconditional social minimum to address the needs of victims of severe destitution is not, therefore, inconsistent with respect for reasonable concerns regarding responsibility for disadvantage.

Responsibility and the Obligation to Assist the Disadvantaged

The Rawlsian argument points not to a defect in the fundamental orientation of luck equality, but rather to a reservation regarding the status of responsibility in an acceptable theory of justice. This argument suggests that luck equality has applied the notion of responsibility too aggressively, and that it is not appropriate to hold a victim responsible for choices that place basic needs at risk. A close examination of Dworkin's insurance argument has revealed no reason to doubt this conclusion.

If we accept this view, however, we must qualify considerably the central luck egalitarian formulation that "*genuine* choice excuses otherwise unacceptable inequalities."[44] Rather, the Rawlsian view that I have presented suggests that *no choice that a person makes can justify certain extreme inequalities*. The Rawlsian argument might seem to justify the stronger claim that no choices that could lead to such inequalities could be genuine. Rawls's argument is not, however, intended to offer a standard for judging the genuineness of choices, but rather to identify just principles to regulate the basic structure of society. According to this argument, such principles should require assistance for victims of extreme inequalities, not because the choices generating those inequalities were not genuine, but because the resulting inequality is in great part the product of bad brute luck. The preferences grounding the choice may defensibly be described as genuine – it may be reasonable to describe them, following Arneson, as ideally considered preferences reflecting a strongly risk-seeking disposition. Nevertheless, while genuine, such preferences and the choices that they ground are strongly affected by brute luck, and should not justify a decision to withhold assistance. Rawls's argument in fact suggests that it may be the role of brute luck in determining outcomes that justifies Scanlon's related argument that persons may be morally responsible for acts without being fully responsible for their consequences.[45]

But could such a view undermine legitimate concerns of justice regarding responsibility? The principal concern suggested by Dworkin is that an acceptable theory of justice must, in determining a just distribution of social goods, hold persons accountable for the costs to others of the choices that they make.[46] Would adopting the Rawlsian approach discussed above allow victims of severe inequality to impose costs unfairly on other members of society? The Rawlsian argument suggests that the answer is *no*. It would be appropriate to view the assistance to the victims as unfairly appropriated only if an impartial consideration of the interests of all members of society determined that the provision of assistance was unfair. But it was precisely such an impartial consideration that determined that assistance was not unfair and was, in fact, an obligation of justice.

The Rawlsian view would thus exempt from luck equality's critical scrutiny an entire category of choices and outcomes. In cases involving deficits of basic needs, egalitarian justice could, under this view, disregard the connection between choice and disadvantage. Such an *unconditional* guarantee of a social minimum, Rawls argues, is an essential feature of an acceptable liberal constitution (PL 228–29; see TJ 243).

The unconditional guarantee of a social minimum is therefore a special case in which justice as fairness suspends the general requirement that "what a person is entitled to depends on what he does" (TJ 74). In cases of severe deprivation, Rawls argues, special considerations justify qualifying this general requirement. While this qualification of his general view constitutes an important element of justice as fairness and has important policy implications, the basic commitment of justice as fairness – as reflected in the principle of fair equality of opportunity – is to secure opportunity in a manner that incorporates concerns regarding responsibility in the character and structure of basic social and economic institutions.

Conclusion

According to a conventional understanding of justice as fairness, a well-ordered society must secure basic liberties, prevent overt discrimination, ensure that the educational system is designed to eliminate class barriers, and then maximize the well-being of the least advantaged through tax and transfer policy. According to this view, justice as fairness requires that officers of the state must determine in advance the distribution of social goods required by justice and must secure that distribution primarily through tax and transfer policy. Thus, the conventional view presents Rawls's account of distributive justice as an allocative theory.

Such an understanding of justice as fairness is particularly misleading because of the character that it assigns to Rawls's theory. According to this view, the policies required to secure distributive justice will be designed primarily to redistribute income through tax and transfer programs in satisfaction of the difference principle. Since the principle of fair equality of opportunity is the more fundamental requirement of Rawls's theory, however, the policies required to secure distributive justice will primarily emphasize education, training, and manpower policy. Policies to redistribute income will play at most a secondary role.

The principle of fair equality of opportunity requires that persons with similar abilities and skills should have equal opportunity to succeed. The principle requires not merely the enforcement of legal protections of formal equal opportunity, but that *all* persons should have a *fair* chance to attain success. Persons who are similarly motivated and endowed should have equal prospects of success regardless of their initial social position. In order to implement this principle, just institutions must guarantee equal opportunity in education and in economic activities. In addition, the principle requires that the appropriate branches of government must secure conditions that make possible reasonably full employment and free choice of occupation.

Most significantly, Rawls's account of fair equal opportunity under this principle requires that if the distribution of social goods is unequal and if those who receive less advantageous shares are under a disadvantage which could be removed by further reform or social action, then such reform or social action is a requirement of justice. Fair equality of opportunity, if fully implemented, would require "imaginative social reform" to address *any* deficits of education or training and any inequalities of access to health care or advantageous environmental factors that might result in unequal ability to compete for advantageous positions.

Far from advocating social arrangements in which a centralized decision process determines the shares of goods that individuals receive, then, Rawls argues for a conception of justice under which the justice of a distribution "cannot be judged at all" until persons have actually participated in economic institutions and have generated their legitimate claims. Just institutions are thus designed primarily to provide individuals with the equal liberty and opportunity to achieve advantageous social positions through the provision of education, training, health care, nutrition, and any other services required by "imaginative social reform" in order to address the disadvantageous effects of environmental factors.

Notes

1 "[A]ssuming that there is a distribution of natural assets, those at the same level of talent and ability and who have the same willingness to use them, should have the same prospects of success regardless of their initial place in the social system." Rawls (1968), p. 161.
2 See Tawney (1952), p. 73.
3 Tawney (1952), pp. 74–75.
4 Tawney (1952), p. 75.
5 Tawney (1952), p. 71.
6 Sidgwick ([1907] 1981), p. 285, my emphasis.
7 Sidgwick ([1907] 1981), p. 285.

Conclusion 185

8 Tawney (1952), p. 73.
9 Tawney (1952), p. 74.
10 Tawney (1952), p. 74.
11 Tawney (1952), pp. 73–74.
12 Tawney (1952), p. 73.
13 Tawney (1952), pp. 73–74.
14 Tawney (1952), p. 74.
15 Williams (1962), p. 125.
16 Williams (1962), p. 125.
17 Williams (1962), p. 127.
18 Williams (1962), p. 127, my emphasis.
19 Williams (1962), p. 127.
20 Williams (1962), p. 127.
21 Williams (1962), p. 127.
22 Williams (1962), p. 127.
23 Williams (1962), p. 127.
24 Nozick (1974), pp. 153–55.
25 Rawls (n.d.-a), p. 57.
26 Scheffler (2010), p. 177.
27 Nozick (1974), p. 208.
28 Dworkin (2000), p. 113.
29 Dworkin (2000), p. 114.
30 Cohen (2011), p. 12.
31 Roemer (1996), p. 246.
32 Roemer (1996), p. 172.
33 Dworkin (2000), p. 114.
34 "The role of the principle of fair opportunity is to ensure that the system of cooperation is one of pure procedural justice" (TJ 76).
35 Arneson defines ideally considered preferences as "those [preferences] I would have if I were to engage in thorough-going deliberation about my preferences with full pertinent information, in a calm mood... making no reasoning errors." Arneson (1989), pp. 82–83.
36 Cohen (2008), p. 3.
37 Dworkin (2000), p. 77.
38 Dworkin (2000), p. 74.
39 Dworkin (2000), p. 75.
40 Rawls argues that the possession of these primary goods is a condition necessary "to enable persons to pursue their determinate conceptions of the good" (PL 307).
41 In view of the high cost of losing gambles and the low cost of insurance, Dworkin notes, the best (though not entirely satisfactory) explanation of the choice to gamble is that people (1) "mistake the actual odds" or

(2) "attach value to uncertainty for its own sake" (96). Since Dworkin also stipulates that persons considering the gamble of not purchasing insurance at the hypothetical resources auction know (at least roughly) the odds of injury (77), persons who fail to purchase insurance must be motivated by mere preference for risk. Moreover, since Dworkin concedes the lack of an available reflective justification for such a preference, the preference can only be viewed as unreflective and the product of genetic heredity or the influence of environment. Dworkin (2000), pp. 77, 96.

42 "The essential thing is not to allow the principles chosen to depend on special attitudes towards risk" (TJ 149).

43 Dworkin defines bad brute luck as "a matter of how risks fall out that are not... deliberate gambles." Dworkin (2000), p. 73. Unlike buying a stock that loses value, being hit by "a falling meteorite whose course could not have been predicted" is a matter of bad brute luck. As Rawls points out, the risk of inheriting risk-seeking preferences resembles the risk of being hit by a meteorite more closely than it resembles the deliberate gamble involved in the purchase of stock.

44 Cohen (2011), p. 29, emphasis mine.

45 Scanlon (1998), p. 292.

46 Dworkin (2000), pp. 69, 81, 89.

7 Democratic Equality

Democratic equality is the conception of distributive justice that is realized through the joint implementation of the two constitutive parts of Rawls's second principle of justice: the principle of fair equality of opportunity and the difference principle. Rawls designs this conception to mitigate the influence on life chances of factors that are arbitrary from the moral point of view – in particular, natural and social endowments. The fair equality of opportunity principle aims to neutralize the influence of social endowments on life chances, while the difference principle aims primarily to reduce the influence of natural endowments. The conception assumes, as a background condition, the satisfaction of Rawls's first principle guaranteeing to each person an equal right to a fully adequate scheme of basic liberties (PL 291). In addition, the two principles of democratic equality are ranked in lexical order, and fair equality of opportunity is assigned strict priority over the difference principle (TJ 73, 266).

While the two principles are ranked in lexical order, Rawls emphasizes that the principles operate as a unit (TJ 73, JAF 46n10[1]). That is, each principle interacts with and qualifies the character and proper operation of the other principle. In developing this notion, Rawls seems particularly concerned to establish that the proper implementation of the second principle of justice should not establish a meritocracy. In addition, Rawls aims to establish that the joint operation of the principle of fair equality of opportunity and the difference principle provides the basis for a form of social life in which social institutions are constituted in a manner than abstains "from the exploitation of the contingencies of nature and social circumstance" (TJ 156).

Moreover, Rawls's account of democratic equality goes beyond providing an account of justice in distribution and sets out a normative ideal of justice that incorporates an account of the structure and character of relations that are appropriate for members of society viewed as free and equal moral beings. In his account of democratic equality, I will therefore argue, Rawls anticipates the concerns of relational egalitarians like Elizabeth Anderson and Samuel Scheffler who argue that a plausible account of distributive egalitarianism must be anchored in a more general conception of equality as a social and political ideal.

This chapter will examine the character and requirements of the conception of distributive justice realized through the joint implementation of the two principles that combine to constitute Rawls's second principle of justice. First, I will examine the manner in which the principles operate as a unit to determine the character of just institutions. Second, I will examine the character of the resulting conception of distributive justice.

The Principles Operate as a Unit

Fair equality of opportunity and the difference principle are ranked in lexical order, and democratic equality assigns strict priority to fair equality of opportunity (TJ 65, 77, 243, 266; JAF 67). Each of the two principles, nevertheless, qualifies and transforms the aims and meaning of the other principle. The principle of fair equality of opportunity alone, Rawls states, secures *a form* of pure procedural justice. The form of procedural justice secured by that principle, however, fails to address adequately concerns about arbitrary influences on life chances unless the effects of that principle are qualified by the operation of by the difference principle. In regulating the distribution of social goods, Rawls argues, the difference principle transforms both the aims of fair equality of opportunity and social understandings of the aims of just social policy generally.

This chapter will examine Rawls's account of the manner in which the two components of the second principle operate as a unit. First, I will set out Rawls's justification for the view that social arrangements realize an acceptable form of pure procedural justice only when the requirements of fair equality of opportunity are qualified by the difference principle. Second, I will discuss the manner in which the combined operation of the two components of the second principle expresses an understanding of *genuine* equal opportunity in which the difference principle transforms social understandings of the nature of equal opportunity. Third, I will examine Rawls's justification for assigning fair equality of opportunity lexical priority over the difference principle. Fourth, I will argue that Rawls's account of the interaction of the two components of the second principle addresses Bernard Williams' concerns regarding the proper scope of equal opportunity. Finally, I will assess the implications for institutional arrangements in a well-ordered society of Rawls's account of the interaction between fair equality of opportunity and the difference principle.

Pure Procedural Justice, Meritocracy, and Arbitrariness

Since fair equality of opportunity is lexically prior to the difference principle, the institutions of a just society must satisfy this principle before any other considerations relating to justice in the distribution of goods – concerns, that is, arising under the difference principle – may be considered. In modeling a well-ordered society, the first consideration – therefore – must be to design institutions that ensure that all persons with similar levels of talent and motivation enjoy the same prospect of success, regardless of their initial social position (TJ 63).

Implementation of the fair opportunity principle, Rawls asserts, ensures that the system of cooperation realized is characterized by *a form* of pure procedural justice (TJ 76). That is, full implementation of the fair opportunity principle, in the context of a background political culture in which basic liberties are secured, ensures that social endowments do not determine life chances, so that – in such an arrangement – opportunities are distributed fairly, all enjoy free choice of occupation, and economic institutions in general satisfy the fundamental requirements of fairness. Thus, a certain conception of pure procedural justice – the conception associated with the liberal equality conception of distributive justice – is realized once the fair opportunity principle has been implemented.

Full realization of an *acceptable* conception of pure procedural justice, however, involves the realization of a condition in which the resulting distribution of social goods is just, whatever it happens to be. As Rawls notes in Section 13, while the liberal equality conception of distributive justice secures pure procedural justice "to some extent at least," such a conception "still leaves too much to social and natural contingency" (TJ 69). In order to address these remaining contingent influences on life chances, it is necessary to ensure that the distribution realized also satisfies the difference principle. In imposing this requirement, Rawls addresses two concerns. First, as he notes, implementation of the fair opportunity principle in combination merely with the principle of efficiency (in the liberal equality interpretation of the second principle) will allow arbitrary factors – in particular, the distribution of natural endowments – to influence life chances decisively. Such an interpretation of the two principles, then, fails "to mitigate the influence of...contingencies...on distributive shares" (TJ 63). Second, Rawls is concerned to ensure that "the democratic equality interpretation of the two principles will not lead to a meritocratic society" (TJ 91, see TJ 86²). In a meritocracy, the arbitrary distribution of a particular natural endowment – talent – determines or significantly influences life chances. A meritocracy therefore allows natural contingency to play a large and unjustifiable role in determining the distribution of social goods and opportunities. In addition, the existence of conditions of meritocracy encourages an unattractive social understanding of equal opportunity – under such conditions, "[e]qual opportunity [merely] means an equal chance to leave the less fortunate behind in the personal quest for influence and social position" (TJ 91). The view that distributive justice requires merely a meritocracy, therefore, constitutes "a danger for the...interpretations of the principles of justice" (TJ 91), since a meritocratic view understands equal opportunity to require nothing more than opportunity to compete for individual advantage in a zero-sum economy.

Transformation of Social Aims

Rawls argues that the two principles, taken together, express an understanding of *genuine* equal opportunity in which the difference principle, while lexically subordinate to the principle of fair opportunity, nevertheless transforms both the operation of that principle and the proper understanding of its aims. While the fair opportunity principle, considered in isolation, would seem to require equal attention to inequalities of opportunity at every level of income and wealth, consideration of the factors that justify the difference principle justifies the conclusion that "to provide genuine equality of opportunity, society must give more attention to those with fewer native assets and to those born into the less favorable social positions" (TJ 86). The difference principle therefore qualifies the application of the fair opportunity principle to require that in providing education and other services to ensure equal opportunity, society should devote more attention to the needs of the least advantaged. Since "inequalities of birth and natural endowments are undeserved," Rawls argues, "greater resources should be spent on the education" of the less well-endowed and less fortunate, "at least over a certain time of life" (TJ 86).

In addition to transforming important features of the operation of the fair opportunity principle, the difference principle "transforms the aims of society" (TJ 91) in a manner that fundamentally changes public understanding of the goals and meaning of equal opportunity. In particular, equal opportunity no longer means equal opportunity "to leave the less fortunate behind" (TJ 91). Rather, the difference principle "transforms the aims of the basic structure so that the total scheme of institutions no longer emphasizes social efficiency and technocratic values" (TJ 87) to the exclusion of reciprocity and fraternity. In particular, the difference principle's requirement of priority for the claims of the least advantaged to receive education and other services under the fair opportunity principle "expresses a conception of reciprocity" (TJ 88) implicit in the difference principle's transformation of the notion of opportunity.

Similarly, the difference principle qualifies the fair opportunity principle in order to ensure that the least advantaged realize an adequate share of the social bases of self-respect. Policies designed to enhance opportunity must also aim to secure conditions in which the least advantaged are able to realize "the confident sense of their own worth" (TJ 92). In order to facilitate the realization of such a sense, the difference principle requires not only that the education provided under fair equality of opportunity must be directed first to the least advantaged, but also that such education not be limited to functional training judged according to the "return as estimated in productive trained abilities" (TJ 92), nor should the value of such training "be assessed solely in terms of economic efficiency" (TJ 87). Rather, such forms of education must be allotted "according to their worth in enriching the personal and social life of citizens" (TJ 92). Each citizen must enjoy equal opportunity with all others, not merely to participate in economic institutions, but also to acquire the culture and knowledge necessary to permit each to participate equally in society's social and cultural life.

In this context, while all enjoy equal opportunity to prosper, all also "gain from their good fortune only on terms that improve the situation of those who have lost out" (TJ 87). The difference principle thus provides an interpretation not only of the notion of reciprocity, but also of the principle of fraternity – "the idea of not wanting to have greater advantages unless this is to the benefit of others who are less well off" (TJ 90). Public affirmation of the second principle thus constitutes affirmation of the notion of fraternity. In acknowledging the conception, the more favored acknowledge that they "are not to gain merely because they are more gifted," but rather "in ways that help the less fortunate as well" (TJ 87).

This understanding of the joint operation of the fair opportunity principle and the difference principle does not, however, require an interpretation of equal opportunity as requiring "that society is to make the same proportionate contribution to each person's realizing the best life which he is capable of" (TJ 446). Such an understanding would, Rawls notes, be seriously problematic for a number of reasons. First, such an understanding "requires a method of estimating the relative goodness of plans of life" (TJ 447). Second, such a suggestion "presupposes some way of measuring what counts as an equal proportionate contribution to persons with different contributions of their good" (TJ 447). More decisively, however, under such an approach, "the greater abilities of some may give them a stronger claim on social resources irrespective of compensating advantages to others" (TJ 447). This approach is unacceptable, then, primarily because it would allow the distribution of natural endowments to determine or strongly influence the distribution of social goods. Full realization of pure procedural justice requires a system that is regulated by an understanding of the fair opportunity principle that is strongly qualified by the difference principle in order to ensure that arbitrary factors do *not* determine life chances.

Reciprocity, Moral Psychology, and Stability

Rawls argues that the commitment to reciprocity that is embedded in the structure of institutions regulated by justice as fairness provides a firmer basis for the stability of those institutions than would be provided under viable alternative conceptions of justice. This argument reflects Rawls's view that the character of public institutions "profoundly influence[s] the social feelings" (TJ 431). In particular, "the manner in which institutions and the actions of others [living under those institutions] affect our good" (TJ 432) has a decisive influence on the orientation of individuals toward their institutions. Rawls thus argues from the assumption that a person's sense of justice is strengthened by her perception of "the manifest intention of others to act for [her] good" (TJ 433).

In a society well-ordered by justice as fairness, both the public conception of justice and the character of the institutions ordered by that conception reflect a joint intention to "abstain from the exploitation of the contingencies of nature and social circumstance" (TJ 156). In affirming a conception of justice embodying this intention, "persons express their respect for one another in the very constitution of their society" (TJ 156). The design of basic institutions in such a society thus reflects the collective intention to further the good of each other person to the full extent required by respect for the idea of fairness. A basic structure regulated by the principles of justice as fairness "manifests...men's desire to treat one another not as means only but as ends in themselves" (TJ 156). Since justice as fairness encourages in each person a concern with the well-being of other members of society that extends to the full extent required by fairness, Rawls concludes, the sense of justice rooted in justice as fairness should be extremely stable.

In order to support his claim that justice as fairness provides a firmer foundation for stable social institutions than the viable alternatives, Rawls develops a comparison between institutions ordered by justice as fairness and institutions ordered by a utilitarian conception of justice. The concern that members of society manifest for any particular individual's good is, Rawls argues, "far stronger" (TJ 437) under justice as fairness than under a utilitarian conception. Under a utilitarian conception, the liberties, opportunities, and claims to a fair share of social goods may all be "overridden for the sake of a larger sum of benefits" (TJ 437). Such an arrangement, Rawls notes, will not "inspire the less advantaged to have friendly feelings" toward those who benefit at their expense, and the loyalty of the less advantaged to institutions that encourage such apparently unfair arrangements will be correspondingly weak. As Rawls notes, "[n]o reciprocity is at work in this case and the appeal to utility may simply arouse suspicion" (TJ 437).

Justice as fairness, in contrast, assures each individual that their just claims will not be neglected or overridden in this way. Since institutions regulated by justice as fairness reflect "a more unconditional caring for our good" than utilitarian institutions, institutions regulated by justice as fairness are likely to produce "a closer affiliation with persons and institutions" (TJ 437). The resulting attachment of persons to institutions, Rawls concludes, should therefore be stronger than under utilitarian institutions. A consideration of the relative qualities of institutions under these contrasting conceptions of justice, Rawls concludes, suggests that the institutions of justice as fairness will generate a more firmly rooted sense of justice and – therefore – more stable social relations than the most viable alternative conception.

Arneson and the Priority of Fair Equality of Opportunity

Rawls, in arguing that the two requirements of the second principle operate as a unit, anticipates and addresses Richard Arneson's argument that fair equality of opportunity would require egalitarians to assign priority to concerns about unequal opportunity among highly skilled workers, all of whom are well compensated, in preference to concerns regarding significant poverty among the less skilled. The most serious problem, Arneson argues, is the lexical priority of fair equality of opportunity over the difference principle.[3] This assignment of priority requires that society should expend no resources to improve the position or holdings of the worst-off members of society (except with regard to liberties) so long as social resources could be employed to improve – "even by the tiniest fraction"[4] – the degree to which equal opportunity is realized. Thus, Arneson argues, if we could, through an enormous investment, marginally improve the competitive success of students in the upper middle class relative to even more affluent students with equal talent, the fair equality of opportunity principle would require that we do so before we made any effort to assist the least advantaged. Moreover, Arneson asserts, in focusing judgments of justice exclusively on equalizing opportunity for those *of similar talents*, the principle would teach us to neglect the significant benefits that the "untalented" might realize from education or training.

In summary, Arneson argues that fair equality of opportunity would require policies that (1) neglect the needs of the worst off, (2) squander social resources enhancing the competitive position of the better off, and (3) deny life-enhancing education and training to the "untalented." Rawls, however, anticipates and addresses all of these concerns. The philosophically interesting point, however, is not the fact that Rawls anticipates Arneson's objections, but rather the contrast between Arneson's approach to reasoning about justice – which leads him to view the concerns he raises as decisive objections to an equal opportunity principle – and Rawls's approach – which leaves him the flexibility to address these concerns while maintaining the integrity of his theoretical commitments.

Fair equality of opportunity, Arneson claims, assigns absolute priority to the project of equalizing opportunity, even if doing so forces us to (1) neglect the pressing needs of the badly off and (2) squander resources on persons who enjoy significant social advantages and who therefore do not need or deserve additional assistance. Rawls, however, explicitly rejects such an interpretation of the requirements of his principle. Genuine equality of opportunity, Rawls argues, "must give more attention to those with fewer assets and to those in less favorable social positions" (TJ 86). Moreover, the assistance to the less well off is not to be limited to training designed to enhance "productive trained capacities" (TJ 92), but must ensure to the less favored the means to realize "the confident sense of their own worth" that is necessary to ensure the social bases of self-respect (TJ 91–92). Only if the least advantaged are put in a position to participate in society as equals will progress be made toward genuine equal opportunity. Implementation of the fair equality principle thus requires the assignment of priority to the needs of the least advantaged. Thus, the principle will neither neglect the pressing needs of the least advantaged nor squander social resources on members of the middle class who require no assistance.

But, Arneson could respond, the fair opportunity principle only assigns priority to the *education and training* of the least advantaged, not to their other basic needs (e.g., nutrition, health care, shelter). In fact, he might continue, despite assigning priority to the *education and training* of the least advantaged, the fair opportunity principle would still assign priority to enhancing the competitive position *of the well-to-do* before addressing any of the *basic needs* of the least advantaged. And the fair opportunity principle, despite assigning priority to educating and training the *talented* worst off in order to improve their competitive position, assigns no value to the benefits that education and training could provide to the *untalented*. Finally, Arneson could argue, Rawls offers *no justification* for the position that the fair opportunity principle should assign priority to the education and training of the least advantaged. Priority to the needs of the least advantaged is required only by the difference principle, and that principle is lexically subordinate to the fair opportunity principle. Rawls's position that the fair opportunity principle should assign priority to the competitive position of the least advantaged, Arneson, could conclude is both (1) inadequate as a response to his objections and (2) unjustified by Rawls's actual arguments.

While these responses on behalf of Arneson seem initially plausible, they all reflect a failure to appreciate the ways in which the elements of Rawls's conception of justice operate together as – and must be understood as – a unified conception. It is this understanding of justice as a unified conception, rather than merely a collection of discrete principles, that distinguishes the basic orientation of theories of relational equality from that of theories of luck equality. An examination of the Rawlsian response to each of these objections will therefore illustrate the fundamental qualities of relational equality's approach to moral reflection that distinguish this view of equality most clearly from luck equality.

Consider, first, the objection that the fair equality principle assigns priority to the education and training of the least advantaged, not to their other basic needs. This objection treats the opportunity principle as though it operated in isolation from any other requirements of justice. As Rawls emphasizes, however, the opportunity principle operates as part of a conception whose elements complement and qualify each other. In particular, the fair equality of opportunity principle is lexically subordinate to the first (liberty) principle, and the first principle requires the provision of "a social minimum providing for the basic needs of all citizens" (PL 228; see JAF 44n7) as a constitutional essential necessary to ensure the worth of liberty. Rawls, in fact, suggests that it might be appropriate to assign a principle providing for basic needs lexical priority over the liberty principle (JAF 44n7).[5] While the fair opportunity principle does not, itself, guarantee provision for the basic needs of the worst off, then, it operates as part of a conception of justice that requires provision for those basic needs as a precondition for interventions to secure equal opportunity. Arneson's objection that the fair opportunity principle is problematic because it would neglect the basic needs of the worst off therefore fails.

Second, consider Arneson's claim that the fair opportunity principle would neglect the untalented. This claim seems plausible if one views the principle as exclusively designed to guarantee equal opportunity to compete in the market. Rawls argues explicitly, however, that training under the principle is to be assessed not merely "in terms of economic efficiency and social welfare" (TJ 87) but in terms of its contribution "in enriching the personal and social life of citizens" (TJ 92). The principle thus justifies – in fact, requires – the provision of training to the least advantaged that is not designed to improve their competitive advantage, but rather to enhance the ability of each member of society "to enjoy the culture of his society and to take part in its affairs" (TJ 87). This education would be available to all of the least advantaged, not merely the talented. Moreover, such training – designed to enable members of society to participate in society as equals – presumably corresponds to the kind of training that Arneson claims would enhance the lives of the untalented. Arneson's claim that the fair opportunity would neglect the untalented, thus, fails.

But, Arneson could respond, Rawls's gloss upon the equal opportunity principle – his claim that the principle should ensure equal opportunity to participate in society as an equal – seems required neither by the literal language of the principle nor by the concern with arbitrary influences on the distribution of goods that justifies acceptance of the principle. Rawls, however, justifies his interpretation of the requirements of the fair opportunity principle precisely by appealing to the concerns that justify acceptance of the second principle of justice. The justification of that principle, Rawls notes, is the notion that "since inequalities of birth and natural endowment are undeserved, these inequalities are to be somehow compensated for" (TJ 86). In particular, this compensation is to "take into account" the effects of endowments and social position on the distribution of "the essential primary good of self-respect" (TJ 91). The second principle therefore requires that "the confident sense of their own worth should be sought for the least favored" (TJ 92). As long as it is kept in mind that the underlying goal of equal opportunity is *joint participation in society as equals*, and not equal opportunity to leave others behind, proper implementation of the second principle will include policies designed to enhance the ability of each member of society "to enjoy the culture of his society and to take part in its affairs" (TJ 87), regardless of the member's level of skill. Implementing the second principle according to this understanding both gives effect to the motivation that justifies acceptance of the principle and, in addition, helps to ensure that promotion of the goal of equal opportunity does not produce a meritocracy – a form of social arrangement that Rawls views as both unjust and psychologically unstable.[6]

Finally, while Arneson assumes that democratic equality would address the needs of the least advantaged only after all efforts necessary to implement the fair opportunity principle have been made, Rawls – as discussed above–emphasizes that (1) the liberty principle requires attention to the basic needs of the least advantaged before the fair opportunity principle is given effect and that (2) the difference principle qualifies the operation of the fair opportunity principle to require that, while providing education and services to ensure equal opportunity, society should assign priority to assisting the least advantaged (TJ 86). This assistance to the less well off is not to be limited to training designed to enhance "productive trained capacities" (TJ 92), but must ensure to the less favored the means to realize "the confident sense of their own worth" that is necessary to ensure the social bases of self-respect (TJ 91–92). This assignment of priority to the needs of the least advantaged represents an aspect of the general effect of democratic equality – viewed as a unit – in transforming both the aims of fair equality of opportunity and social understandings of the aims of just social policy generally in a manner that represents the shared social commitment jointly to abstain "from the exploitation of the contingencies of nature and social circumstance" (TJ 156).

Arneson's objections to the fair opportunity principle thus reflect a failure to recognize the integrated nature of Rawls's approach to moral reflection. Arneson adopts a piecemeal approach to moral reasoning that focuses exclusively on individual principles and then applies deductive reasoning to derive practical conclusions that follow directly from each principle. Rawls asserts instead that the justification of claims of justice "rests upon the entire conception and how it fits in with and organizes our considered judgments" (TJ 507). His theory identifies a set of the most central considerations relating to judgments of justice and incorporates this set of considerations in an account of moral reflection, employing priority rules to regulate their influence on moral judgment.

Structure and Priority

While the principles operate together as a unit, the fair opportunity principle is nevertheless assigned strict priority over the difference principle. This assignment of priority is principally significant because it establishes that just social policies may not pursue increased fairness in the distribution of goods through policies that reduce equality of opportunity. Even if it were possible to improve everyone's quality of life by accepting certain inequalities of opportunity – that is, it if were "possible to improve everyone's situation by assigning certain powers and benefits to positions despite the fact that certain groups are excluded from them" (TJ 73) – such an arrangement would be "strictly forbidden by the principle of fair equality of opportunity" (TJ 73). That principle, Rawls asserts, "expresses the conviction that if some [advantageous positions] were not open on a basis fair to all, those kept out would be right in feeling unjustly treated *even though they benefited from the greater efforts of those who were allowed to hold them*" (TJ 73, my emphasis). Inequalities in opportunity, then – even inequalities that appear to produce benefits that improve the quality of life of the least advantaged – are strictly unjust unless it can be shown that "to eliminate these inequalities would so interfere with the social system and the operations of the economy that...*the opportunities* of the disadvantaged would be even more limited" (TJ 265, my emphasis).

This assignment of priority is justified – in fact required – Rawls argues, because depriving a person of equal opportunity excludes the person "from experiencing the realization of self which comes from a skillful and devoted exercise of social duties" (TJ 73).[7] While Rawls's statement of his justification is, in this case, less than ideally perspicuous, his concern is clear. A person is best able to realize his or her potential as a free and equal being if he or she is free to explore and exploit opportunities that make it possible for him or her to develop and realize his or her talents and capabilities. If some persons have access only to limited opportunities, then they will have less than an equal opportunity to realize their potential as persons. Such inequality of opportunity, Rawls judges, reflects a profound failure to respect persons as equals and is therefore strictly forbidden by fair equality of opportunity unless the elimination of these inequalities would generate an arrangement in which the opportunities of the least advantaged would be even more limited.

Rawls later expressed doubts about the absolute quality of the lexical priority of fair equality of opportunity, considering the possibility "that either a weaker priority or a weaker form of the opportunity principle would be better" (JAF 163n44). However, Rawls is perhaps excessively cautious in considering such a qualification of his view, since the priority of the fair equality principle over the difference principle in *A Theory of Justice* is deliberately diluted by the interaction of the two principles – for example, by the influence of the difference principle both on the distribution of goods (e.g., education and training) required by the fair equality principle and by the difference principle's transformative effect on social understanding of that distribution.

Bernard Williams and the Proper Scope of Equal Opportunity

In Sections 46 and 77 of *Theory*, Rawls considers a question raised by Bernard Williams in his examination of the notion of equal opportunity. In "The Idea of Equality" – as discussed in Chapter 6 – Williams develops an expansive understanding of the notion of equal opportunity. In Williams's account, equality of opportunity – if fully implemented – would require "imaginative social reform" to address *any* deficits of education or training and any inequalities of access to health care or advantageous environmental factors that might result in unequal ability to compete for advantageous positions. This expansive view of equal opportunity is justified, Williams argues, by the consideration that a social system fails to secure equal opportunity if the distribution of a social good is unequal and those who receive less advantageous shares "are under a disadvantage which could be removed by further reform or social action."[8]

Williams notes, however, that the same logic that requires that we "abstract the individual from some effects of his environment"[9] – that is, to view those effects and their impact on the individual as things for which it is not reasonable to hold the person responsible – can seem to require extreme and even implausible conclusions. How far, Williams asks, should this line of reasoning be pursued? If brain surgery – available to the privileged but not to the poor – could correct for deficits of ability, would equal opportunity require subsidies to provide the operation to the poor? Such reasoning might seem to reduce persons to "pure subjects or bearers of predicates."[10]

Underlying this line of inquiry, Williams notes, is a tension between two ideas of equality. The first idea relates to concerns regarding the fair distribution of goods. The second idea relates to the notion of respect for the integrity persons independent of any consideration of the distribution of goods. A single-minded concern with the first idea of equality might seem to require the provision of surgery to correct for genetic defects, while consideration of the second might seem to forbid such a policy.[11] The task of reconciling these ideas of equality is so intimidating, Williams notes, that "there is a strong temptation, if one does not abandon the idea [of equality] altogether, to abandon some of its elements."[12] This temptation, Williams argues, should be resisted. The discomfort that we face in addressing such a tension within the ideal of equality "is just that of genuine political thought."[13] The problems that one faces in explicating the idea of equality, Williams concludes, are significant but are nevertheless no greater than the problems one faces in explicating the concept of liberty or "any other... substantial political ideal."[14]

Williams, in an uncharacteristically optimistic mood, suggests that his concerns may be resolved by "genuine political thought." Rawls attempts to rise to Williams's challenge – that is, to address Williams's concerns – in a number of passages of *Theory*. First – it is important to note – Rawls's account of the liberty principle would absolutely forbid any policy that required surgery to correct any aspect of the person's genetic endowments. The principle's protection of integrity of the person would simply bar any requirement that a person submit unwillingly to surgery. Williams does not discuss such a case, but Nozick – perhaps inspired by Williams's discussion of this issue – does discuss the possibility that compulsory surgery to correct for genetic defects might be required by the difference principle.[15] Nozick's argument involves a confusion, however, reflecting Nozick's failure to note that the liberty principle – which would strictly forbid such compulsory surgery – is assigned strict priority over the difference principle (which, in any case, could not plausibly be construed to require such compulsory surgery). As Rawls emphasizes, Williams's second idea of equality – the idea of the integrity of the person viewed as a moral being – is the more fundamental notion and "is defined by the first principle of justice and ... owed to human beings as moral beings" (TJ 447). The first principle's priority over the second, Rawls notes, "enables us to avoid balancing these conceptions of equality [Williams's first and second ideas of equality] in an ad hoc manner" (TJ 447). Moreover, Rawls notes, "the argument from the original position shows how this precedence comes about" (TJ 447).

Rawls explicitly addresses Williams's question regarding "how far the notion of equality of opportunity can be carried" (TJ 265) in

Sections 46 and 77 of *Theory*. Rawls notes first that "following the difference principle and the priority rules it suggests reduces the urgency to achieve perfect equality of opportunity" (TJ 265). An acceptable conception of justice, Rawls thus suggests, aims not at "perfect" equal opportunity, but rather at a more complex conception that encompasses a principle of equal opportunity that is constrained by the more privileged considered judgment regarding respect for the inviolability of the person, but which is also modified by the requirements of the difference principle. In particular, the difference principle, by altering social understandings of the notion of equal opportunity (to include opportunity for culture, and not merely for earning power) and by transforming social understandings of the inequalities that remain in a well-ordered society (to reflect the understanding that such inequalities are to everyone's advantage) reduces or eliminates the sense that any remaining inequalities are unjust.

Thus, while a single-minded concern with the first idea of equality might, as Williams suggests, seem to require counterintuitive conclusions (e.g., mandatory surgery to correct for weak genetic endowments of talent; abolition of the family), "there is much less urgency to take this course" (TJ 448) when the idea of equal opportunity is viewed within the context of a theory of distributive justice that places equality in a proper balance with other considered judgments of justice (e.g., judgments relating to liberty, fairness, integrity of the person, reciprocity, fraternity). In particular, the sense that inequalities that result from differences in backgrounds within the family or from differing endowments of talent must be completely eliminated is diminished once the effect of the difference principle in mitigating those inequalities and in transforming social understandings of both opportunity and inequality itself are taken into account: "[t]he acknowledgment of the difference principle redefines the grounds for social inequalities ... and when the principles of fraternity and redress are allowed their appropriate weight, the natural distribution of assets and the contingencies of social circumstances can be more easily accepted" (TJ 448). The conception of justice, viewed as a whole, seems likely to "transform our perspective on the social world and to reconcile us to the dispositions of the natural order and the conditions of human life" (TJ 448) in a manner that seems adequate to resolve Williams's concerns regarding the tension necessarily associated with the two competing ideas of equality.

Just Institutions

Rawls's account of suitable background institutions for a well-ordered society provides some indication of the manner in which the principles of justice would work as a unit to regulate basic social institutions. The interaction of the principles would determine the nature and status of institutional features securing a social minimum, ensuring equal opportunity, and regulating inequalities in the distribution of goods.

First, a social minimum is required, as a constitutional essential, under the liberty principle's guarantee of the worth of liberty (PL 228–29). Constitutional essentials, such as the guarantee of a social minimum, are elements of the basic structure that "specif[y] and [secure] citizens' equal basic rights and liberties" (PL 229; see TJ 243). Rawls, in fact, seriously considers preceding the liberty principle with a lexically prior principle requiring the guarantee of a social minimum: the liberty principle "may be preceded by lexically prior principle requiring that basic needs be met" (JAF 44n7). This minimum is a necessary feature of just social institutions and "is the responsibility of the transfer branch" (TJ 244).

The fair opportunity principle then applies, prior to the difference principle, to require guarantees of employment, free choice of occupation, "similar chances of education and culture for persons similarly motivated" (TJ 245), real equal access to high quality education and training, all other forms of "imaginative social reform"[16] required to ensure real equal opportunity, and the policing of the conduct of firms to prevent "restrictions and barriers to the more desirable positions" (TJ 243). These requirements of fair equality of opportunity are implemented by the stabilization, distribution, and allocation branches. The stabilization branch aims to realize "reasonably full employment" (TJ 244) so that "the free choice of employment . . . [is] supported by strong effective demand" (TJ 244). The distribution branch secures the revenues necessary to "provide revenue for . . . the establishment of fair equality in education and the like" (TJ 247). In addition to policies to equalize opportunity in education, interventions required to realize equal opportunity would include policies providing job training (TJ 270), medical care (JAF 67) and protections designed to ensure that "the burdens of bearing, raising, and educating children does not fall more heavily on women" (JAF 11). Such policies would presumably include subsidized jobs, apprenticeship programs, public service employment, case management, and the remaining repertoire of programs associated with labor policy in the United States and Western Europe. The allocation branch keeps the price system competitive and prevents the "formation of unreasonable market power" (TJ 244) that might allow privileged economic elites to monopolize opportunity.

The economic relations established under such institutions would, however, still allow arbitrary factors to exercise an undue influence over life chances and might – without further regulation by the difference principle – establish conditions that might lead to a meritocratic society. In order to satisfy the requirements of justice, basic economic institutions must also, therefore, satisfy the difference principle. The requirements of the difference principle are implemented by the transfer and distribution branches. The transfer branch maintains the social minimum which is required by the first principle, but whose level is determined through application of the difference principle. The distribution branch, as noted above, "raise[s] the revenues that justice requires" (TJ 246). These funds, Rawls notes, provide for "the transfer payments necessary to satisfy the difference principle" (TJ 246).

It is important to note, however, that while the preceding language might suggest that the difference principle requires primarily income transfers, Rawls emphasizes that the difference principle operates to a significant extent to make "all-purpose means available to the least advantaged members of society to achieve their ends" (PL 326). Like the fair opportunity principle, then, the difference principle operates in large part to create conditions within which persons are free to pursue their own ends and have the capacity to exploit that freedom. The difference principle thus complements and interacts with the implementation of the fair opportunity principle by (1) requiring that policies designed to realize equal opportunity assign priority to the needs of the least advantaged, but also (2) providing assistance (under the difference principle) in the form of all-purpose means designed to improve the capacity of the less fortunate to realize equal opportunity (not, that is, primarily in the form of income assistance). In addition, as discussed above, the difference principle requires that assistance to the less advantaged under the fair opportunity principle must provide opportunity for culture and education in the liberal arts, not merely training that generates skills rewarded in the market.

The two principles thus operate as a unit to determine the general form and character of basic social institutions. In this process, each of the two principles qualifies and transforms the aims and meaning of the other principle. While the principle of fair equality of opportunity secures a form of pure procedural justice, the form of procedural justice secured by that principle would fail to address adequately concerns about arbitrary influences on life chances unless the distribution of goods were also regulated by the difference principle. Similarly, while the difference principle directs the attention of policy makers to the needs and interests of the least advantaged, the interaction of the difference principle with the fair equality principle requires that the aid provided to the least advantaged should focus, in significant part, upon improving opportunity rather than on supplementing income directly. Finally, in regulating the distribution of goods, the difference principle transforms both the aims of fair equality of opportunity and social understandings of the aims and proper functions of just social institutions.

Character of the Conception

The broad outlines of the structure of Rawls's account of distributive justice are thus clearly ascertainable. At the base level, democratic equality guarantees an absolute right to a social minimum covering basic human needs. This guarantee is unconditional and required by the liberty principle, which is lexically prior to fair equality of opportunity and the difference principle. Once the most extensive system of equal basic liberties compatible with a similar system of liberty for all is guaranteed, social cooperation for mutual benefit operates within institutions that are designed to ensure that all persons, regardless of their original social position, enjoy real equal opportunity to develop their talents and employ them productively. Finally, the difference principle ensures that (1) institutions assign priority to realizing opportunity for the least advantaged persons; (2) opportunity is understood in terms of the chance to realize equal citizenship, not the opportunity to leave others behind; and (3) the inequalities permitted to the more fortunate under circumstances that satisfy the preceding conditions are to everyone's advantage.

This section explores the significance and implications of the theory's structure. First, I will discuss the similarity in structure and substance between democratic equality and the capabilities approach. Second, I will argue that democratic equality – as a conception of distributive justice with a conception of egalitarian justice at its core – performs a function whose necessity has been noted in the recent egalitarian literature. That is, democratic equality locates questions of egalitarian justice within the context of a wider conception of distributive justice. Third, I will discuss the manner in which democratic equality – in providing the wider context of a full theory of distributive justice – responds to Nozick's criticisms of Bernard Williams's article, "What is Equality?"

Democratic Equality and the Capabilities Approach

Once the structure of Rawls's view is clearly understood, the degree to which democratic equality and the capabilities approach – in particular, in the account developed by Martha Nussbaum – are compatible is clearly apparent. In this subsection, I will suggest that the two approaches are not merely compatible; they are complementary. Each approach addresses concerns suggested by a careful consideration of the other theory. In order to develop this argument, I will first outline the elements and structure of Nussbaum's account of the capabilities approach here.

Nussbaum's account of the capabilities approach identifies three categories of capabilities: (1) *basic capabilities*, defined as innate forms of cognitive equipment; (2) *internal capabilities*, defined as developed states of the person necessary for the performance of important functionings; and (3) *combined capabilities*, defined as internal capabilities combined with external conditions suitable for their realization. *Basic capabilities* perform an essential role in the realization of any human form of life; a person who is deprived of the capability to see, hear, or reason has been deprived of one of the qualities that make a life essentially human. An acceptable theory of equality must therefore aim to secure threshold levels of the preconditions for realizing these basic capabilities for all persons. Access to adequate nourishment, health care, and education should, the capabilities approach argues, be among the unconditional guarantees of an acceptable egalitarian theory. Complete realization of *internal capabilities* is not the subject of a similar commitment. The capabilities approach, in itself, merely argues for the obligation to secure each person's capacity to choose a form of life, rather than a guarantee of the full realization of the person's set of internal capabilities. The egalitarian's obligation to assist is therefore limited to assuring access to the social bases of the internal capabilities (e.g., access to various forms of education, training, free choice of occupation) necessary to ensure that each person realizes the capacity to choose freely the kind of life that they wish to pursue. This obligation is, nevertheless, significant and substantial. Finally, different sets of internal capabilities will require different kinds of external conditions to be realized as *combined capabilities*. Nussbaum argues for an egalitarian obligation to guarantee a carefully specified set of combined capabilities.[17] In particular, even if a person has completely realized her internal capabilities, she will not possess the opportunity to employ them productively if she has internalized a norm that prevents her from applying her capabilities practically (e.g., a norm requiring that a wife should sacrifice her career to that of her husband). A distribution of social goods will not satisfy the necessary conditions of justice under the capabilities approach if the choices of many citizens are determined by habituated preferences that induce their bearers to suppress their genuine preferences to realize at least a threshold level of capabilities.

The capabilities approach thus argues in favor of securing necessary conditions of justice relating to (1) threshold levels of basic capabilities, (2) access to the social bases of internal capabilities, and (3) external conditions that secure the integrity of the process of preference formation. Finally, the capabilities approach does not claim to provide a complete account of the necessary conditions of justice.[18] Rather, far from assuming that egalitarian obligation to assist is exhausted by necessary conditions derivable from capabilities analysis, the capabilities approach encourages evaluation of equality in terms of the capabilities metric as a basis for judgments implementing the requirements of broader accounts of justice.[19]

The structural similarities between democratic equality and the capabilities approach are, thus, striking. Both democratic equality and the capabilities approach view the guarantee of a social minimum as a foundational commitment. Both approaches aim to guarantee opportunity, not outcomes. And both approaches focus on the realization of the individual's capacity to act effectively to realize their ends.

The most striking similarity may be the focus of both theoretical approaches on opportunity rather than outcomes. Democratic equality aims to secure conditions in which each person enjoys the opportunity to succeed to the extent permitted by her abilities. Similarly, the capabilities approach measures success in improving quality of life in terms of improved opportunity to function. In both cases, the individual must act to exploit these opportunities in order to enjoy improved quality of life. In both cases, the approach seems well described by Dworkin's phrase characterizing the fundamental goal of egalitarian justice: securing "freedom to choose what form of life to lead."

As a result, both approaches reflect an attitude toward responsibility that is closer than has been generally appreciated to Dworkin's notion that egalitarian justice must hold persons responsible for inequalities that result from their voluntary and genuine choices. Thus, in Rawls and Nussbaum, as in Dworkin, a person is responsible for disadvantage that is the product of his or her free choices after equal opportunity has been assured. The claims of justice for assistance that remain legitimately available to a person in such a position are sharply reduced in both theories.

Rawls and Nussbaum's views diverge from Dworkin's approach, however, in the significance that they assign to the conclusion that a person is responsible for her disadvantage. In Dworkin's theory of equality of resources, a person whose free and genuine choices caused her disadvantage has exhausted the claims to assistance that she may legitimately assert – her destitution is simply her problem. In Rawls and Nussbaum, the situation is viewed differently. A person whose choices have caused her disadvantage is, first, still entitled to the social minimum, which is guaranteed to all persons irrespective of their choices and degree of responsibility for disadvantage. Nussbaum has focused her arguments so centrally on the urgency of supplying such a minimum guarantee that much of the rest of her theory has been obscured. Rawls does not provide such vivid rhetorical support for the social minimum requirement, but he does describe the social minimum as (1) an essential institutional fundamental (TJ 243), (2) a constitutional essential (PL 228–29), and (3) a guarantee that should perhaps be embodied in a principle lexically prior to the liberty principle (JAF 44n7). Rawls's less vivid rhetorical presentation of this requirement may perhaps reflect the view that the justification for requiring such a social guarantee is more directly evident – and would therefore seem to require less supportive argumentation – than the justification for the second principle of justice. Rawls's firm commitment to requiring the guarantee of a social minimum as an element of the foundational level of the basic structure, however, cannot be doubted.

It is relevant to note and address here a confusion in the literature regarding the status of the difference principle in Rawls's account of political liberalism. It has been widely noted that, in *Political Liberalism*, Rawls states that – while the social minimum is a constitutional essential that should be protected at the constitutional level – the difference principle is not a constitutional essential, and the requirements of this principle must therefore be addressed at the legislative stage (PL 228–29). This distinction, it has been suggested, reflects an alteration in the status of the difference principle within justice as fairness.[20] Such an interpretation of Rawls's language in *Political Liberalism*, however, reflects a confusion. Rawls has maintained the view that the second principle is addressed at the legislative stage consistently since he presented his account of the difference principle in *A Theory of Justice*. As Rawls notes at the beginning of Chapter 4 of *A Theory of Justice*, citizens must be prepared to make three kinds of social judgments, those regarding (1) the justice of constitutional arrangements, (2) the justice of legislation and policy, and (3) "the grounds and limits of political duty and obligation" (TJ 171–72). These three forms of judgment, Rawls argues, must be addressed at different stages of "a several-stage sequence" (TJ 172). The stages in this sequence are the constitutional stage, the legislative stage, and the judicial and administrative stage (TJ 173–75). In this sequence, Rawls argues, issues relating to liberty interests are to be addressed at the constitutional stage, while "[t]he second principle comes into play at the stage of the legislature" (TJ 175). Far from qualifying the status of the difference principle, then, the language in *Political Liberalism* simply and literally repeats the view that Rawls developed in *Theory*.

In addition to the social minimum guarantee, persons whose free and genuine choices have caused their disadvantage continue – in democratic equality and the capabilities approach – to be entitled to assistance in the form of primary goods and services necessary to enable them to pursue their ends. As discussed in Chapter 6, fair equality of opportunity, if fully implemented, would require "imaginative social reform" to address *any* deficits of education or training and any inequalities of access to health care or advantageous environmental factors that might result in unequal ability to compete for advantageous positions. The principle does not define a canonical moment after which recipients of assistance are responsible for their own disadvantage and may therefore no longer claim assistance as a requirement of justice. Under fair equality of opportunity, then, a person who has caused her own disadvantage but, in addition, suffers from the effects of environmental factors that prevent her from competing for advantageous positions on an equal basis with others of similar ability and motivation may still claim assistance as a requirement of justice. Moreover, as discussed in Chapter 6, Rawls's argument from the original position appears to establish that no choice that an individual can make can justify certain severe levels of disadvantage. Persons suffering severe disadvantage, then, may legitimately press their claims for assistance without regard for any choices they may have made in the past. Similarly, capabilities equality assesses the justice of social arrangements in terms of the abilities of members of society to be and do various things. Like democratic equality, the capabilities approach defines no canonical moment at which the requirements of justice are absolutely satisfied and beyond which the individual may assert no justifiable claim for assistance. Moreover, like democratic equality, the capabilities approach insists on the individual's absolute right to a specified social minimum, irrespective of any choices the person may have made.

Democratic equality and the capabilities approach thus share an approach to responsibility that incorporates Dworkin's concern that egalitarian justice must take account of the choices that individuals have made in determining the shares of goods to which individuals are entitled, but that rejects Dworkin's conclusion that a concern with responsibility justifies the specification of a canonical moment beyond which the individual may no longer assert claims of justice for assistance. Individuals are held responsible because both democratic equality and the capabilities approach guarantee opportunity, not outcomes. Neither approach, however, would deny assistance to a person who is attempting to employ her abilities productively in the present merely because that person has made disadvantageous (or even irresponsible) choices in the past.

An Ideal of Equality

The most compelling account of distributive justice, Samuel Scheffler argues, will be an account "whose source in an ideal of genuine social equality can be vividly and convincingly demonstrated."[21] Scheffler intends to criticize theories of egalitarian justice – such as those of luck egalitarians like Arneson, Cohen, and Dworkin – that present equality as an "essentially distributive ideal."[22] That is, such theories present egalitarian justice as concerned exclusively with determining the proper distribution over persons of goods measured in some specified currency. Scheffler argues that the luck egalitarian account of equality as a distributive ideal – in particular – supports judgments inconsistent with reliable moral intuitions. For example, many versions of luck equality would accept the view that an indigent defendant should be denied access to legal counsel if her inability to afford such counsel is "the result of poor financial planning on her part."[23] Horror stories of this sort, Scheffler and Elizabeth Anderson[24] argue, undermine confidence in the ideal of equality that grounds the luck egalitarian view. In order to address such concerns, luck egalitarians need to connect their arguments regarding justice in the distribution of goods to a plausible ideal of equality. In the process, Scheffler suggests, luck equality may need to revise its principles and its normative judgments.

The value of anchoring distributive justice in an ideal of equality, Scheffler argues, is that such an approach captures the normative ideal of justice that the notion of a society of equals represents. This notion does not merely express the idea that each person is entitled to an "equal" share of the appropriate currency of egalitarian justice. Rather, the normative ideal of justice that grounds any acceptable account of distributive justice requires not mere equality in the distribution of goods, but also requires that relations among member of society "should have a certain structure and character."[25] This structure would provide a basis for avoiding the horror stories that Scheffler suggests are consistent with the leading accounts of luck equality. An acceptable conception of distributive justice, then, must – in addition to providing an account of justice in distribution – provide an account of this structure.

Democratic equality addresses Scheffler's concern – that is, it goes beyond an account of justice in distribution, and sets out a normative ideal of justice that incorporates an account of the structure and character of relations that are appropriate for members of society viewed as free and equal moral beings. While the fair opportunity and difference principles determine the nature of a just distribution of goods, the liberty principle ensures that the basic rights and liberties of citizens enjoy full and unconditional protection and that – in particular – those rights guarantees ensure that all members of society are treated fairly. The liberty principle thus performs important work in realizing the idea – implicit in social contract – that in a just social order, the laws must be incapable of doing wrong to anyone. In addition, the function of the second principle in transforming social goals and social understandings of the meaning of success ensure that all persons are guaranteed equal citizenship, not merely equal opportunity to leave others behind in a zero-sum form of economic competition. Thus, Rawls's theory, as Scheffler notes, "shows how... a plausible form of distributive egalitarianism can be anchored in a more general conception of equality as a social and political ideal."[26]

Scheffler's conclusion – that the more general conception of equality provided by Rawls's theory provides a necessary anchor for discussions of egalitarian justice – was, in essence, the view that resolved a controversy in the egalitarian literature of the 1970s involving Bernard Williams, Robert Nozick, and Amy Gutmann. The controversy was generated by Williams's argument, in "The Idea of Equality," that the idea of equality, properly explicated, has powerful normative implications. Such an explication, Williams argues, must work from the intuition that equality requires that people should be treated alike under relevantly similar circumstances. Egalitarian justice therefore requires that for every difference in the way people are treated, some general ground of differentiation must be given. Moreover, Williams continues, such a ground will not justify unequal treatment unless it shows why the stated basis for unequal treatment (e.g., race, gender, class) is relevant to the distribution of goods. The requirements of equality, then, are satisfied only if a relevant reason can be provided that justifies differential treatment.

Williams's application of this standard, however, exposes a weak point in his argument. Applied to the sphere of health care, Williams suggests, his approach requires that inequality in the provision of medical services can be justified only if such inequality is a necessary element of a policy that reduces ill health more effectively than a policy that does not require such unequal provision. It is "a necessary truth," Williams claims, that "the proper ground of distribution of medical care is ill health."[27] According to this view, then, any argument offered to justify the unequal distribution of medical care must demonstrate that the unequal distribution effectively serves the goal of reducing ill health. The relevant reason capable of justifying inequalities in the provision of health care, Williams thus suggests, can be identified simply through an assessment of the character of the social practice of medicine.

In response to this argument, however, Nozick notes that the process of identifying a relevant reason to regulate a particular practice – in Williams's approach – is more dependent than Williams concedes upon the assumptions that any person attempting to apply the idea of equality to a practice will need to make regarding the character of the practice. For example, Williams asserts that it is "a necessary truth" that the character of the practice of medicine requires the distribution of medical services on the grounds of ill health. But suppose, Nozick suggests, that medical services are also distributed through another social practice – schmoctoring – in which the relevant reason for distributing medical services is profit.[28] If both practices exist, Nozick inquires, how could one justify the claim that the only relevant reason capable of justifying inequalities in the provision of medical services is ill health? That is, on what grounds could one justify privileging the practice of medicine over the practice of schmoctoring?

While Nozick's critique of Williams initially appeared to present a strong case against Williams's attempt to generate precise practical extensions of the idea of equality – and, by extension, against the project of generating precise practical extensions of moral ideas in general – it is more plausibly viewed, as Gutmann notes, as an indictment of Williams's narrow focus on particular applications of the idea of equality without careful consideration of the concept's connection to more general social principles. The internal purposes of a practice, Gutmann notes, are often properly construed in light of broader social purposes. In order to provide defensible accounts of relevant reasons to regulate particular practices, Williams's account of equality must therefore be "situated within a theory of justice that reconciles these purposes when they conflict."[29]

Situating Williams's account of equality within the structure of Rawls's theory of justice would thus provide the basis for a response to Nozick's objection. To see how this would work, suppose that an individual urgently requires a medical service that he cannot afford, and that his society's medical practitioners – who endorse the schmoctoring interpretation of their practice – refuse to provide him with the service unless he pays for it in full. If the society is in general regulated by a Rawlsian public conception of justice, then members of that society will affirm the considered judgment that access to valuable social goods should not be determined by arbitrary factors such as level of income or wealth. In a society well-ordered by a Rawlsian public conception of justice, members of the medical profession would – on reflection – recognize that the schmoctoring interpretation of their practice is inconsistent with the considered judgments of justice that they affirm and would therefore cooperate to generate an acceptable arrangement providing urgently needed medical services to poor patients. Rawls's account of justice thus provides the required justification for privileging the practice of medicine over the practice of schmoctoring.

More generally, a general theory of justice sets out criteria that provide the basis for assigning priority to certain interpretations of practices and thus facilitates the identification of relevant reasons that could justify or require the rectification of inequalities in distribution. The identification of relevant reasons and development of criteria of distribution based upon those reasons could also ensure rejection of the view that an indigent defendant should be denied access to legal counsel because of her inability to afford such counsel. Thus, consideration of the Williams/Nozick controversy and Rawls's contribution to the resolution of that controversy illustrates the specific character of the contribution to ethical thought that a general theory of justice performs in regulating more specific analyses of moral questions.

Conclusion

Democratic equality constitutes, in Rawls's view, the most satisfactory interpretation of the requirements of distributive justice. This conception is made up of the principles that most adequately address the influence of arbitrary factors – in particular natural and social endowments – on life chances. The specific character of this conception is determined not merely by the content of its constitutive principles, however, but also by (1) the structural relation between these principles and (2) the consequences of their interaction. While the two principles are ranked in lexical order, Rawls – in addition – specifies that the principles operate as a unit; that is, each principle necessarily interacts with and qualifies the character and proper operation of the other principle. Interaction between the two principles ensures that (1) implementation of the principle of fair equality of opportunity does not establish a meritocracy and (2) the joint operation of the principles provides the basis for a form of social life in which social institutions are constituted in a manner than abstains from the exploitation of the contingencies of nature and social circumstance.

The interaction between the difference principle and fair equality of opportunity transforms the aims of the basic structure so that the total scheme of institutions no longer emphasizes social efficiency to the exclusion of reciprocity and fraternity. In particular, in qualifying the requirements of the fair opportunity principle to require priority for the needs of the least advantaged, the difference principle expresses a conception of reciprocity implicit in the difference principle's transformation of the notion of opportunity. Similarly, the interaction between the difference principle and the fair opportunity principle ensures that the least advantaged realize an adequate share of the social bases of self-respect. The conception of distributive justice realized through the interaction of these principles, viewed as a whole, thus seems likely to "transform our perspective on the social world and to reconcile us to the dispositions of the natural order and the conditions of human life" (TJ 448).

In addition, democratic equality offers an a approach to responsibility for disadvantage that incorporates Dworkin's concern that justice must hold persons responsible for willful extravagance without adopting either Dworkin's compensatory approach to distributive justice or his harsh line-drawing approach to responsibility. In fact, like the capabilities approach – with which democratic equality shares many structural features – democratic equality would exempt from scrutiny the choices and behavior of the most severely disadvantaged.

Finally, democratic equality addresses the concern – expressed by Scheffler and others – that an acceptable account of egalitarian justice must go beyond an account of justice in distribution and must set out a normative ideal of justice that incorporates an account of the structure and character of an egalitarian society. In particular, the function of the second principle in transforming social goals and social understandings of the meaning of success ensures that all persons are guaranteed equal citizenship, not merely equal opportunity to leave others behind in a zero-sum form of economic competition. Thus, Rawls's theory, as

Scheffler notes, "shows how... a plausible form of distributive egalitarianism can be anchored in a more general conception of equality as a social and political ideal."[30]

Notes

1 The two principles are intended "to apply in tandem and to work as a unit" (JAF 46n10).
2 "I should like to forestall the objection to the principle of fair opportunity that it leads to a meritocratic society" (TJ 86).
3 Arneson (1999), pp. 81–83.
4 Arneson (1999), pp. 81–82.
5 The liberty principle "may be preceded by a lexically prior principle requiring that basic needs be met, at least insofar as their being met is a necessary condition for citizens to understand and to be able fruitfully to exercise the basic rights and liberties" (JAF 44n7). "[A] social minimum providing for the basic needs of all citizens is... also [a constitutional] essential" (PL 228–29).
6 As noted above, Rawls is concerned to ensure that "the democratic equality interpretation of the two principles will not lead to a meritocratic society" (TJ 91, see TJ 86). A meritocracy, Rawls argues, allows natural contingency to play a large and unjustifiable role in determining the distribution of social goods and opportunities.
7 See Taylor (2011), pp. 73–91, for a defense of the priority of the fair equality principle grounded in the interest in self-realization through work.
8 Williams (1962), p. 127.
9 Williams (1962), p. 146.
10 Williams (1962), p. 147.
11 Williams (1962), p. 148.
12 Williams (1962), p. 148.
13 Williams (1962), p. 149.
14 Williams (1962), p. 149.
15 Nozick (1974), p. 206.
16 This requirement is discussed in the preceding chapter.
17 Nussbaum (2000), p. 85; see pp. 70-86.
18 Nussbaum (2000), pp. 75, 86.
19 Nussbaum (2000), p. 86.
20 See, e.g., Holmes (1993).
21 Scheffler (2010), p. 207.
22 Scheffler (2010), p. 200.
23 Scheffler (2010), p. 201.

24 Anderson (1999).
25 Scheffler (2010), p. 202.
26 Scheffler (2010), p. 199.
27 Williams (1962), p. 121.
28 Nozick (1974), p. 235.
29 Gutmann (1980), p. 102.
30 Scheffler (2010), p. 199.

8 | *Ideal Theory and Practical Judgment*

In *A Theory of Justice*, Rawls develops an account of justice designed to regulate the basic institutions of a *well-ordered* society – a society in which the behavior of all members is effectively motivated by the sense of justice, so that "everyone is presumed to act justly" (TJ 8). Rawls thus develops his arguments from the assumption of strict compliance. Rawls, it is important to note, does not assume that the behavior of people in any existing society meets the standard of strict compliance. Rather, strict compliance is a simplifying assumption adopted to facilitate Rawls's aim of articulating the contents of the sense of justice of a reasonable person. This development of the argument in the form of ideal theory is justified, Rawls argues, because ideal theory "provides... the only basis for the systematic grasp of [the] more pressing" issues of social justice (TJ 8). Only by abstracting away from issues of partial compliance, that is, is it possible to isolate and analyze without confusion the questions relevant to the resolution of conflicts regarding these pressing issues.

In *The Idea of Justice*,[1] however, Amartya Sen criticizes Rawls's reliance upon an ideal theoretic approach. Rawls's strategy, Sen argues, introduces several problems into his argument. Most significantly, Rawls's choice to develop his argument while working from the assumptions of ideal theory leads him to develop an account of justice designed to identify a *single* set of institutions that most closely fits the considered judgments of reasonable members of society. Not only is such a goal unachievable, Sen argues, but also an approach designed to identify a single set of best justified institutions will necessarily neglect the interactive relationship among motivation, behavior, and institutions.

I will argue that Sen's objections reflect a misunderstanding of Rawls's argument. Rawls does not aim to describe a uniquely just set of institutions. Rather, his approach is both more flexible and more practical than Sen suggests. Far from aiming for completeness in moral judgment, Rawls's theory sets out an open-ended framework that identifies the considerations fundamentally relevant to judgment, but that assigns considerable autonomy to persons individually and collectively in determining the specific requirements of justice. While the principles of justice as fairness identify relevant considerations, the resolution of questions of justice ultimately requires careful reflection relating those considerations to the complex set of facts facing the policy-maker in the relevant context. In designating principles – rather than rules – as the fundamental standard of justice, I will argue, Rawls indicates his intention to design a flexible approach that regulates reasoning about justice but that does not aspire to determine judgments of justice in advance. After responding to Sen's specific objections, I will – in the next chapter – examine the potential of Rawls's ideal theory approach to provide a flexible analytic framework to address practical issues.

Ideal Theory and Practical Analysis

Sen raises five objections to Rawls's reliance upon an ideal theoretical approach. First, Sen argues, Rawls's approach commits him to the goal of specifying a unique account of perfectly just institutions. Second, Rawls's focus on institutional design distracts him from the task of assessing the normative presuppositions of his approach. Third, Rawls's institutional fundamentalism leads him to show insufficient concern regarding the consequences that implementing perfectly just institutions may produce. Finally, Sen argues, an ideal approach to moral reasoning unrealistically aims for completeness in moral judgment. I will argue that these objections all reflect a confusion regarding the status of ideal reasoning in Rawls's thought.

A Unique Set of Just Institutions

In *A Theory of Justice*, Sen claims, Rawls aims to identify the specific institutional structure that is best suited for "a perfectly just society" (262; see 82ff.). This kind of "institutional fundamentalism" (83), Sen argues, "ride[s] roughshod over the complexity of societies" (83).

Rawls, however, can quite persuasively reject this objection. Far from attempting to set out a blueprint for a unique set of just institutions, Rawls's comments on the nature of just institutions are quite general and simply set out guidelines that just institutions should meet. Rawls develops his views on institutions for a just society most carefully in Chapters 4–6 of *A Theory of Justice*. In these chapters, Rawls discusses a number of requirements that must be met by (1) a just constitution (Chapter 4), (2) a just legislative process (Chapter 5), and (3) a just process for the implementation of just legislation (Chapter 6). Thus, in Chapter 4, he argues that a just constitution must protect a system of equal basic liberties for each person that is as extensive as is compatible with a similar guarantee for every other member of society. While Rawls offers general recommendations for the form of institutional arrangements that meet this requirement (e.g., each member of society should enjoy equal opportunity to determine the outcomes of elections; wealth should be widely distributed; political parties are to be made independent of the influence of wealthy private individuals), he offers few specific institutional proposals and nothing resembling a blueprint that just institutions must meet.

In Chapters 5 and 6, Rawls sets out standards that just institutions must meet – legislation should be enacted by a democratic legislature; governmental institutions should aim to secure reasonably full employment, competitive markets, and equal opportunity; a basic social minimum must be provided to those unable to support themselves. Again, however, the requirements are quite loose and could be implemented through many forms of institutional arrangement. A democratic legislature, for example, could take the form of (1) a parliament or (2) a unicameral or bicameral legislative branch in a system characterized by separation of powers. A government could secure full employment through aggressive fiscal policy, subsidies to employers, education and training policies, public service employment, or a policy that combines some or all of these elements. A policy designed to provide social minimum could take the form of a negative income tax, a family allowance, or a means-tested entitlement.

Rawls, in fact, emphasizes the open-ended nature of his inquiry. It is not always clear, Rawls states, "which of several constitutions, or economic or social arrangements would be chosen" on due reflection (TJ 176). Under such conditions, "justice is to that extent likewise indeterminate" (TJ 176). Not only is the choice of institutions under appropriate principles open-ended, but also reflection regarding the choice of the principles that regulate the choice of institutional arrangements may itself be unavoidably indeterminate. "We must recognize the possibility," Rawls cautions, "that there is no way to get beyond a plurality of principles [of justice]" (TJ 36). At best, due reflection may reduce the indeterminacy.

Thus, Sen's first objection – that Rawls aims to set out a definitive account of just institutions – presents a distorted view of Rawls's analysis. Rawls does not attempt to provide a precise blueprint for perfectly just institutions. His comments on institutions simply provide a general set of criteria that acceptable institutions must satisfy.

Far from offering a blueprint, Rawls's comments on institutions in fact present a political conception that is similar in significant respects to Martha Nussbaum's notion of a thick vague moral conception – a conception that is thick in the sense that it focuses on specific aspects of human life but vague in the sense that it "admits ... of many concrete specifications"[2] and may therefore be specified in a manner sensitive both to particular aspects of the background political culture and to the actual consequences of having the proposed institutions in place. Such an approach may simultaneously be informed by the self-understandings of social beings and yet be flexible enough to be realizable in diverse political cultures.

Normative Presuppositions

Rawls's approach, Sen argues, fails to provide an account of a deliberative framework within which the normative presumptions underlying arguments justifying the proposed institutional arrangements are made explicit and carefully examined. Yet this claim seems odd as a criticism of Rawls. In *A Theory of Justice*, Rawls devotes extensive and explicit attention to the normative presuppositions of arguments about justice. His discussion of political justification focuses precisely on the status of reliable normative presuppositions – that is, considered judgments of justice – in moral reflection and on the relation between these presuppositions and justifiable political judgments. In particular, his decision procedure explicitly *models* the normative propositions that justice (1) should not be arbitrary, (2) should respect the inviolability of the person, and (3) should be impartial. All judgments formed in the original position – including judgments relating to the choice of institutions – therefore develop the practical implications of a specified set of normative presuppositions.

Sen's second objection – the objection that Rawls's approach fails to identify and examine the normative presuppositions of the arguments for these institutions – therefore fails. Rawls's method focuses centrally on the assessment of the normative presuppositions of arguments for particular institutions.

Insensitivity to Consequences

Rawls, Sen argues, is an institutional fundamentalist. Institutional fundamentalism presents institutions as good in themselves, rather than as "possibly effective ways of realizing acceptable or excellent social achievements" (83). Thus, Sen argues, Rawls's institutional fundamentalism often "prevents critical examination of the actual consequences of having the recommended institutions" (83). While institutions can plausibly be viewed as part of the subject-matter of justice, he concludes, an acceptable theory must also focus attention on the practical consequences of establishing the institutional arrangements that are under consideration.

As a consequence of his institutional fundamentalism, Sen argues, Rawls's approach is necessarily insensitive to the practical consequences of establishing these preferred institutions – since the reflection that guides the choice of institutions, in Rawls's approach, focuses *solely* on the requirements of justice, the choice of institutions will necessarily ignore practical consequences. In particular, Sen claims, Rawls's view that liberty interests may never be compromised to address injustice in distribution is unrealistically absolute precisely because of this feature of Rawls's approach. Otherwise, a reasonable person would surely judge that some liberty interests might justifiably be compromised in order to prevent such bad outcomes as severe famines or epidemics. Moreover, Sen argues, the absolute commitment to liberties that is generated through Rawlsian ideal theory provides no basis for the mediation of conflicts between liberties, when they occur.

While Sen insists that Rawls's approach is necessarily inattentive to practical consequences, however, note that Rawls's concern with stability – which occupies a central place in all of Rawls's work after 1990 – is precisely a concern with the practical consequences of the institutions that Rawls proposes. In asking whether a well-ordered society under justice as fairness could stable, Rawls focuses specifically on the possible effects of his institutional proposals on the behavior of members of that society.

Ideal Theory and Practical Analysis 223

While Sen appears to concede that the concern with stability in Rawls's later work does reflect sensitivity to practical consequences, Sen suggests that this concern arises only in Rawls's later work as a possible corrective to the ideal character of his earlier work (11). Rawls's concern with stability and the practical and theoretical significance of the fact of reasonable pluralism, however, is clearly present in *A Theory of Justice* as well as in his later work. In Chapter 9 of *Theory*, Rawls focuses precisely on the question of whether a person's pursuit of her individual good would lead her to affirm the principles of justice as fairness or to violate their requirements in the pursuit of the good. In order to address this question, Rawls (1) employs the account of practical rationality that he has developed in Chapter 7 to test the fit between the requirements of justice and an individual's good, (2) examines the question of how conflicts between an individual's perceived good and the requirements of justice should be analyzed, and (3) proposes an account of unity of the self to address and resolve such conflicts. All of these arguments concern the practical consequences of Rawls's institutional proposals. Sen's general claim that Rawls's approach is insensitive to the practical consequences of establishing these preferred institutions therefore fails. Rawls devotes significant attention to the practical consequences of establishing proposed institutions, both in *Theory* and in his later work.

Sen, however, also offers the more specific objection that the absolute priority that Rawls's theory assigns to liberty interests would encourage moral agents to neglect the consideration of practical consequences of policies that privilege liberties absolutely – consequences that might include the failure to implement adequate policies to address the effects of famines and epidemics. The inflexibility of the first principle, Sen suggests, thus illustrates the rigidity of an approach that relies upon an ideal theoretic approach.

While Sen argues persuasively that the need to prevent or alleviate famines or epidemics could justify policies with the same priority as those that protect liberty interests, Rawls explicitly endorses the same view. The first (liberty) principle guarantees not merely the protection of liberties, but also the social minimum share of goods necessary to enjoy those liberties (PL 228). Social arrangements that fail to protect members from serious infringements of the capacity to enjoy or exercise basic liberties – due to poverty, hunger, ignorance, disease, or other causes – fail to provide adequate protections for the liberties guaranteed under the first principle. Indeed, as discussed in Chapter 7, Rawls suggests that the liberty principle "may be preceded by a lexically prior principle requiring that basic needs be met, at least insofar as their being met is a necessary condition for citizens to understand and to be able fruitfully to exercise the basic rights and liberties" (JAF 44n7).

Rawls, in fact, argues explicitly that in conditions in which "social circumstances do not allow the effective establishment of basic rights, one can concede their limitation" (TJ 132). Presumably, the most plausible justification for the claim that social circumstances do not allow the effective establishment of basic rights would be the (true) claim that the funds necessary for the establishment of basic rights are more urgently needed to provide members of society with basic resources necessary for survival or to address essential health needs. Rawls thus concedes that the priority of liberty interests does not justify the failure to implement adequate policies to address the effects of famines and epidemics.

Sen's objection that the priority assigned to liberty by justice as fairness would require neglect of other pressing interests – such as hunger, disease, or destitution – fails. The social minimum – which is required by the first principle and therefore shares the priority assigned the interests protected by that principle – would require attention to precisely these interests.

Sen, however, develops an additional criticism relating to the status of liberty interests in justice as fairness. Rawls, Sen argues, assigns priority to liberty interests without specifying a manner of resolving conflicts among liberties (97). Rawls's failure to describe an approach to resolving conflicts among liberty interests, Sen asserts, again exemplifies the inflexibility that makes Rawls's theory insensitive to practical problems.

Rawls, however, provides an explicit account of the manner in which conflicts among liberty interests may be resolved. In a just constitutional order, Rawls argues, the state may regulate or restrict certain aspects of liberty in order to protect more fundamental aspects of liberty. Following Kant, Rawls argues that a basic liberty may be limited "only for the sake of liberty itself" (TJ 179) – that is, only to ensure that that some other basic liberty is properly protected. The basic liberties, Rawls argues, are to be assessed as a whole – that is, as a single system (TJ 178). Each liberty is to be defined so that the central applications of each can be simultaneously secured. In order to ensure that the system of liberties as a whole effectively secures the core applications of each basic liberty, the scheme is to be assessed from the standpoint of the representative equal citizen, and the various liberties are to be broadened or narrowed to reflect the ways in which they affect one another.

Rawls notes that liberties may be limited in three ways: (1) the constitution may define freedom of participation more or less extensively, (2) the constitution may allow inequalities in political liberties, and (3) larger or smaller amounts of social resources may be devoted to insuring the worth of freedom (TJ 196–97). The *extent* of the principle of participation, for example, is determined by the extent to which the constitution restricts the application of the bare majority rule. A bill of rights generally removes certain liberties from majority regulation altogether, and separation of powers and judicial review also restrict the power of the legislature. These and other permissible restrictions on the extent of the principle of participation must bear equally on all persons. These restrictions are justified because they protect the other freedoms. Thus, restrictions on majority rule in a constitution are justified to the extent that the arrangements structured by the constitution ensure the protection of basic liberties, in particular, by mitigating the defects of the majority principle (TJ 201).

Inequalities in *political liberty* must be justified, Rawls argues, in the same way. Such inequality is justified, Rawls argues, if – when viewed from the point of view of a representative citizen assessing the total system of freedom – the inequality would be acceptable, on due reflection, to the persons who are to suffer the lesser liberty because of the greater protection of their other liberties that results from the restriction (TJ 203). The most obvious political inequality, Rawls states, is the failure to implement the precept of one person one vote. John Stuart Mill, Rawls notes, was willing to argue for the violation of this precept on the grounds that political inequality would benefit those with lesser liberty. In particular, Mill argued that persons with greater education and intelligence should have extra votes. Such an arrangement, Mill argued, is in the interest of each because assigning more influence to better-informed voters was likely to increase the justice of legislation. For this argument to be successful, Rawls asserts, Mill would have to argue persuasively that this arrangement would in fact be acceptable to those persons whose franchise was restricted because the arrangement improved the security of other more fundamental liberties.[3]

Rawls thus gives serious consideration to the problem of conflicts among liberties and offers a plausible approach to the resolution of those conflicts. Sen's argument that Rawls's ideal form of analysis yields a rigid and absolute requirement of respect for liberty that leaves no room for compromise therefore fails.

Sen argues that Rawls's assignment of lexical priority to liberty interests generates an approach that (1) is necessarily insensitive to practical consequences, (2) would provide an inadequate response to bad outcomes such as famine or epidemic, and (3) provides no basis for resolving conflicts among liberties. As discussed above, however, Rawls's analysis (1) devotes significant attention to practical consequences, (2) explicitly requires policies to address the effects of famine or epidemic as part of the enforcement of the liberty principle, and (3) requires balancing among liberties in order to produce an adequate scheme of liberties.

Completeness in Moral Judgment

Rawls's "totalist" approach to moral reasoning, Sen argues, unrealistically views incompleteness in judgments about justice as a failure (103). Rawls, Sen claims, aims "to identify the transcendentally just social arrangement" (102), an aim that requires a complete comparative ranking of feasible institutional arrangements. From the totalist perspective that Sen attributes to Rawls, Sen notes, incompleteness is viewed as a defect that undermines the plausibility of a theoretical position.

Sen criticizes the notion that a theory of justice must aim for this sort of completeness. Incompleteness may be unavoidable, he notes, for a number of reasons. Information sufficient to ground complete judgments may simply not be available. Even if sufficient information could be obtained, it may be impossible to craft a definitive resolution to conflicting claims grounded in conflicting basic assumptions about value or legitimacy. If society is characterized by a plurality of inconsistent views about value, as Rawls concedes, then – Sen concludes – incompleteness is neither a surprising nor a problematic feature of a theory of justice. Rawls's pursuit of completeness, Sen concludes, undermines the plausibility of his philosophical project.

If Rawls were in fact committed to the pursuit of completeness in moral or political judgment, Sen's criticism would be quite persuasive.

But Sen's argument presents a distorted account of Rawls's method. Even setting aside Rawls's concern in his later work on political liberalism – work that Sen describes as a corrective to Rawls's earlier totalist approach – to address the fact of reasonable pluralism, Rawls manifests throughout his work a strong awareness of the significance of pluralistic disagreement, combined with a rejection of the view that completeness in practical judgment is possible. In his "Remarks on Justification" in *A Theory of Justice*, Rawls emphasizes the limited scope of the claims that he aims to justify. The aim of moral philosophy, he emphasizes, is "to look for possible bases of agreement where none seem to exist . . . to extend the range of some existing consensus and to frame more discriminating moral conceptions for our consideration" (TJ 509). While Rawls's theoretical project is designed to identify the principles that match the considered judgments of justice of reasonable and rational persons in reflective equilibrium, he explicitly refuses to assume that "the principles that characterize one person's considered judgments are the same as those that characterize another's" (TJ 44). Rather, Rawls emphasizes that "[w]e cannot take for granted that there must be a complete derivation of principles" of justice (TJ 35).

The aim of *A Theory of Justice*, then, is *not* to set out a complete and definitive account of justice, but rather to provide "a guiding framework designed to focus our moral sensibilities and to put before our intuitive capacities more limited and manageable questions for judgment" (TJ 46). If the resulting theory "tends to reduce disagreements and to bring divergent convictions in line," Rawls concludes, "then it has done all that one may reasonably ask" (TJ 46). As in *Political Liberalism*, Rawls's aim in *A Theory of Justice* is "to look for possible bases of agreement" and "to extend the range of some existing consensus" (509), not to outline a blueprint offering a complete resolution of the central questions in moral or political philosophy.

Rawls, in fact, describes his project – in *A Theory of Justice* – as simply the attempt to formulate "a set of principles which, when conjoined to our beliefs and knowledge of the circumstances" (TJ 41), would lead us to the judgments that would be required by the sense of justice. Commentators who write as though Rawls presented his theory as a complete and definitive blueprint for political morality fail to note that the choosers in the original position choose *principles* of justice, not *rules* of justice. Principles are formally distinct from rules, and perform a more modest role in guiding judgment. Rawls's reliance on this more limited normative standard, in fact, defines the role that Rawls intends his theory to play in regulating judgments of justice.

Rawls discusses the distinction between rules and principles in "Outline of a Decision Procedure for Ethics." Rules, Rawls notes, are maxims that express the results of applying moral principles to particular types of cases.[4] Principles, in contrast, are "general directives" that, when applied to specific cases, generate a judgment corresponding to "our preferences expressed in considered judgments."[5] Principles thus state the reasons to resolve an issue one way or another that ground more particular considered judgments. Principles function primarily to justify judgments, while rules function to regulate behavior and constitute practices.

Rawls's understanding of the distinction between rules and principles is thus consistent with the account of the logical distinction between rules and principles that Ronald Dworkin develops in his legal theory.[6] Since Dworkin's analysis clarifies some implications of Rawls's distinction between rules and principles, it is therefore useful to review the relevant elements of Dworkin's account. Rules apply in an all-or-nothing fashion and determine the judgment with regard to any issue to which they apply, Dworkin notes, while principles do not exercise such a decisive influence. Principles, rather, state a reason to decide one way or another that may or may not have decisive weight in resolving a contested issue. Since principles do not necessarily determine a contested issue, more than one principle may apply to the same question. Multiple principles of varying weights may apply to the same issue, and when multiple principles *do* apply, a final judgment is determined by the principle with the greatest weight (see TJ 37). Since rules, in contrast, apply in an all-or-nothing fashion and therefore determine judgment in any case to which they apply, only one rule may apply to any particular question. Principles thus *raise* issues for reflection, while rules *settle* issues and *end* reflection.

Rawls's principles of justice as fairness function in precisely this manner. Each principle identifies a reason to decide contested questions of justice one way rather than another. The first principle requires that the fact that a policy is necessary to ensure protection of a basic liberty constitutes a centrally important consideration in political reflection. Under the second principle, the fact that implementation of a policy would improve or undermine (1) equal opportunity and/or (2) fairness in the distribution of goods is also a centrally important consideration.

Ideal Theory and Practical Analysis

If a policy enhances liberty but also undermines both equal opportunity and fairness, then the liberty principle, the principle of fair equality of opportunity, and the difference principle are all centrally relevant to the resolution of the question. In such a case, Rawls's first priority rule dictates the proper resolution by assigning decisive weight to the liberty principle (unless the failure of equal opportunity or fairness is so significant that the guarantee of a social minimum is seriously compromised). Thus, Rawls's principles identify the basic considerations that are relevant to questions of justice, and each principle connects the relevant consideration to judgment – each principle, that is, indicates the way in which effects on liberty, opportunity, and fairness constitute reasons to decide one way or another. Finally, Rawls's priority rules determine the respective weight of each of the principles and thus identify the considerations that should be decisive in resolving the contested question. Since the principles operate together as a unit, however, the application of the priority rules is not absolute. The requirements of the difference principle, for example, are relevant to the determination of the size and nature of the social minimum that is required under the first principle.

Note that even a principle with decisive weight does not require a *particular* outcome. Rather, that principle identifies the considerations that should have the greatest weight in resolving a contested question. The resolution of the contested question, however, is determined by reflection in applying that consideration to the specific facts. Suppose, for example, that the contested question involves an assessment of an environmental policy that (1) is necessary to ensure breathable air but that (2) undermines equal opportunity because it reduces the number of quality jobs available to members of the working class while increasing employment for consultants and attorneys involved in implementing the policy. In order to avoid the undesirable distributive results of this policy, the fair equality principle would require the adoption of some policy to offset the reduction in equal opportunity. The principle does not, however, identify one uniquely just policy response. Rather, an acceptable policy response could take the form of retraining and relocating displaced workers, subsidies to employers to encourage hiring, stimulative fiscal policy, or some other program designed to equalize opportunity. The fair equality principle identifies effects on opportunity as a consideration of justice that counts as a reason in favor of adopting a policy, but does not determine the specific nature of the policy adopted.

Thus, the process of applying the principles will not in most cases point to a single uniquely just outcome. Rather, a number of possible outcomes may be consistent with the proper application of the principle. In such cases, as Rawls notes, it is not clear "which of several constitutions, or economic or social arrangements would be chosen" on due reflection (TJ 176). The requirements of justice are, to that extent, indeterminate.

Far from aiming for completeness in moral judgment, then, Rawls's theory sets out an open-ended framework that identifies the considerations fundamentally relevant to judgment, but that assigns considerable autonomy to persons individually and collectively in determining the specific requirements of justice. The principles identify relevant considerations, but the resolution of questions of justice ultimately requires careful reflection relating those considerations to the complex set of facts facing the policy-maker in the relevant context. In designating principles – rather than rules – as the fundamental standard of justice, then, Rawls indicates his intention to design a flexible approach that regulates reasoning about justice but that does not aspire to determine judgments of justice in advance.

Conclusion

Sen argues that Rawls's approach is designed to specify a unique account of perfectly just institutions. Rawls's approach, Sen argues, (1) commits him to the goal of specifying a unique account of perfectly just institutions, (2) fails to devote adequate attention to assessment of the normative presuppositions of his approach, (3) shows insufficient concern regarding the consequences that implementing perfectly just institutions may produce, and (4) unrealistically aims for completeness in moral judgment. I have argued that these objections fail. Rawls's ideal theory approach does not commit him to the goal of specifying a unique account of perfectly just institutions. Rawls's approach provides an explicit method for assessing the normative presuppositions of his approach. Rawls is sensitive to the consequences of implementing his institutional proposals. Finally, Rawls does not aim for completeness in moral judgment.

While Rawls's explicit adoption of an ideal theoretical approach has invited misconstruction, Rawls's approach is ideal only in the sense that the discussion abstracts away from issues of partial compliance.

There is no effort to sketch a unique set of perfectly just institutions. Far from aiming for completeness in moral judgment, Rawls's theory sets out an open-ended framework that identifies the considerations fundamentally relevant to judgment, but which assigns considerable autonomy to persons individually and collectively in determining the specific requirements of justice.

Notes

1 Sen (2009). Page numbers in this chapter will refer to this work.
2 Nussbaum (1990), p. 217.
3 Mill's argument is interesting, Rawls suggests, because it enables one to see why political equality has sometimes been regarded as less essential than equal liberty of conscience or liberty of the person. To the extent that one assumes that it is the sole purpose of government to secure the common good, one may be persuaded that government by the more educated or intelligent is acceptable if that arrangement most effectively realizes the common good. However, if one does not view the purposes of government as entirely instrumental, Rawls suggests, this conclusion may seem less justifiable.
4 Rawls (1951), p. 17.
5 Rawls (1951), p. 9.
6 See Dworkin (1977), pp. 22–28.

9 | Poverty, Inequality, and Justice

In Chapter 8, I argue that Rawls aims to offer a general framework for political judgment rather than a precise blueprint for just institutions or policy. Nevertheless, application of the principles that constitute justice as fairness to specific social institutions and circumstances will ground significant substantive judgments regarding institutions and policy. This chapter examines the nature of the judgments that the principles would justify in the context of the social conditions currently existing in the United States. Such a focus illustrates both (1) the potential of justice as fairness to contribute to egalitarian thought and (2) the manner in which the principles provide a framework rather than a blueprint.

This chapter focuses, in particular, on poverty and income inequality in the United States. The first section discusses the nature of the policy judgments that justice as fairness would justify to address these conditions. The second section assesses a recent major policy initiative affecting antipoverty policy in the United States.

Poverty and Inequality in the United States

The most salient feature of current social and economic conditions in the United States is the inequality of income and wealth. In 2012, Census Bureau data indicate that members of the wealthiest 20 percent of households received 51 percent of total income, while the top 5 percent received 22.3 percent of total income.[1] The poorest 20 percent of households, in contrast, received 3.2 percent of income. Extreme as the income inequality reflected in that data might seem, an updated study of income data by economists Emmanuel Saez and Thomas Piketty indicates that the Census data seriously *understate* income inequality in the United States. Saez and Piketty's analysis found that the top 1 percent of earners received 23.5 percent of income, while the top 10 percent received over 50 percent of income.[2] This unequal distribution, moreover, is the product of a continuous and ongoing pattern of income redistribution from the lower quintiles to the wealthiest earners. According to Census Bureau data, the share of total income received by the top 5 percent of earners increased from 15.6 percent in 1969 to 22.3 percent in 2012, while the income share of the lowest quintile declined steadily from 5.6 percent of income in 1969 to its current level of 3.2 percent.[3] Between 1973 and 2003, the average real income of the bottom 90 percent of earners fell by 7 percent, while the income of the top 1 percent increased by 148 percent.[4] During this period, Census Bureau data indicate that the income share of the top 1 percent increased from 7.74 percent to 19.34 percent.[5]

The distribution of *wealth* is even more asymmetrical. The members of the top quintile of households in 2005 possessed 84.4 percent of wealth. The top 1 percent alone possessed 33 percent of wealth, while the bottom 40 percent possessed 0.7 percent.[6] Moreover, wealth inequality has increased dramatically in recent decades. In 1983, the richest 1 percent possessed on average 1,500 times the wealth of the bottom 40 percent of households. In 2001, the wealth of the richest 1 percent was almost 4,400 times the wealth of the bottom 40 percent.[7]

Such dramatic and steadily increasing inequality could be justified under the difference principle only on the grounds that permitting such inequality was to the benefit of the least advantaged. Yet the available evidence does not appear to support such a claim. As the share of the highest quintile increased from 40.6 percent to 50.4 percent of income between 1969 and 2005, the share of the lowest quintile fell from 5.6 percent to 3.4 percent. In fact, the share of the lowest three quintiles fell from 35.7 percent to 26.6 percent between 1969 and 2005 – the lowest 60 percent of the distribution, that is, lost 22.4 percent of its income share during this period. Moreover, as noted above, the average real income of the bottom 90 percent of earners fell by 7 percent between 1973 and 2003. The percentage of Americans living in poverty during this period remained consistently between 12 and 13 percent until 2010, when the percentage rose to 15 percent.[8] The available evidence, then, shows no sign that inequalities in favor of the more fortunate during this period worked as part of a scheme that benefited the least advantaged.

The inequality in income distribution parallels inequality in access to secondary education, higher education, and employment. Not only has the quality gap between the secondary educational opportunity available to less and more advantaged students not decreased, but also the quality gap has increased significantly. A recent study based upon data compiled by the Department of Education examined the academic achievement gap between children from high- and low-income families and found that the gap between the academic achievement of children from families with incomes at the ninetieth percentile of family and those from families at the tenth percentile has increased by 75 percent between the early 1940s and 2001.[9] Indeed, the study notes that "[t]he relationship between family socioeconomic status characteristics and student achievement is one of the most robust patterns in educational scholarship."[10]

Opportunity in higher education is characterized by similar inequality. Higher family income is associated by a much greater probability that a child will enter college and an even greater probability of college completion. A study based upon data compiled by the US Bureau of Labor Statistics found that the probability of college entry for children in the top quartile in 1982 was 80 percent, while the probability for children in the bottom quartile was 29 percent. The contrast in completion rates was even more extreme: 54 percent of children from the top quartile completed college, while the completion rate for children from the lowest quartile was 9 percent.[11] Children of higher income families are thus more than twice as likely to enter college and six times as likely to complete college as children of lower income families.

Inequality in the opportunity to attend highly selective colleges is even more acute. Seventy-four percent of students attending highly selective colleges are from families in the top quartile, while 3 percent of students attending these colleges are from the lowest quartile.[12]

Finally, less skilled workers are experiencing increasing difficulty in securing employment, and economic mobility is extremely limited. The labor force participation rate of nonelderly men with only a high school diploma fell from 92 percent on 1979 to 83 percent in 2007, while the rate for nonelderly men without a high school diploma fell from 79 percent to 73 percent in the same period. The labor force participation rate for nonelderly women with a high school diploma rose from 61.7 percent in 1979 to a high of 69.9 percent in 1997, but declined to 66.8 percent by 2007. Among nonelderly women without a diploma, the labor force participation rate rose from 44 percent in 1979 to 50 percent in 2000, but declined to 47.8 percent by 2007. Employment opportunity has thus declined significantly for less skilled nonelderly men since 1979. Less skilled nonelderly women improved upon their weak labor market position between 1979 and 2000, but their position deteriorated after 2000.

Moreover, contrary to conventional wisdom, social mobility in the United States is limited. A recent study found that about 60 percent of persons in the bottom quintile of the population remained in that quintile nine years later.[13] Studies of social mobility report "high levels of [intergenerational income] persistence in the United States."[14] Indeed, the Economic Mobility Project reports that "there is a stronger link between parental education and children's economic, educational, and socio-economic outcomes" in the United States than in any of the other countries (e.g., Australia, Canada, Denmark, Finland, France, Germany, Italy, Sweden, the United Kingdom) investigated.[15]

Basic social institutions in the United States thus fail to meet the minimum standards for a just society. The distribution of income, wealth, and opportunity is characterized by dramatic and steadily increasing inequality, and the available evidence suggests that permitting such inequality has not benefited the least advantaged. Moreover, the living conditions of a significant portion of the population fall below standards for any reasonable social minimum; and many of the poorest members of society lack access to adequate food, shelter, and medical services.[16]

A variety of forms of social policy are required to address the institutional inadequacies that have produced these failures to satisfy the requirements of justice. Policies that supply income transfers and policies that provide services such as health care and food are both necessary to address the failure of current market institutions to guarantee a social minimum. Policies that improve access to education, training, and employment are required to address the societal failure to ensure equal opportunity. And some combination of collective bargaining, wage subsidies, and earned income credits are necessary to ensure fair compensation.

Note that the priority of the first principle requires that attention must be addressed first to the failure to ensure a basic social minimum to address the needs of persons who are destitute, starving, homeless, and without access to medical care. The most fundamental deprivation involves the lack of food, shelter, and clothing. The first principle therefore assigns priority to the provision of assistance to address these forms of deprivation. Note, however, that an intervention addressing these forms of deprivation could many take the forms, including (1) a means-tested income transfer program, (2) a negative income tax, (3) a policy combining family allowances and relief to single adults, or (4) a policy combining one or more of the three preceding approaches with in-kind relief (e.g., food stamps, housing subsidies). Policy makers for a well-ordered society regulated by justice as fairness would be likely to reject a means-tested policy approach, since participants in means-tested programs usually suffer significant social stigma. Such a policy would therefore fail to ensure a satisfactory share of the primary good of self-respect.[17] Policies involving family allowances and policies involving a negative income tax would both, however, appear to be consistent with justice as fairness.

The destitute also lack access to adequate health care services, and any set of policies designed to secure a social minimum would need to address this lack. A policy to address this problem could also, however, take many forms – a single payer system, a system based upon subsidies to the private sector, an employer mandate, or one of the many other policy approaches that have been considered or implemented as national health policies.

After policies are enacted to secure a social minimum, the fair equality of opportunity principle requires policies to ensure that persons with similar abilities and motivation enjoy similar chances of success. Most obviously, fair equality of opportunity requires equal access to high quality education, and the interaction of the fair opportunity principle and the difference principle requires that attention must be directed first to the condition of the least advantaged. Again, a wide range of policy options are available. An early intervention compensatory education program such as Head Start would seem a natural candidate for inclusion among these policy options, but many options are available for the implementation of even this single program. Three models – the child-centered model, the cognitively oriented model, and the direct instruction model – have been employed as the basis of program curricula. The first two models are grounded in Piagetian theory, while the third is grounded in the sharply contrasted theory of B. F. Skinner.[18] Policy makers would therefore need to assess these models to determine – in their considered judgments, on due reflection – which would most effectively reduce inequality in opportunity. In addition, they would need to decide whether the program should continue to be provided only to children between kindergarten and third grade, or whether services should be extended to grades 4–6 as was contemplated by the Follow-Through Program enacted in 1966.[19] Moreover, adequate policies to improve educational quality should extend beyond the most disadvantaged neighborhoods served by Head Start and, in addition, should provide services to students through junior high school and high school. Some compensatory services to these groups are currently provided in the United States under Title One of the Elementary and Secondary Education Act, but the act provides services only to schools in poor neighborhoods. Moreover, policy makers attempting to implement the most acceptable form of this program would face choices regarding theoretical models and curricula similar to those that arise in the case of Head Start. Finally, while the choice of model and curriculum should be determined by probability of success in improving the quality of education provided, such a calculation may generate different conclusions in different contexts – so that conclusions reached under Rawls's approach will vary with context as Sen recommends.

Policy makers attempting to reduce inequality in educational opportunity would face many other complex choices. For example, since elite private schools are gatekeeper institutions that ration access to institutes of higher education, it would seem that fair equality of opportunity should require wider access to elite private schools. Multiple policy options are available in this case as well. Elite private schools could be required to admit a certain percentage of disadvantaged students in each cohort; the state could provide subsidies to schools that admit disadvantaged students; or the state could subsidize or sponsor the creation of additional schools of similar quality.

Complex decisions would also face policy makers regarding higher education. Opportunities for higher education are provided to only a minority of the eligible population in the United States. In 2009, according to Census Bureau data, only 30 percent of adults had completed a college degree. Another 21 percent had attended college without completing a degree.[20] While access to higher education could be improved by providing improved financing options, any policy designed to provide access for a significant percentage of those currently not attending college would need to increase the number and/or size of colleges of high quality. In addition, policies providing support and remedial skill training would be necessary to increase the rate of program completion.

As discussed in Chapter 6, however, fair equality of opportunity would require policies that extend far beyond the guarantee of equal opportunity in education. In addition to a fiscal policy designed to produce full employment, the fair equal opportunity principle would require effective policies to ensure equal opportunity to obtain employment. The United States has experimented with a number of policies designed to equalize opportunity. The Comprehensive Education and Training Act united a number of programs employing traditional approaches including on-the-job training, public service employment, work experience, and classroom training. Some approaches (e.g., on-the-job training) were more effective than others, but the program impacts of even the most successful programs were modest.[21] A number of more intensive programs (Job Corps, Supported Work, Youth Employment and Demonstration Projects) have produced "very significant increases in employment and earnings."[22] Moreover, most of the Western European democracies have implemented employment and training programs that are more extensive than any of the manpower policies that have been enacted in the United States and seem in many cases to be quite effective in improving access to employment. Germany, for example, attempts to promote employability during the school-to-work transition through a formalized apprenticeship program that provides training to a large percentage of students during high school.[23] Similarly, in Sweden, a majority of students receive training through the vocational education system.[24] Policy makers would therefore face a wide range of choices in implementing the fair opportunity principle to improve access to employment. As in the case of educational policy, the choice of policy would be dictated by a judgment regarding which policy, in the specific local social and economic context, would most effectively reduce inequality of opportunity. And, as in the case of judgments regarding education policy, that judgment will differ as the specific features of the economic context vary. Far from requiring a single form of intervention, then, institutions for manpower policy will also be highly context specific.

Finally, once policies implementing the fair equality principle to the fullest extent possible were implemented, the difference principle would require attention to remaining inequalities of income and wealth that result from the inequality in the compensation provided by the market for the employment of human capital. Such inequalities are justifiable under the difference principle only if they function as part of a scheme that benefits members of the least advantaged class. Policy makers could employ a range of policies to ensure that remaining inequalities meet this requirement. Rawls argues that implementation of the fair opportunity principle will do much of the work in securing a fair distribution: "[t]he idea is that given the equal basic liberties and fair equality of opportunity, the open competition between the greater numbers of well-trained and better educated reduces the ratio of shares until it lies within an acceptable range." In the conditions of free competition among better qualified workers secured by the prior principles, "the more advantaged cannot unite as a group and then exploit their market power to force increases in their income."[25] If such arrangements are not completely effective in securing a fair distribution, however, other policy options – including income taxes, inheritance taxes, transfers, and the creation of additional earning opportunities for the less fortunate – may be appropriate (TJ 242–47).

Welfare "Reform": A Case Study

This section examines the degree to which the framework for reflection that Rawls supplies sets out criteria that can be employed to identify the merits or flaws of concrete social policy. In particular, this section assesses the degree to which the 1996 legislation that restructured the provision of income assistance to the disadvantaged in the United States satisfies the criteria of justice as fairness. This discussion will both apply the criteria of justice as fairness to concrete policy and examine the manner in which the reasoning of policy makers may misapply those criteria.

Changes in Policies of Income Support

Before 1996, Aid to Families with Dependent Children (AFDC) constituted the United States's largest federal income transfer program designed to assist the destitute. While AFDC provided targeted assistance to poor recipients, however, the program was not available to all poor persons. Rather, assistance under the program was available only to women without a source of income and with dependent children under the age of eighteen. The program was not generous. In 1988 – shortly before the program was replaced by the Temporary Assistance for Needy Families program (TANF) – the real value of the median state's maximum AFDC payment was 46 percent of the 1988 federal poverty threshold.[26] Nor was the program designed to realize progress toward equal opportunity – AFDC provided no services designed to enhance employability, and participation in the program carried sufficient stigma to deter many potential employers from hiring aid recipients.

The program was therefore clearly problematic. It provided no services designed to improve opportunity, it provided a stipend low enough to ensure that the limited set of persons who qualified to receive benefits continued to live in grinding poverty, and participation in the program conferred a stigma that constituted an obstacle to improved opportunity. Critics of the program also argued that recipients of assistance formed stable and long-term preferences for dependency upon state support. The available data, however, provide little support for this last claim. In particular, 70 percent of recipients returned to work within four years of first receiving aid.[27]

While the program was problematic, it also constituted the only source of support for several million women and young children. In 1988, 3.7 million households with 7.3 million children received benefits under the program.[28] While the program did little to reduce poverty and nothing to equalize opportunity, then, it did prevent malnutrition, starvation, and absolute destitution for millions of households. In the absence of a more adequate policy, AFDC constituted at least a timid step toward a satisfactory policy designed to secure an adequate social minimum.

Federal legislation enacted in 1996, however, altered the program in ways that seriously reduced its already tenuous effectiveness in securing an adequate social minimum. The 1996 legislation imposed time limits on participation in the AFDC program, capped total federal spending on welfare, and required participation in "work activities" as a condition of assistance.

The 1996 legislation is widely viewed as a major policy success. In the first years after its enactment, the number of persons receiving income assistance dropped by over 50 percent. In addition, many states initially reported that 60 percent of those leaving welfare were employed. With reliance on income transfers declining and a majority of those leaving welfare apparently working, welfare reform was described as "one of the most successful experiments in social policy of the last 25 years."[29]

The data, however, suggest a rather different story. The post-1996 income of poor single-parent families has dropped; and the Center on Budget and Policy Priorities reports that the new policies have pushed hundreds of thousands of children into poverty. But most significantly, the claim that a majority of people leaving welfare are employed is highly misleading.

The idea that the deep and intractable problems of poor single-parent families could have been rapidly solved through time limits and brief and inexpensive training programs is, in fact, implausible. The poor single mothers who relied upon income assistance from AFDC generally suffer from crippling disadvantages that undermine their attempts to enter the work force. A 1997 study found that 47 percent of persons first enrolling in AFDC had not completed high school, and 39 percent had not worked in the past year.[30] In addition, since most lack access to adequate day care, they can accept employment only during certain hours; and they may have to cancel job interviews on short notice. Transforming this population into self-sufficient members of the labor market would have required an extraordinary investment of public resources.

The work training programs required by the 1996 legislation involve no such investment. In all but the most ambitious programs, welfare recipients are merely required to attend a four-week job readiness program in which participants discuss and are lectured on appearance, attitude, and self-presentation. The programs are designed to improve employability by altering expectations and behavior. But a four-week program that provides little or no real instruction or training cannot erase serious deficits in skills, education, and work experience. These programs do not even begin to address the problems that make it so difficult for welfare recipients to enter the work force.

As a result, persons leaving welfare ("leavers") since 1996 have experienced high levels of poverty, unemployment, and underemployment. Although a number of studies have reported that 50 percent to 60 percent of leavers are employed, those studies are designed to determine whether leavers have worked at all, not whether they are continuously employed and earning enough to pay for basic needs. The studies employ one of the three following criteria to define the class of employed leavers: (1) any earnings at all in a calendar quarter, (2) at least $100 earned in a calendar quarter, or (3) at least $500 earned in a calendar quarter.[31] Most studies employ the first two criteria. Thus, the category of "employed" leavers includes a high proportion of people whose earnings are too low to cover even the most urgent food and rent expenses.

A household requires income of twice the official poverty line in order to meet basic needs.[32] Most leavers receive incomes well below the poverty line. The Urban Institute studied and synthesized numerous state studies of postwelfare employment and earnings during the first post-TANF exit quarter range in 1997. In the fifteen states, cities, and counties surveyed, median quarterly earnings varied from a low of $1,941 to a high of $3,416.[33] In eleven of the fifteen areas surveyed, quarterly earnings were below $3,000. The median across-the-studies earnings per quarter varied from a low of $2,575 (in the second quarter following departure) to $2,712 (in the fourth quarter).[34] Even if leavers were employed in all four quarters at the higher (fourth quarter) median rate, their maximum annual earnings would be $10,848 – about 20 percent below the poverty line for a family of three[35] ($13,330 in 1997). Other studies have confirmed these findings. A 2001 study of state reports of leaver earnings by the National Campaign for Jobs and Income Support found median annual earnings ranging from $1,400 (West Virginia) to $9,800 (Illinois).[36] A 2000 study for the Institute for Research on Poverty, studied the earnings of leavers in three years after program exit, and found that median annual earnings increased from $8,608 in the first year to $10,924 in the third year.[37] Even the higher earnings in year three, however, remain about 20 percent below the poverty line.

Moreover, as Brauner and Loprest note, most estimates of annual leaver earnings almost certainly "overestimate leavers' true earnings."[38] Generally, estimates of leaver annual earnings *simply quadruple quarterly earnings*. Many leavers are not, however, able to maintain employment in all four quarters. The Urban Institute's Final Synthesis of studies of outcomes for leavers found that "only 37 percent of leavers worked in all four postexit quarters. The 'all-four-quarters' employment rates range from a low of 25% in Iowa to a high of 47% in Cuyahoga County."[39] The state of Washington, Braun and Loprest note, reported that leavers worked an average of thirty-four weeks per year.[40] Cancian et al., analyzing results for leavers in Wisconsin, found that leavers "who were employed were employed for an average of 3.0 quarters."[41] Leavers who were employed three quarters at $2,575 would have annual earnings of $6,725 – just over half of the poverty threshold. Reports from Iowa, South Carolina, and Texas show similar results, suggesting that leaver annual earnings were generally far below the poverty threshold.[42] These results may help to explain (1) SIPP data indicating a significant increase (from 24.4 to 33.3 percent) in the percentage of leavers with incomes below 50 percent of the poverty line after 1996[43] and (2) findings that between 50 percent and 75 percent of leavers remain poor two to three years after leaving welfare.[44]

Note, in addition, that the data regarding earnings take into account only leavers who are considered to be "employed." Approximately 40 percent of leavers are not considered "employed," even under the "any earnings in a calendar quarter" criterion. These leavers, by definition, have no known source of income. Some of these leavers return to welfare, but a number of studies report the presence of a growing class of "disconnected" leavers with no known source of income.[45] As many as one-quarter of all single mothers leaving TANF were disconnected for at least a four-month period in 2009.[46]

But, it might be objected, these studies analyze data from only the first few years after enactment of TANF. Such short-term assessments could reasonably be expected to understate the improvements of condition realized by leavers who could not be expected to move directly from welfare into jobs of high quality. Longer-term data, this objection would continue, would presumably reveal improvements in leavers' living conditions as they established themselves in the labor market.

This objection points to a real problem – the lack of longer-term outcome evaluations. As noted in the Urban Institute's Final Report to the Department of Health and Human Services on the impact of TANF on leavers, "it is still rare to find studies using data any later than 2002."[47]

Sufficient data are, however, available to contradict the suggestion that the earnings of leavers increased over time. Analyzing data from the National Survey of America's Families, the Survey of Income and Program Participation, and the Current Population Survey, the Urban Institute's Final Report determined that there was, on average, no increase in the earnings of leavers between 2001 and 2005. In fact, their analysis found that leavers suffered a significant increase in poverty during this period.[48] This increase in poverty paralleled decreasing rates of employment among leavers. The Urban Institute's Final Report found a 15 percent drop in employment among leavers between 2000 and 2005.[49]

It is therefore not surprising that the number of households whose earnings (including all available government assistance) fall into the "extreme poverty" category – persons living on an income equal to or less than 13 percent of the official poverty line – increased dramatically in the period following the enactment of TANF. A total of 409,000 households fell into this category in 1996 (before the enactment of TANF), while 613,000 households (including 1.17 million children) fell into this category in 2011.[50] The significant increase in the poverty rate among female-headed households (from 33 percent in 2000 to 40.9 percent in 2012)[51] undoubtedly constitutes a significant component of this increase. Indeed, hundreds of thousands of children have been shifted into deep poverty through the direct effect of the 1996 legislation: in 1995, AFDC lifted out of poverty 62 percent of children who would otherwise have been below half of the poverty line, but by 2005, TANF lifted out of poverty just 21 percent of children who would have been below half of the poverty line.[52]

But if the 1996 legislation failed to improve the employability of welfare recipients, why has the number of persons receiving benefits dropped so sharply? While the available data are incomplete, a significant body of research offers evidence to support two explanations. First, tough new administrative rules are apparently deterring or deflecting new claims while normal program attrition reduces the number of existing welfare recipients. Before the 1996 legislation, large numbers of persons left welfare each year. Fifty-six percent of welfare participants left the program within one year, and 80 percent left within five years. It would therefore be possible to produce massive reductions in participation simply by sustaining the pre-reform rate of program exits while blocking new applications. The total number of new welfare applications approved between 1994 and 1997 declined by more than one-third, suggesting that just such a mechanism is at work.[53]

Second, the aggressive use of sanctions to drop participants from the program has produced a large number of involuntary exits. Welfare participation has dropped most sharply, not in the states with the most extensive training and placement programs, but in states that impose sanctions that require dropping entire families from the program for the first failure to comply with program rules. Between 1994 and 1997, approximately 25 percent of the caseload reduction was the direct result of the application of sanctions. Moreover, the states with the strictest sanctions experienced caseload declines as much as

25 percent greater than those reported by states with the least stringent sanctions.[54]

It is not surprising that the states, faced with capped federal funding under the 1996 reforms, have found it easier to deter new applicants and to drop families from the program than to move people from welfare to work. No known training programs could perform such a task. All of the training programs offered under welfare reform–job readiness, job search, work experience and on-the-job training – have been in use since the 1960s, and we know pretty well what they can and cannot do. Some are more effective than others; but a 1980 study found that only 25 percent of participants in Job Corps, the most effective of the training programs, remained employed full-time eighteen months after completing the program.[55] This means that 75 percent of the people who complete even the best training programs still have serious difficulty in obtaining employment. It would be unrealistic, then, to believe that we could simply put welfare recipients into even the best of these programs and expect their employment problems to disappear.

And yet the authors of the 1996 reforms seem to have believed that these training programs could make aid recipients readily employable. On the basis of this belief, they changed policy in a way that quickly made millions of people ineligible for continued income assistance. Why did the legislators have such confidence in the effectiveness of these programs? Because of the results of a social experiment conducted during the 1980s: the Work Incentive Program demonstration projects (the "WIN demos"). This experiment tested the impact on welfare recipients of providing an array of training programs similar to those provided by the 1996 reforms.

Demonstration projects under the experiment were conducted by nineteen states, but the programs had a measurable and nontrivial effect on employability in only two states. In the first two years after program participation, program participants in these two states appeared to earn about $500 per year more than persons who left AFDC without similar training. It was not a tremendous effect – it would not lift anyone out of poverty. But if the effect were stable and increasing, then the program might plausibly be said to have changed the employment prospects of participants.[56]

Before putting much faith in these programs, however, a policy analyst would want to see impact reports over a much longer period (at least three to five years). In 1991, the five-year impact reports became available. Unfortunately, but predictably, the impacts of the demos turned out to be unstable. In the case of the San Diego WIN demo – which had been the most dramatic success story – the decline was particularly sharp. At the end of two years, the reports had shown participants in the demos earning $500 per year more than nonparticipants. After four years, however, they were earning only $300 more; and at the end of five years, they were earning only $150 more. The impact had declined by two-thirds in five years.[57]

Since few of the persons surveyed earned above the minimum wage, even at the high point of their earnings, the decline in earnings is unlikely to have resulted from a large reduction in wages levels. Rather, these figures tell us that, after five years, people were working significantly fewer hours. The most natural interpretation of the results is that large numbers of people were losing jobs. The bottom line was that even the best of the WIN demos did not have a sustainable impact on employability. People who had difficulty getting and keeping full-time jobs before they participated in the programs had about the same problems five years later. The WIN demos, then, actually demonstrated the *ineffectiveness* of the training programs that the 1996 legislation count on to do so much.

Assessment

Viewed from the perspective of justice as fairness, the changes in the welfare program undermined the justice of social institutions with regard to the first principle and were ineffective in promoting opportunity, as required by the second principle. The program undermined the already limited policy efforts to guarantee a social minimum, as required by the first principle, in order to fund programs to improve opportunity; and the programs to improve opportunity were ineffective and diverted spending from more effective antipoverty programs.

The income support provided through the AFDC program constituted a limited social effort to secure a social minimum for persons unable to secure employment. The program was inadequate to the task, since (1) the real value of AFDC payments in most states was well below the poverty threshold throughout the program's history and (2) many persons who in fact met the program's criteria were denied aid.[58] Moreover, the program provided little or no assistance to impoverished males; and the program provided no assistance to impoverished adults of either sex who did not have dependent children. Nevertheless, AFDC *did* provide assistance to millions of destitute households. In particular, the support protected millions of children from the threat of homelessness and malnutrition.

The 1996 legislation significantly reduced the income support under AFDC that served to secure a social minimum to a small subset of the poor in order to fund programs to improve employability. Thus, in order to fund programs intended to increase opportunity, the legislation deliberately reduced support for basic needs required in order to secure the social minimum – a shift in priorities that is strictly forbidden by the justice as fairness. The guarantee of a social minimum is required by the first principle, while the promotion of equal opportunity is required by the second. Since the first principle is strictly prior to the second, justice fairness would forbid changes in policy that sacrifice the provision of a social minimum in order to improve opportunity. Rawls, as discussed above, suggests that it might be appropriate to assign lexical priority over the first (liberty) principle to a principle providing for basic needs (JAF 44n7). The guarantee of a social minimum, Rawls suggests in this passage, may constitute the most fundamental requirement of distributive justice. From the standpoint of justice as fairness, then, the 1996 legislation was unjust, and would have remained unjust even if the programs to improve opportunity had been effective.

As discussed above, however, the work training programs required by the 1996 legislation do not even begin to address the problems that make it so difficult for welfare recipients to enter the work force. As a result, implementation of the legislation significantly increased poverty among the poorest female-headed households without producing any improvement in opportunity. Even if the enactment of the legislation had not been clearly unjust under the first principle of justice, its effect in increasing poverty among the least advantaged members of society would clearly establish that the legislation is unjust under the second principle.

Finally, while this example involves a case in which Rawls and many of his critics would agree in criticizing the legislation in question, it is important to emphasize that Rawls and many of these critics would not agree upon (a) the scope of the duty of justice owed to persons harmed by the legislation or (b) the justification of that duty. Rawls, for example, argues for an unconditional requirement to guarantee minimum support to each disadvantaged person, while a utilitarian approach would fine-tune the level of support provided to ensure certain utility consequences. In Rawls's theory, the provision of such minimum assistance is justified as necessary in order "for citizens to understand and to be able fruitfully to exercise the basic rights and liberties" (JAF 44n7), while in a utilitarian conception, the minimum is justified as necessary to optimize aggregate or average utility. The contrast between the respective underlying rationales justifies the difference in the nature of the respective duties to provide assistance. In Rawls's theory, only a social minimum that is sufficient to secure the value of basic liberties is acceptable; an unconditioned guarantee of a certain level of support is thus required. In utilitarian theory, a social minimum is to be designed to secure optimum utility in the relevant circumstances; utilitarian theory thus generally justifies a guarantee that is (1) less secure and (2) conditioned on certain utility consequences. The example thus illustrates the specific character of a representative duty of justice in Rawls's theory and the form of justification that the theory provides for such a duty.

Conclusion

The discussion in the first section focuses on three of the policy areas to which justice as fairness would assign the highest priority – the guarantee of a social minimum; equality of opportunity in education; and equality of opportunity in employment. In each case, justice as fairness provides the basis for a specific substantive critique of current policy. In each case, however, it is clear that justice as fairness would not prescribe a unique blueprint for policy or institutions. Instead, Rawls's approach would identify central considerations that must be addressed, as a matter of justice, and would provide a framework to regulate reflection regarding the choice of a policy to address needs in each area. Nevertheless, an analysis employing justice as fairness provides the basis both for a critique of current policy and efforts to reform policy in order to improve the justice of our institutions.

The second section examines an important recent piece of legislation from the perspective of Rawls's analytic framework. Assessed from this perspective, the 1996 legislation that replaced AFDC with TANF fails to satisfy the criteria of just legislation both because the legislation significantly weakened the nation's already inadequate programs designed to secure a social minimum and because the policy changes were badly designed to increase opportunity among the least advantaged members of society.

This chapter has thus focused upon a number of issues relevant to an effort to apply justice as fairness, and in particular the second principle, to assess the justice of the distribution of income, wealth, and opportunity in the United States. The chapter does not aim to provide a comprehensive discussion of the relevant set of issues. Such a comprehensive treatment would require a full account of the policies necessary to realize the institutional arrangement that Rawls calls "property-owning democracy." Rawls argues that the institutions of a property-owning democracy will "work to disperse the ownership of wealth and capital, and thus to prevent a small part of society from controlling the economy, and indirectly, political life as well" (JAF 139). The institutions of such a society, Rawls claims, will achieve this result, not through redistributive tax and transfer, policies, but rather by "ensuring the widespread ownership of productive assets and human capital... against a background of fair equality of opportunity" (JAF 139). A full account of the practical implications of the second principle would therefore need to provide an account of the necessary and sufficient conditions for realizing a property-owning democracy. Such an account would need to provide a thorough account of the policy approaches required (1) to address inequalities of access to advantageous environmental factors that result in unequal ability to compete for advantageous positions (as required by fair equality of opportunity) and (2) to prevent unfair inequalities in compensation (as required by the difference principle). Such an account would also need to explore approaches to ensuring widespread ownership of productive assets. While the focus of this chapter is limited, however, it illustrates the potential of justice as fairness to ground policy judgments that are specifically substantive, yet which do not attempt to define a specific blueprint for policy.

Notes

1 US Census Bureau (2012), Table 2, p. 10.
2 Saez (2008).
3 US Census Bureau (2012), Table 2, p. 10.

4 Bouchey and Weller (2005), p. 31.
5 The World Top Income Database, Paris School of Economics, available at http://topincomes.parisschoolofeconomics.eu/#Database.
6 Bouchey and Weller (2005), pp. 38–39.
7 Bouchey and Weller (2005), pp. 38–39.
8 US Census Bureau (2012), Table B-1, p. 52.
9 Reardon (2011), p. 95.
10 Reardon (2011), p. 92.
11 Bailey and Dynarski (2011), pp. 120–21.
12 A total of 9 percent of students attending highly selective colleges are from the bottom half of the distribution. Research by Anthony P. Carnevale and Stephen J. Rose, cited in Stiglitz (2012), p. 308n83.
13 Gottschalk and Spolaore (2002).
14 Jantti (2009), p. 196.
15 Economic Mobility Project of the Pew Charitable Trusts (2011), p. 2. See Huggett and Yaron (2011).
16 See U.S Census Bureau (2012).
17 As discussed in Chapter 4, the adequacy of the share of self-respect realized by members of society is a fundamental consideration for the choosers in the original position.
18 The Cognitively Oriented model attempts to stimulate the development of attitudes positively related to academic achievement, such as (1) persistence in tasks, (2) motivation to achieve, and (3) resistance to distraction. To achieve these goals, the intervention (1) emphasizes underlying processes of thinking and language development and (2) omits training in specific skills, such as reading and arithmetic. The child-centered model assumes that children have certain innate tendencies toward growth which only need certain opportunities to occur. The model emphasizes stimulation of intellectual development, and discourages the teaching of specific skills. The direct instruction model emphasizes the acquisition of specific skills necessary for learning. Thus, Direct Instruction curricula focus on the mastery of three curriculum components: reading, arithmetic, and language. See Wang and Ramp (1987).
19 See Wang and Ramp (1987).
20 US Census Bureau (2009), Table 1, p. 6.
21 A major survey of CETA program results was conducted continuously between 1975 and 1981 by Westat, Incorporated. The results were issued in a series of Continuous Longitudinal Manpower Surveys (CLMS). In addition, the Department of Labor and the Congressional Budget Office commissioned reanalyses of program results utilizing CLMS data. See Barnow (1987). The CLMS reports identified statistically significant positive impacts on earnings. While positive impacts were measurable, they

were not large. Overall, CETA programs increased earnings by $200–$600. Impacts were not evenly distributed over men and women. Minority women and, to a slightly lesser extent, white females experienced impacts which greatly exceeded impacts on male participants in all programs except on-the-job training (OJT). Impacts on male participants in each program except OJT, and to a lesser extent, public service employment, were not statistically different from zero. Other analyses generally confirmed Westat's findings (Barnow 1987), although two studies found negative impacts. None of the analyses, however, identified impacts significantly larger than those identified by Westat.

22 Bassi and Ashenfelter (1986), p. 143.
23 Osterman (1988), pp. 113–14.
24 Osterman (1988), p. 114.
25 Rawls (2001), p. 67.
26 Levitan (1990), p. 49.
27 Bane and Ellwood (1994), p. 32.
28 Levitan (1990), p. 49.
29 Pear (2013).
30 Page and Larner (1997), Table 1, p. 22.
31 Acs et al. (2001), p. 24.
32 Acs et al. (2001), p. 3. Basic needs are defined to include food, rent and utilities, medical, child care, and transportation expenses.
33 Acs and Loprest (2004), p. 33.
34 Acs et al. (2001), p. 28.
35 The median number of children in leaver families is two. See Loprest (1999).
36 National Campaign for Jobs and Income Support (2001).
37 Cancian et al. (2000), Table 8, p. 36.
38 Brauner and Loprest (1999), p. 6.
39 Acs and Loprest (2004), p. 24.
40 Brauner and Loprest (1999), p. 6.
41 Cancian et al. (2000), p. 14.
42 Brauner and Loprest (1999), p. 6.
43 Acs and Loprest (2007), p. 83.
44 Blank (2002).
45 Loprest (2011); Blank (2007); Turner et al. (2006).
46 Loprest (2011).
47 Acs and Loprest (2007), p. 17.
48 Acs and Loprest (2007).
49 Acs and Loprest (2007), p. 76.
50 Shaefer and Edin (2014).
51 National Women's Law Center (2013), p. 8.

52 Trisi and Pavetti (2012), p. 7.
53 Schramm and Soss (2001), p. 59; see Maloy et al. (1998).
54 Schramm et al. (2009), p. 400. See Goldberg and Schott (2000) and Rector and Youssef (1999).
55 See Barnow (1987).
56 Bassi and Ashenfelter (1986); Goldman et al. (1986); Friedlander et al. (1985).
57 Gueron and Pauly (1991).
58 See Patterson (1981), pp. 78–96, for a helpful discussion of the history of the practices if individual states in the administration of AFDC programs.

References

Acs, G., and P. Loprest. 2004. *Leaving Welfare: Employment and Well-Being of Families That Left Welfare in the Post-Entitlement Era*. Kalamazoo, MI: Upjohn Institute.
 2007. *Final Report: TANF Caseload Composition and Leavers Synthesis Report*. Washington, DC: Urban Institute.
Acs, G., P. Loprest, and T. Robert. 2001. *Final Synthesis Report of Findings from ASPE's "Leavers" Grants*. Washington, DC: Urban Institute.
Agarwala, B. K. 1986. "In Defence of the Use of Maximin Principle of Choice under Uncertainty in Rawls's Original Position." *Indian Philosophical Quarterly* 13/2: 250–54.
Alejandro, R. 1988. *The Limits of Rawlsian Justice*. Baltimore, MD: Johns Hopkins University Press.
Allais, M. 1979. "The Foundations of a Positive Theory of Choice Involving Risk and a Criticism of Postulates and Axioms in the American School," in M. Allais and Otto Hagen, eds., *Expected Utility Hypotheses and the Allais Paradox*. Dordrecht: Reidel, pp. 27–148.
Anderson, E. 1999. "What Is the Point of Equality?," *Ethics* 109/2: 287–337.
Angner, E. 2004. "Revisiting Rawls: *A Theory of Justice* in the Light of Levi's Theory of Decision," *Theoria* 70/1: 3–21.
Arneson, R. J. 1989. "Equality and Equal Opportunity for Welfare," *Philosophical Studies* 56: 77–93.
 1999. "Against Rawlsian Equality of Opportunity," *Philosophical Studies* 93: 77–112.
Arrow, K. J. 1973. "Some Ordinalist-Utilitarian Notes on Rawls's Theory of Justice," *Journal of Philosophy* 70: 245–63.
Baier, K. 1989. "Justice and the Aims of Philosophy," *Ethics* 99: 771–90.
Bailey, M. J., and S. M. Dynarski. 2011. "Inequality in Post-Secondary Education," in Duncan and Murnane, *Whither Opportunity*, pp. 117–32.
Bane, M. J., and D. Ellwood. 1994. *Welfare Realities: From Rhetoric to Reform*. Cambridge, MA: Harvard University Press.
Barnow, B. 1987. "The Impact of CETA Programs on Earnings: A Review of the Literature," *Journal of Human Resources* 22: 157–93.

Barry, B. 1973. *The Liberal Theory of Justice*. Oxford: Oxford University Press.
1989. *Theories of Justice*. Berkeley, CA: University of California Press.
Bassi, L. J., and O. Ashenfelter. 1986. "The Effect of Direct Job Creation and Training Programs on Low-Skilled Workers," in Danziger and Weinberg, *Fighting Poverty*, pp. 133–51.
Binmore, K. 1994. *Game Theory and the Social Contract: Vol. I. Playing Fair*. Cambridge, MA: MIT Press.
Blank, R. M. 2002. "Evaluating Welfare Reform in the United States," *Journal of Economic Literature* 40/4: 1105–66.
2007. "Improving the Safety Net for Single Mothers Who Face Serious Barriers to Work," *The Future of Children* 17/2: 183–97.
Blinder, A. S. 1987. *Hard Heads, Soft Hearts*. Reading, MA: Addison-Wesley.
Blocker, H. G., and E. H. Smith (eds.). 1980. *John Rawls' Theory of Social Justice: An Introduction*. Athens, OH: Ohio State University.
Bouchey, H., and C. E. Weller. 2005. "What the Numbers Tell Us," in Lardner and Smith, *Inequality Matters*, pp. 27–40.
Brauner, S., and P. Loprest. 1999. *Where Are They Now? What States' Studies of People Who Left Welfare Tell Us*, New Federalism Series A, No. A-32, Washington, DC: The Urban Institute.
Buchanan, A. 1980. "A Critical Introduction to Rawls' Theory of Justice," in Blocker and Smith, *John Rawls' Theory of Social Justice: An Introduction*, pp. 5–41.
Cancian, M., and S. Danziger (eds.). 2009. *Changing Poverty, Changing Policies*. New York, NY: Russell Sage Foundation.
Cancian, M., et al. 2000. *Before and after TANF: The Economic Well-Being of Women Leaving Welfare*. Madison, WI: Institute for Research on Poverty.
Chambers, S. 1996. *Reasonable Democracy: Jürgen Habermas and the Politics of Discourse*. Ithaca, NY: Cornell University Press.
Charney, E. 1998. "Political Liberalism, Deliberative Democracy, and the Public Sphere," *American Political Science Review* 92/1 (March): 97–110.
Cohen, G. A. 1989. "On the Currency of Egalitarian Justice," *Ethics* 99/4: 906–44.
2008. *Rescuing Justice and Equality*. Cambridge, MA: Harvard University Press.
2011. *On the Currency of Egalitarian Justice and Other Essays in Political Philosophy*. Princeton, NJ: Princeton University Press.
Cohen, J. 1989. "Democratic Equality," *Ethics* 99/4: 736–50.
1993. "Moral Puralism and Political Consensus," in Copp, Hampton, and Roemer, *The Idea of Democracy*, pp. 270–91.

Copp, D., J. Hampton, and J. Roemer, eds. 1993. *The Idea of Democracy*. Cambridge: Cambridge University Press.

Corrado, G. 1980. "Rawls, Games, and Economic Theory," in Blocker and Smith, *John Rawls' Theory of Justice: An Introduction*, pp. 71–109.

Daniels, N. 1996. *Justice and Justification: Reflective Equilibrium in Theory and Practice*. Cambridge: Cambridge University Press.

Danziger, S. H., and D. H. Weinberg (eds.). 1986. *Fighting Poverty: What Works and What Doesn't*. Cambridge, MA: Harvard University Press.

Doppelt, G. 1989. "Is Rawls's Kantian Liberalism Coherent and Defensible?" *Ethics* 99: 811–51.

Duncan, G. J., and R. J. Murnane (eds.). 2011. *Whither Opportunity: Rising Inequality, Schools, and Children's Life Chances*. New York, NY: Russell Sage Foundation.

Dworkin, R. 1977. *Taking Rights Seriously*. Cambridge, MA: Harvard University Press.

  2000. *Sovereign Virtue*. Oxford: Oxford University Press.

Economic Mobility Project of the Pew Charitable Trusts. 2011. "Does America Promote Mobility as Well as Other Nations?," http://economicmobility.org/assets/pdfs/CRITA_FINAL.pdf.

Ellsberg, D. 1961. "Risk, Ambiguity, and the Savage Axioms," *Quarterly Journal of Economics* 75: 643–99.

Estlund, D. 1998. "The Insularity of the Reasonable: Why Political Liberalism Must Admit the Truth," *Ethics* 108: 252–75.

Freeman, S. 1994. "Political Liberalism and the Possibility of a Just Democratic Constitution," *Chicago-Kent Law Review* 69: 619–68.

  2003. "Introduction: John Rawls – An Overview," in *The Cambridge Companion to Rawls*. Cambridge: Cambridge University Press, pp. 1–61.

  2007. *Rawls*. London: Routledge.

Friedlander, D., G. Hoerz, D. Long, and J. Quint. 1985. *Maryland: Final Report of the Employment Initiatives Evaluation*. New York: Manpower Development Research Corporation.

Galston, W. A. 1989. "Pluralism and Social Unity," *Ethics* 99: 711–26.

Gauthier, D. 1974. "Justice and Natural Endowment: Towards a Critique of Rawls's Ideological Framework," *Social Theory and Practice* 3: 3–26.

Goldberg, H., and L. Schott. 2000. *A Compliance Oriented Approach to Sanctions in State and County TANF Programs*. Washington, DC: Center on Budget and Policy Priorities.

Goldman, B., D. Friedlander, and D. Long. 1986. *California: Final Report on the San Diego Job Search and Work Experience Demonstration*. New York, NY: Manpower Development Research Corporation.

Goldman, H. S. 1980. "Rawls and Utilitarianism," in Blocker and Smith, *John Rawls' Theory of Justice*, pp. 346–94.
Gottschalk, P., and E. Spolaore. 2002. "On the Evaluation of Economic Mobility," *Quarterly Journal of Economics* 69: 191–208.
Gueron, J., and E. Pauly. 1991. *From Welfare to Work*. New York, NY: Russell Sage.
Gutmann, A. 1980. *Liberal Equality*. Cambridge: Cambridge University Press.
Habermas, J. 1995. "Reconciliation through the Public Use of Reason: Remarks on John Rawls's Political Liberalism," *Journal of Philosophy* 92 (March): 109–31.
Hampton, J. 1989. "Should Political Philosophy Be Done without Metaphysics?," *Ethics* 99: 791–815.
  1994. "The Common Faith of Liberalism," *Pacific Philosophical Quarterly* 75: 186–216.
Hardin, R. 1988. *Morality within the Limits of Reason*. Chicago, IL: University of Chicago Press.
Hare, R. M. 1989. *Essays on Political Morality*. Oxford: Oxford University Press.
Harsanyi, J. C. 1976. "Can the Maximin Principle Serve as a Basis for Morality? A Critique of Rawls's Theory," in *Essays on Ethics, Social Behavior and Scientific Explanation*. Dordrecht, Netherlands: D. Reidel, pp. 37–63.
Hausman, D. M., and M. S. McPherson. 1996. *Economic Analysis and Moral Philosophy*. Cambridge: Cambridge University Press.
Herman, B. 1989. "Justification and Objectivity: Comments on Rawls and Allison," in Eckhardt Forster (ed.), *Kant's Transcendental Deductions*. Stanford, CA: Stanford University Press, pp. 131–44.
Hill, T. E. 1994. "The Stability Problem in Political Liberalism," *Pacific Philosophical Quarterly* 75: 333–52.
  2002. *Human Welfare and Moral Worth: Kantian Perspectives*. Oxford: Oxford University Press.
Holmes, S. 1993. "John Rawls and the Limits of Tolerance: The Gatekeeper," *The New Republic*, October 11, 39–47.
Huggett, M., G. Ventura, and A. Yaron. 2011. "Sources of Life-time Inequality," *American Economic Review* 101/7: 2923–54.
James, A. 2005. "Constructing Justice for Existing Practice: Rawls and the Status Quo," *Philosophy & Public Affairs* 33/3: 281–316.
  2007. "Constructivism about Practical Reasons," *Philosophy and Phenomenological Research* 74/2: 302–25.
Jantti, M. 2009. "Mobility in the United States in Comparative Perspective," in Cancian and Danziger, *Changing Poverty, Changing Policies*, pp. 180–200.

Julius, A. J. 2003. "Basic Structure and the Value of Equality," *Philosophy & Public Affairs* 31: 321–55.
Kaufman, A. 1999. *Welfare in the Kantian State*. Oxford: Oxford University Press.
Klosko, G. 1993. "Rawls's 'Political' Philosophy and American Democracy," *American Political Science Review* 87: 348–59.
   1994. "Rawls's Argument from Political Stability," *Columbia Law Review* 94: 1882–97.
   1997. "Political Constructivism in Rawls' *Political Liberalism*," *American Political Science Review* 91: 635–46.
Korsgaard, C. M. 1996. *The Sources of Normativity*. Cambridge: Cambridge University Press.
   2008. *The Constitution of Moral Agency*. Oxford: Oxford University Press.
Krasnoff, L. 1999. "How Kantian Is Constructivism?," *Kant-Studien* 90: 385–409.
Kukathas, C., and P. Pettit. 1990. *Rawls: A Theory of Justice and Its Critics*. Stanford, CA: Stanford University Press.
Kymlicka, W. 1989. "Liberal Individualism and Liberal Neutrality," *Ethics* 99: 883–905.
   1990. *Contemporary Political Philosophy: An Introduction*. Oxford: Oxford University Press.
Lardner, J., and D. A. Smith (eds.). 2005. *Inequality Matters*. New York, NY: New Press.
Levi, I. 1967. *Gambling with Truth*. New York, NY: A. Knopf.
   1974. "On Indeterminate Probabilities," *Journal of Philosophy* 71: 391–418.
   1980. *The Enterprise of Knowledge: An Essay on Knowledge, Credal Probability and Chance*. Cambridge, MA: MIT Press.
   1984. *Decisions and Revisions: Philosophical Essays on Knowledge and Value*. Cambridge: Cambridge University Press.
   1986. "The Paradoxes of Allais and Ellsberg," *Economics and Philosophy* 2: 23–53.
Levitan, S. A. 1990. *Programs in Aid of the Poor*. 6th ed. Baltimore, MD: Johns Hopkins University Press.
Loprest, P. J. 1999. *Families Who Left Welfare: Who Are They and How Are They Doing? Assessing the New Federalism: An Urban Institute Program to Assess Changing Social Policies*. Washington, DC: Urban Institute.
   2011. *Disconnected Families and TANF*. OPRE Research Brief #02. Washington, DC: Urban Institute.
Maloy, K. A., L. A. Pavetti, P. Shin, J. Darnell, and L. Scarpulla-Nolan. 1998. "Description and Assessment of State Approaches to Diversion

Programs and Activities under Welfare Reform." http://aspe.os.dhhs.gov/hsp/isp/diverzn/.

Martin, R. 1985. *Rawls and Rights*. Lawrence, KA: University of Kansas Press.

McClennen, E. 1990. *Rationality and Dynamic Choice: Foundational Explorations*. Cambridge: Cambridge University Press.

Mouffe, C. 1996. "Democracy, Power, and the 'Political,'" in S. Benhabib (ed.), *Democracy and Difference*. Princeton, NJ: Princeton University Press, pp. 245–56.

Murphy, L. 1999. "Institutions and the Demands of Justice," *Philosophy & Public Affairs* 27: 251–91.

National Campaign for Jobs and Income Support. 2001. *Poverty amidst Plenty: Unspent TANF Funds and Persistent Poverty*. Washington, DC: Center for Community Change.

National Women's Law Center. 2013. *Insecure and Unequal: Poverty and Income among Women*. Washington, DC: National Women's Law Center.

Neal, P. 1994. "Does He Mean What He Says? (Mis)Understanding Rawls's Practical Turn," *Polity* 27/1: 77–111.

Nozick, R. 1974. *Anarchy, State, and Utopia*. New York, NY: Basic Books.

Nussbaum, M. C. 1990. "Aristotelian Social Democracy," in R. B. Douglass, G. R. Mara, and H. S. Richardson (eds.), *Liberalism and the Good*. New York: Routledge, pp. 203–52.

  2000. *Women and Human Development: The Capabilities Approach*. Cambridge: Cambridge University Press.

O'Neill [Nell], O. 1975. *Acting on Principle: An Essay in Kantian Ethics*. New York: Columbia University Press.

  1988. "Ethical Reasoning and Ideological Pluralism." *Ethics* 98: 705–22.

  1989. *Constructions of Reason*. Cambridge: Cambridge University Press.

  2008. "Constructivism in Rawls and Kant," in Samuel Freeman (ed.), *The Cambridge Companion to Rawls*. Cambridge: Cambridge University Press, pp. 347–67.

Osterman, P. 1988. *Employment Futures: Reorganization, Dislocation, and Public Policy*. Oxford: Oxford University Press.

Page, S. B., and M. B. Larner. 1997. "Introduction to the AFDC Program," *Welfare to Work* 7/1: 20–27.

Palmer, John, and Gregory Mills. 1982. "Budget Policy," in J. Palmer and I. Sawhill (eds.), *The Reagan Experiment*. Washington, DC: Urban Institute, pp. 59–96.

Patterson, J. T. 1981. *America's Struggle against Poverty: 1900–1980*. Cambridge, MA: Harvard University Press.

Pear, R. 2013. "House Endorses Stricter Work Rules for the Poor," *New York Times*, February 13.
Pogge, T. 1989. *Realizing Rawls*. Ithaca, NY: Cornell University Press.
  2000. "On the Site of Distributive Justice: Reflections on Cohen and Murphy," *Philosophy & Public Affairs* 29: 137–69.
Rawls, J. 1951. "Outline of a Decision Procedure for Ethics," *Philosophical Review* 60/2: 177–97. Reprinted in Samuel Freeman (ed.), *John Rawls: Collected Papers* (Cambridge, MA: Harvard University Press, 1999), pp. 1–19.
  1955. "Two Concepts of Rules," *Philosophical Review* 64/1: 3–32. Reprinted in Samuel Freeman (ed.), *John Rawls: Collected Papers* (Cambridge, MA: Harvard University Press, 1999), pp. 20–46.
  1958. "Justice as Fairness," *Philosophical Review* 67/2: 164–94. Reprinted in Samuel Freeman (ed.), *John Rawls: Collected Papers* (Cambridge, MA: Harvard University Press, 1999), pp. 47–72.
  1963a. "Constitutional Liberty and the Concept of Justice," in *Nomos*, vol. VI, *Justice*. New York, NY: Atherton Press, pp. 98–125. Reprinted in Reprinted in Samuel Freeman (ed.), *John Rawls: Collected Papers* (Cambridge, MA: Harvard University Press, 1999), pp. 73–95.
  1963b. "The Sense of Justice," *Philosophical Review* 72/3: 281–305. Reprinted in Samuel Freeman (ed.), *John Rawls: Collected Papers* (Cambridge, MA: Harvard University Press, 1999), pp. 96–116.
  1964. "Legal Obligation and the Duty of Fair Play," in Sidney Hook (ed.), *Law and Philosophy: A Symposium*. New York, NY: New York University Press, pp. 3–18. Reprinted in Reprinted in Samuel Freeman (ed.), *John Rawls: Collected Papers* (Cambridge, MA: Harvard University Press, 1999), pp. 117–29.
  1967. "Distributive Justice," in Peter Laslett and W. G. Runciman (eds.), *Politics, Philosophy, and Society*. Oxford: Blackwell. Reprinted in Samuel Freeman (ed.), *John Rawls: Collected Papers* (Cambridge, MA: Harvard University Press, 1999), pp. 130–53.
  1968. "Distributive Justice: Some Addenda," *Natural Law Forum* 13: 51–71. Reprinted in Samuel Freeman (ed.), *John Rawls: Collected Papers* (Cambridge, MA: Harvard University Press, 1999), pp. 154–75.
  (1971) 1999. *A Theory of Justice*. Cambridge, MA: Harvard University Press.
  1971. "Justice as Reciprocity," in S. Gorowitz (ed.), *John Stuart Mill: Utilitarianism, with Critical Essays*. Indianapolis, IN: Bobbs Merrill. Reprinted in Reprinted in Samuel Freeman (ed.), *John Rawls: Collected Papers* (Cambridge, MA: Harvard University Press, 1999), pp. 190–224.

1975. "The Independence of Moral Theory," *Proceedings and Addresses of the American Philosophical Association* 48: 5–22. Reprinted in Samuel Freeman (ed.), *John Rawls: Collected Papers* (Cambridge, MA: Harvard University Press, 1999), pp. 286–302.

1980. "Kantian Constructivism in Moral Theory," *Journal of Philosophy* 77: 515–72. Reprinted in Samuel Freeman (ed.), *John Rawls: Collected Papers* (Cambridge, MA: Harvard University Press, 1999), pp. 303–58.

1985. "Justice as Fairness: Political, not Metaphysical," *Philosophy & Public Affairs* 14 (1985): 223–52. Reprinted in Samuel Freeman (ed.), *John Rawls: Collected Papers* (Cambridge, MA: Harvard University Press, 1999), pp. 388–414.

1987. "The Idea of an Overlapping Consensus," *Oxford Journal of Legal Studies* 7: 1–25. Reprinted in Samuel Freeman (ed.), *John Rawls: Collected Papers* (Cambridge, MA: Harvard University Press, 1999), pp. 421–48.

(1993) 1996. *Political Liberalism*. New York, NY: Columbia University Press.

1999. *The Law of Peoples*. Cambridge, MA: Harvard University Press, including the paper "The Idea of Public Reason Revisited."

2000. *Lectures on the History of Moral Philosophy*. Cambridge, MA: Harvard University Press.

2001. *Justice as Fairness: A Restatement*. Cambridge, MA: Harvard University Press.

N.d.-a. "Justice as Fairness: A Guided Tour." Unpublished manuscript.

N.d.-b. "Lectures on Kant's Ethics." Unpublished manuscript.

Raz, J. 1990. "Facing Diversity: The Case of Epistemic Abstinence," *Philosophy & Public Affairs* 19: 3–46.

Reardon, S. F. 2011. "The Widening Academic Achievement Gap between the Rich and the Poor: New Evidence and Possible Explanations," in Duncan and Murnane, *Whither Opportunity*, pp. 91–116.

Rector, R. E., and S. E. Youssef. 1999. *The Determinants of Welfare Caseload Decline*. Report 99–04. Washington, DC: Heritage Foundation.

Roemer, J. 1996. *Theories of Distributive Justice*. Cambridge, MA: Harvard University Press.

Saez, E. 2008. "Striking It Richer: The Evolution of Top Incomes in the United States," *Pathways Magazine*, Winter.

Sandel, M. (1982) 1998. *Liberalism and the Limits of Justice*. Cambridge: Cambridge University Press.

Scanlon, T. M. 1976. "Nozick on Rights, Liberty, and Property," *Philosophy & Public Affairs* 6/1: 3–25.

1998. *What We Owe to Each Other*. Cambridge, MA: Harvard University Press.

2003. "Rawls on Justification," in Samuel Freeman (ed.), *The Cambridge Companion to Rawls*. Cambridge: Cambridge University Press, pp. 139–67.

Scheffler, S. 1994. "The Appeal of Political Liberalism," *Ethics* 105: 4–22.

2003. "Rawls and Utilitarianism," in Samuel Freeman (ed.), *The Cambridge Companion to Rawls*. Cambridge: Cambridge University Press, pp. 426–59.

2006. "Is the Basic Structure Basic?," in C. Snypowich (ed.), *The Egalitarian Conscience: Essays in Honor of G. A. Cohen*. Oxford: Oxford University Press, pp. 102–29.

2010. *Equality & Tradition: Questions of Value in Moral and Political Theory*. Oxford: Oxford University Press.

Schramm, S., and J. Soss. 2001. "Success Stories: Welfare Reform, Policy Discourse, and the Politics of Research," *Annals of the American Academy of Political and Social Science* 577: 49–65.

Schramm, S., J. Soss, R. C. Fording, and L. Houser. 2009. "Deciding to Discipline: Race, Choice and Punishment at the Frontlines of Welfare Reform," *American Sociological Review* 74: 398–422.

Sen, A. 1985. "Rationality and Uncertainty," *Theory and Decision* 81: 109–27.

2009. *The Idea of Justice*. Cambridge, MA: Harvard University Press.

Shaefer, H. L., and K. Edin. 2014. *Rising Extreme Poverty in the United States and the Response of Federal Means-Tested Transfer Programs*. Washington, DC: National Poverty Center.

Sidgwick, H. (1907) 1981. *The Method of Ethics*. Indianapolis, IN: Hackett.

Skorupski, John. 1989. *John Stuart Mill*. London: Routledge.

Stiglitz, J. E. 2012. *The Price of Inequality*. New York, NY: W. W. Norton.

Tawney, R. H. 1952. *Equality*. Totowa, NJ: Rowman & Littlefield.

Taylor, C. 1989. "Cross-Purposes: The Liberal-Communitarian Debate," in N. Rosenblum (ed.), *Liberalism and the Moral Life*. Cambridge, MA: Harvard University Press, pp. 159–82.

Taylor, R. 2011. *Reconstructing Rawls: The Kantian Foundations of Justice as Fairness*. University Park, PA: Pennsylvania State University Press.

Trisi, T., and L. Pavetti. 2012. *TANF Weakening as a Safety Net for Poor Families*. Washington, DC: Center on Budget and Policy Priorities.

Turner, L. J., S. Danziger, and K. S. Seefeldt. 2006. "Failing the Transition from Welfare to Work: Women Chronically Disconnected from Employment and Cash Welfare," *Social Science Quarterly* 87/2: 227–49.

US Census Bureau. 2000. *Statistical Abstract of the United States*. Washington, DC: US Census Bureau.

2009. *Current Population Reports: Educational Attainment in the United States*. Washington, DC: US Department of Commerce.

2012. *Current Population Report: Income, Poverty, and Health Insurance Coverage in the United States.* Washington, DC: US Department of Commerce.

Van Parijs, P. 2003. "Difference Principles," in Samuel Freeman (ed.), *The Cambridge Companion to Rawls.* Cambridge: Cambridge University Press, pp. 200–240.

Wang, M. C., and E. A. Ramp. 1987. *The National Follow-Through Program: Design, Implementation, and Effects.* Philadelphia, PA: Temple University Center for Research.

Wenar, L. 1995. "Political Liberalism: An Internal Critique," *Ethics* 106 (October): 32–62.

Williams, A. 1998. "Incentives, Inequality and Publicity," *Philosophy & Public Affairs* 27/3: 225–47.

Williams, B. W. 1962. "The Idea of Equality," in P. Laslett and W. G. Runciman (eds.), *Politics, Philosophy, and Society: Second Series.* Oxford: Basil Blackwell, pp. 110–31.

1985. *Ethics and the Limits of Philosophy.* Cambridge, MA: Harvard University Press.

Wingenbach, E. 1999. "Unjust Context: The Priority of Stability in Rawls's Contextualized Theory of Justice," *American Journal of Political Science* 43/1: 213–32.

Wolf, C. 2000. "Fundamental Rights, Reasonable Pluralism, and the Moral Commitments of Liberalism," in V. Davion and C. Wolf (eds.), *The Idea of a Political Liberalism.* Lanham, MD: Rowman and Littlefield, pp. 103–4.

Young, I. M. 1995. "Rawls's *Political Liberalism*," *Journal of Political Philosophy* 3 (June): 181–90.

Index

acceptability, 38
    changes in principles of justice, 28–29
    criteria, 27
    reflective equilibrium and, 83
    standard of, 27
Acting on Principle (O'Neill), 99
administrative stage, 209
affirmative action, 5, 52
Aid to Families with Dependent Children (AFDC), 239–40, 241, 246–47
allocation branch, 165
allocative justice, 167, 175, 176
Anderson, Elizabeth, 1, 188
Angner, Erik, 122
arbitrariness, 141–44, 189–90
Arneson, Richard, 1, 167, 174, 182, 194–98, 211

bad brute luck, 181, 182
Barry, Brian, 109, 113–14, 117–18, 119–20
basic capabilities, 206–07
basic rights
    establishment of, 224
    invasion of, 10
    principles of justice and, 148–49
    public reason and, 61
    social circumstances and, 224
    social minimum and, 203
basic structure of society, 145–50
    objection, 150
    private behavior within, 147–48, 149
    Rawls's specification for, 149
    regulation of, 10
    two coordinate roles of, 10, 11
Bayesian criterion, 109, 122–24

Bayesian expected-utility maximization rule, 109
Binmore, Ken, 109, 120
Buchanan, Allen, 113–14, 117–18
Burke, Edmund, 47
Bush tax cuts, 152–54

capabilities approach, 206–10
Center on Budget and Policy Priorities, 241
CETA program, 164
Chambers, Simone, 35
Charney, Evan, 63–65
child-centered model, 236
choice under certainty, 120–21
civil constitution, 80
class hierarchy, 35
cognitive oriented model, 236
Cohen, G. A., 241
    ambiguities, 133–45, 154
        basic structure as second ambiguity, 145–50
        difference principle as first ambiguity, 136–45
    basic structure objection, 138, 146, 150
    criticism of Rawls's theory of justice, 16–17
    on disagreements with Rawls, 176
    incentives argument, 136, 138
    luck egalitarianism and, 167, 211
    on moral desert, 170–71
    on moral judgements, 75–76
    on principles of justice, 95
    on Rawls's constructivism, 15, 86–91
    on share of goods, 175–76
    theory of equal access to advantage, 174

263

combined capabilities, 206–07
completeness, in moral judgement, 226–30
comprehensive doctrines
   appeal to authority of, 62–63
   political conception in, 32–33, 41
   reasonable vs. unreasonable, 63–65
Comprehensive Education and Training Act, 238
conception of justice, 47, 196
   acceptability of, 115
   allocative, 166–67
   construction of, 80–81
   definition of, 115
   just distribution and, 166
   maximin argument and, 110
   overlapping consensus in, 48
   politically liberal theory as, 60
   principles of, 47
   satisfactory minimum and, 116, 117
   stability requirement in, 47–49
consensus
   establishing and preserving, 31
   overlapping, 31, 32, 33, 37, 48, 53–54
   political conception as focus of, 29–30
considered judgments, 5–6
   conditions for, 5
   due reflection and, 5, 14, 38
   fact-insensitive principles associated with, 95
   foundational, 94–95
   levels of generality, 5–6
   moral justification and, 77
   original position and, 24
   as provisional fixed points, 34
   reflective equilibrium and, 83–84
constitutional reforms
   first principle of justice and, 67
   in well-ordered society, 66–67
constitutional stage, 209
constructivism, 15
   ethical. *See* ethical constructivism
   facts and, 86–91
   Kantian, 76, 84–86, 98–99
   political. *See* political constructivism
   social contract and, 79–82
contractarianism, 81, 82–83

Corrado, Gail, 122
Current population Survey, 243

decision procedure
   due reflection and, 5, 177
   elements of, 80
   for ethical problems, 99
   freedom and equality in, 84, 85
   Kantian constructivism and, 96
   modification of, 28–33
   moral judgements and, 75
   normative presuppositions, 221
   original position and, 96, 98
   political constructivism and, 103
   in selection of principles of justice, 6
   structure of, 85, 86
deliberations
   due reflection in, 35, 60
   fundamental ideas as, 34–35
   in original position, 31
   overlapping consensus, 59
   on principles of justice, 81–82
   reasonableness of, 38
   two-stage, 28, 29
   in well-ordered society, 41
deliberators
   basic premises of, 34
   and democratic political culture, 35–36
   and due reflection, 35
   located within a tradition, 34
   of political questions, 34
democratic culture. *See also* political culture
   basic ideas in, 26
   due reflection in, 14
   fundamental ideas in, 35, 36
   provisional fixed points in, 34
   reasonable pluralism in, 30
democratic equality, 9, 17–18, 187–216
   arbitrariness, 189–90
   capabilities approach and, 206–10
   as conception of distributive justice, 205–14
   definition of, 187
   difference principle and, 188–205
   fair equality of opportunity and, 188–205
   ideal of equality, 210–14

Index   265

just institutions and, 203–05
least advantaged and, 198
meritocracy and, 189–90
moral psychology and, 192–94
priority, 198–200
pure procedural justice and, 189–90
reciprocity and, 192–94
scope of equal opportunity and, 200–02
stability and, 192–94
structure, 198–200
transformation of social aims and, 190–92
vs. luck equality, 167–68
deprivation, 4, 183, 235–36
difference principle, 9, 16–17
  acceptable interpretation of, 135
  arbitrariness and, 141–44
  as Cohen's first ambiguity, 136–45
  concerns of justice and, 144
  democratic equality and, 187
  fair equality of opportunity and, 156–57
  inequalities under, 134–35
  informal argument, 133–34
  joint operation with fair equality of opportunity, 188–205
    arbitrariness, 189–90
    just institutions, 203–05
    meritocracy, 189–90
    moral psychology, 192–94
    priority, 194–200
    pure procedural justice, 189–90
    reciprocity, 192–94
    scope of equal opportunity, 200–02
    stability, 192–94
    structure, 198–200
    transformation of social aims, 190–92
  just institutions and, 166
  justice as fairness and, 169–70
  maximin argument and, 120
  position of least advantaged and, 137–41
  private behavior and, 149
  productive employment of talents and, 141–44
  Rawls's restriction on scope of, 147

requirements of, 139
responsibility and, 177–78
selfish maximizing behavior and, 144–45
strict and lax reading of, 136, 137, 144
direct instruction model, 236
disadvantaged, 157–58, 166
  education of, 237
  entrepreneurial class and, 138–39
  guarantee of minimum support to, 248
  responsibility and obligation to assist, 181–83
distribution branch, 159, 165
"Distributive Justice," 81, 82
distributive justice, 2, 156–57
  anchoring, 211
  difference principle and, 169–70
  Dworkin's theory of resource equality and, 173
  fair choice position and, 180–81
  liberal equality conception of, 189
  willful extravagance and, 181
due reflection, 5
  considered judgments and, 5, 14, 27, 38
  on constitutional reforms, 66
  in deliberations, 35, 60
  deliberative forum and, 30
  Kantian constructivism and, 76
  moral justification and, 77
  political conception on, 52
  on political liberalism, 41
  principles of justice and, 67–68
  reasonable persons and, 59
Dworkin, Ronald, 1, 211
  on acceptable account of egalitarian justice, 4
  distinction between rules and principles, 228
  goal of egalitarian justice, 208
  on justice as fairness, 170
  on relation between choice and consequences, 167
  on risks to economic and social mobility, 179–80
  theory of distributive justice, 180–81
  theory of resource equality, 173

economic inequality, 7
Economic Mobility Project, 235
education, 195–96, 203–04, 236–37
egalitarian justice, 212
egalitarianism, 1
    distributive, 167, 188, 212
egotism, 57–58
Elementary and Secondary Education Act, 237
employment, 203–04
endowment of talents, 141–44
equality, 84, 85
    democratic. See democratic equality
    of economic opportunity, 1, 2
    liberal, 8–9
    luck. See luck equality
    original position of, 82, 85
    resource, 173
Estlund, David, 37–38
ethical constructivism, 75–104. See also constructivism; Kantian constructivism; political constructivism
    facts and, 86–91
    Kantian influence on, 78–86
    Kantian objections, 96–102
        choice of principles, 96–98
        hypothetical or possible choice, 100–02
        scope of ethical concerns, 98–100
    moral judgements and, 75
    moral justification and, 77–78
    overview, 75
    removal of Kantian elements from, 102–03
    revision of, 102–03
    social contract and, 79–82
    social practices and, 91–95
expected utility, 123
extreme fundamentalism, 57–58

facts, 86–91
fair choice position, 180–81
fair equality of opportunity, 158–64
    access to education, 160, 161
    access to medical care, 160
    aims of, 158–59
    Arneson's objection to, 198
    claims to goods and, 143–44
    democratic equality and, 167–68, 187
    deprivation and, 236
    difference principle and, 156–57
    environmental influences on prospects and, 161–62
    goal of, 197
    ideal justice and, 161
    implementation of, 189
    joint operation with difference principle, 188–205
        arbitrariness, 189–90
        meritocracy, 189–90
        moral psychology, 192–94
        priority, 194–200
        pure procedural justice, 189–90
        reciprocity, 192–94
        scope of equal opportunity, 200–02
        stability, 192–94
        structure, 198–200
        transformation of social aims, 190–92
    just institutions and, 164–68
    in just society, 159–60
    justice as fairness and, 156–84
    justification of, 197
    liberal equality and, 8–9
    luck equality, 167–68
    neglect of the untalented in, 196–97
    overview, 17
    as principle of justice, 157
    priority of, 194–98
    pure procedural justice and, 172, 188, 189
    required policies for, 194–95
    requirements, 156, 158, 163–64
    responsibility for disadvantage and, 168–83
    scope of, 162–64, 200–02
    scope of guarantees under, 160–61
    social endowments and, 187
    social minimum and, 236–37
    social understanding of, 190
    transformation of social aims and, 190–92
    for welfare, 174
families
    allowances, 235–36

Index

basic structure of society and
    education of children, 161–62,
        233–34
    extreme-poverty, 244
    income support for, 239–40
    incomes of, 233–34
    injustice in, 149–50
    political principles and, 147
    principles of justice and, 148–49
    single-parent, 241
    training programs for, 245
family, 148
family law, 160
Follow-Through Program, 237
freedom, 84, 85
Freeman, Samiel, 123
fully autonomous persons, 32
fundamental ideas, 26–36
    assumptions in, 26
    and ideal external to tradition,
        33–36
    modification of decision procedure,
        28–33
    and political beliefs/convictions,
        26
    as product of political deliberation,
        34–35
    and public opinion, 27–28
fundamental rights, protecting, 66
fundamentalism, 57–58

Galston, William, 37, 39
good, pursuit of, 223
*Groundwork of the Metaphysics of
    Morals* (Kant), 79, 84, 100
Gutmann, Amy, 212, 213

Habermas, Jürgen, 28, 30
Hampton, Jean, 37
Harsanyi, John, 109, 120–21
Hausman, Daniel, 109, 120, 122
Head Start program, 164, 236, 237
higher education, 234, 237
Hill, Thomas, 101–02
Hinton, Timothy, 1
Hume, David, 78
hypothetical consent, 100–02

Idea of Justice (Sen), 218
ideal justice, 161
ideal theory, 18, 218–31

insensitivity to consequences,
    222–26
just institutions and, 219–21
moral judgment and, 226–30
normative presuppositions, 221–22
practical analysis and, 219–30
income distribution, 232–33
incompleteness, 226
"Independence of Moral Theory, The,"
    142
inequalities, 7
    accommodationist approach to, 134
    arrangement of, 139
    conditions for, 8
    difference principle and, 134–35,
        136
    economic, 7
    least advantaged and, 138–39
    social, 7
inequality in the United States, 232–39
informal argument, 133–34
injustice, 142, 149–50
Institute for Research on Poverty, 242
institutional fundamentalism, 219, 222
institutions
    choice of law in, 222
    justice, 219
    preferred, consequences of, 222
insular groups, 37–38
insurance, 179
internal capabilities, 206–07

James, Aaron, 15, 75–76, 91–94
Job Corps, 238
judicial stage, 209
just institutions, 164–68, 219–21
    democratic equality and, 167–68,
        203–05
    just distribution and, 166
    luck equality and, 167–68
    social reforms and, 166
    well-ordered society and, 164
justice, 36–41
    considered judgments of, 5–6
    constructivist approach to, 4
    egalitarian, 212
    nature and requirements of, 3
    political conception of, 29–30
    practical conception of, 23–43
    principles of, 6
    stability and, 50–53

"Justice as Fairness," 79, 81–82
justice as fairness, 6–7, 47
   and allocative conceptions of justice, 166–67
   claims of moral desert of reward and, 170–71
   difference principle and, 169–70
   distribution of social burdens and benefits, 116–17
   distributive justice in, 169–70
   fair equality of opportunity and, 156–84
   functions of, 228–29
   fundamental requirement in, 156–57
   liberty and, 224
   luck equality and, 172–73
   maximin argument and, 109
   not an end-state theory, 169
   outcome, 229
   priority rules, 115–16, 198, 228–29
   pursuit of the good and, 223
   responsibility in
     concerns of justice regarding, 182
     difference principle and, 177–78
     obligation to assist the disadvantaged, 181–83
     pure procedural justice and, 171–77
     social minimum and, 178–81
   restriction of focus of, 175
   social institutions and, 193–94
   strains of commitment and, 10
   in well-ordered society, 193
Justice as Fairness: A Restatement, 115–16, 117, 139–41, 148–49
justification, 5–6, 14–16
   contractarian approach to, 81

Kant, Immanuel, 47, 78–86
Kantian conception of the person
   constructivism and, 98
   social contract and, 84–86
Kantian constructivism, 76, 84–86, 98–99. *See also* constructivism; ethical constructivism; political constructivism
"Kantian Constructivism in Moral Theory," 79, 84–86

Kaufman, Alexander, 1
Krasnoff, Larry, 96, 100
Kukathas, C., 39

labor force, participation rate, 234–35
Law of Peoples (Rawls), 94
least advantaged, 137–41
   entrepreneurial class and, 138–39
   permissible inequalities and, 138–39
legislative stage, 209
less skilled workers, 234–35
Levi, Isaac, 122
liberal equality, 8–9
Liberal Theory of Justice, The (Barry), 120
liberties, 203, 208
   equal right to, 7
   inequalities in, 225
   justice as fairness and, 224
   lexical priority of, 225, 226
   moral agents, 223
   natural, 8
   preferred institutions and, 222
   protection of, 223–24
   restriction of, 224–25
   unacceptable losses of, 180
luck, 142
luck equality, 167–68
   access to legal counsel and, 211
   choices and outcomes in, 182
   individualized treatment of person's circumstances and choices in, 175, 179
   structure of, 173–74
   vs. justice as fairness, 172–73, 174–75

Martin, Rex, 108
Mattravers, Matt, 1
maximin argument, 15–16, 108–26
   account of justice and, 108–09, 110
   Bayesian criterion, 122–24
   choice under certainty and, 120–24
   defenses of, 122
   difference principle and, 120
   expected utility criterion, 123
   maximizing share of goods in, 2
   objections to, 119–20

original position and, 119–20
overview, 111–13
satisfactory minimum and, 9–10, 113–20
McPherson, Michael, 109, 120, 122
medical care, unequal distribution of, 212–13
meritocracy, 8–9, 189–90
Methods of Ethics, The (Sidgwick), 78
Mill, John Stuart, 47, 148–49
minimum wage, 157–58
moral conception, 47, 76, 221, 227
moral considerations, 93–94
moral judgements, 75, 176, 226–30
moral justification, 3, 77–78
  possible grounds for, 3
moral persons, 84–86
moral principles, 97–98
moral psychology, 55, 192–94
moral reasoning, 78, 91, 97, 103, 177, 198
moral reflection, 83
Mouffe, Chantal, 58–64, 65

National Campaign for Jobs and Income Support, 242
National Survey of America's Families, 243
natural liberty, 8
Neal, Patrick, 65–67
normative claims, justifying, 3
normative foundations, 37–39
Nozick, Robert, 167, 169–70, 201, 212, 213
Nussbaum, Martha, 1, 208, 221

objectivity, 14, 41
Okin, Susan, 148
O'Neill, Onora, 96, 98–99, 100–02
on-the-job training, 238
original position, 5, 108
  appeals to moral considerations, 93–94
  deliberation in, 31
  of equality, 82
  equality of moral persons in, 85
  limited authority of, 94
  maximin argument, 9–10, 15–16
  maximin argument and, 120
  Pareto argument, 88

principles chosen in, 24, 28, 30, 67–68, 96, 97–98
principles of justice in, 29, 80, 83, 95
rational choosers of, 88, 133
Rawls's account of reflection in, 28
reasonable persons and, 40–41, 85
satisfactory minimum and, 114
structure of, 94–95
"Outline of a Decision Procedure for Ethics," 79, 82–83
overlapping consensus, 66
  conception of justice and, 48
  deliberations and, 59
  exclusion of nonliberal views in, 59–60
  exclusion of unreasonable views from, 58
  focus of, 31, 48
  justification of, 59–60
  political conception as resource, 33
  political liberalism and, 53–54
  public reason and, 59–60
  stability of, 50–51
  sustaining, 32
  toleration and, 37

Pareto argument, 87–88
Pareto Principle, 87–89
person, fully autonomous, 32
Pettit, P., 39
philosophy, proper task, 39–41
Piagetian theory, 236
Piketty, Thomas, 232
pluralism, simple vs. reasonable, 58
pluralistic societies, 48
plurality voting, 66
political authority, grant of, 57
political beliefs, 25
political conception, 12–13
  and comprehensive doctrine, 32–33
  conflict mediation and, 52
  exclusion of unreasonable views and, 58
  feasibility of, 51
  as focus of consensus, 29–30
  and overlapping consensus, 33
  in well-ordered society, 31–32
  willing agreement of citizens and, 51–52

political constructivism, 177. *See also* constructivism; ethical constructivism; Kantian constructivism
  fundamental ideas, 26
  Kantian elements in, 102–03
  moral reasoning and, 103
  vs. Kantian constructivism, 76, 102–04
political convictions
  objectivity of, 52
    modification of, 27
  persuasiveness of reasons to justify, 40
  political liberalism and, 39–40
political culture, 35
  comprehensive doctrines in, 60
  democratic, 25, 26, 35–36
  fundamental ideas in, 34, 41, 49, 51–53
  moral conception and, 221
  political liberalism and, 11–13, 23
  public, 26, 29, 31
  of well-ordered society, 68–69
political justification, 3
political liberalism, 41
  acceptability, 37–38
  acceptance by insular groups, 37–38
  as basis for political agreement, 23
  consensus in, 29
  criticisms of, 36
  and lack of philosophical ambition, 39
  overlapping consensus and, 53–54
  and political convictions, 39–40
  and political reflection, 23–24
  and political stability, 24
  and reasonable pluralism in democratic society, 30
  securing stability in, 49
  socialization and, 69–70
  stability requirement in, 49
  two stages in exposition of, 31
Political Liberalism, 11–13
  account of reflection in, 28
  account of stability in, 49
  accounts of justice in, 76
  Lecture IV of, 66
  Parts I and II, 31
  pluralistic disagreement in, 48
  Rawls's criterion of objectivity in, 40–41
  Rawls's language in, 209
  standards of reasonableness in, 60
political principles, objective, 24
political reasoning, 24
political stability, 65
political theory, 23
poverty in the United States, 232–39
  extreme, 244
practical conception of justice, 23–43
  and concept of truth, 39
  and essential nature/identity of persons, 24–25
price system, 142–43, 165
primary goods, 114
principle of violation, 79
principles of justice
  acceptable, 81–83, 90, 175
  choice of, 81–82
  constructivist approach to, 88, 90, 95
  deliberations on, 81–82
  due reflection and, 67–68
  fact-dependent, 86–91
  injustice as defined by, 149–50
  intuitive argument for, 88, 95
  practical application of, 18–19
  regulation of basic structure, 7
  rules of justice and, 227–28
  selecting, 6
  strains of commitment and, 10
  in well-ordered society, 68–69
priority rules, 115–16, 198, 228–29
private behavior, 147–48
procedural justice, 4, 172, 188, 189–90
public goods, 142
public institutions, 192
public laws, 80
public opinion, 27–28
public policy, concerns of, 144
public reason, 13
  criterion of reciprocity and, 62
  duty to honor, 62
  issues within scope of, 61
  limits of, 59–60, 65

Index

nature of duty to respect limits of, 61–63
persons subject to limits of, 61
restriction of public discourse and, 61
sincere judgment as central requirement of, 62
public spheres, 65–68
publicity principle, 87, 89
pure justice, 86, 87
pure procedural justice, 189–90
   acceptable conception of, 189–90
   fair equality of opportunity and, 172, 188

rational, 85
rational choice
   contractarian account of, 82
   moral reasoning and, 78
rational egotism, 57–58
Reagan tax cuts, 153–54
reasonable, 85
reasonable comprehensive doctrine
   characterization of, 54
   definition of, 54–55
   lack of precision of, 55
   main features of, 55–56
   reasonable persons and, 55
   state power and, 57
reasonable persons, 85
   definition of, 58–59
   due reflection, 52–53
   judgements of, 38
   qualities of, 54–55
   Rawls's definition of, 27
   on use of state power, 56
   views affirmed by, 54–58
   views of, 59
reasonable pluralism, in democratic culture, 30, 36
reasonable view, 56
reasonableness, 48
   characterization of, 54
   political liberalism and, 53–54
   standard for, 57–58
   standard of, 56–57, 59
reasoning process, 91
reasons, persuasivenesss o, 40
reciprocity, 192–94

reflective equilibrium, 6, 82–84, 92
religious doctrines, 55, 57
Rescuing Justice & Equality (Cohen), 87, 88
resource equality, 173
respect, public expression of, 117
responsibility
   concerns of justice regarding, 182
   difference principle and, 177–78
   obligation to assist the disadvantaged, 181–83
   social minimum and, 178–81
restricted utility principle, 117
Roe v. Wade, 64
Roemer, John, 1, 109, 120, 171
rules of justice, 227–28

Saez, Emmanuel, 232
satisfactory minimum, 10
   conception of justice and, 114–15, 116, 117
   diminishing marginal value, 113–14
   fundamental interests protected by, 118–19
   minimum threshold, 113–14
   objections to, 117–18
   proposed conceptions, 115–16
   protection of liberty interests, 116
Scheffler, Samuel, 1, 188, 210–11, 212
schmoctoring, 213
selfish maximizing behavior, 144–45
Sen, Amartya, 1, 18, 218, 221, 223–24
Sidgwick, Henry, 78, 161, 164
single-parent families, 241
Skinner, B. F., 236
slavery, 35
social aims, transformation of, 190–92
social contract, 79
   constructivism and, 79–82, 103
   Kantian conception of the person and, 84–86
   reflective equilibrium and, 82–84
social endowments, 187
social goods, 4
   distribution of, 9
   fair distribution of, 1
social inequality, 7

social judgments, 209
social life, conflict about ideals of, 39
social minimum, 208
    access to health care services and, 236
    as a constitutional essential, 203
    deprivation and, 235–36
    disadvantaged and, 209–10
    fair equality of opportunity and, 196, 236–37
    income inequality and, 235
    responsibility and, 178–81
    unconditional guarantee of, 183
    welfare and, 247
social mobility, 235
social policies, 164, 188, 198, 240
social practices, 91–95
    arguments from existing practices, 92–93
    authority independent of judgements, 94
    constructive interpretation of, 92
    moral considerations in, 93–94
socialization, 68–70
    citizens' acceptance of political order and, 69
    citizens' resistance to, 68
    political liberalism and, 69–70
    toleration and, 70
society
    basic structure of, 145–50
    consensus among members of, 12
    pluralistic, 48
    private behavior in, 147–48
    Rawls's specification for basic structure of, 135
    well-ordered. *See* well-ordered society
    willing identification of members, 23
stability
    appropriateness of requirement, 53
    fit with views, 50–51
    justice and, 50–53
    kind of fit, 51–53
    limits of public reason and, 60
    overview, 14–15
    principle, 89–90
    principle of, 192–94

Rawls's concern with, 41, 48–49, 222
    satisfaction of requirements, 47–48
    securing, 49
stabilization branch, 165
state power, 56
strains of commitment, 10
Supported Work, 238
Survey of Income and Program Participation, 243
Sweden, 238

talents, productive employment of, 141–44
Tawney, R.H., 159, 161–62, 164
tax cuts, 152–54
Taylor, Robert, 109, 120
Temporary Assistance for Needy Families program (TANF), 239–40, 244
"Theory and Practice" essay, 84
Theory of Justice, A, 1, 5–11, 41–42
    account of objectivity in, 40–41
    account of stability in, 48–49
    aim of, 227–28
    approach to justification in, 30
    arguments for principles of justice in, 88
    conception of justice in, 80
    constructivism in, 76
    decision procedure in, 86
    difference principle in, 136–37, 138
    equal opportunity principle in, 160, 198–200, 201–02
    errors of attribution to Rawls in, 2
    formal argument, 9–11
    informal argument, 7–9
    just institutions in, 219–21
    justification, 5–6
    Kantian conception of the person in, 48
    Kantian constructivism in, 98
    maximin arguments in, 122
    nature of social institutions in, 165
    normative presuppositions in, 221
    original position in, 82, 108–09
    political reasoning in, 24
    presentation of alternatives in, 97
    pursuit of the good in, 223
    reflective equilibrium in, 82–83

regulation of institutions in, 218
"Remarks on Justification," 227
social judgments in, 209
toleration, 70
training, 195–96, 203–04, 238, 245
Treatise of Human Nature (Hume), 78
truth, 36–41
two-stage deliberation, 28
   Rawls's rejection of, 29

Urban Institute, 242, 243
utilitarianism, 80

van Parijs, Philippe, 109

Walrasian auction, 173
wealth distribution, 233
welfare, 239–48
   1996 reforms, 240, 245
   assessment, 246–48
   children recipients of, 240
   demonstration programs, 245–46
   equal opportunity for, 174
   extreme poverty and, 244
   income support, 239–46
   involuntary exits, 244–45
   leavers
      earnings of, 242–43
      employed, 241–42, 243
      statistics, 244

single-parent families on, 241
social minimum and, 247
training programs, 245, 247–48
work training programs, 241
well-ordered society, 18
   constitutional reforms in, 66–67
   deliberations in, 41
   fair equality of opportunity in, 164
   fair opportunity principle and, 189
   fit with views, 50
   justice as fairness in, 193
   Kantian constructivism and, 98–99
   overlapping consensus in, 32
   policies in, 236
   political conception in, 31–32
   political culture of, 68–69
   principles of justice in, 68–69
   regulation of basic institutions in, 218
   views of reasonable citizens in, 41
Wenar, Leif, 54–57, 58, 64
willful extravagance, 181
Williams, Bernard, 162–64, 200–02, 212–13
willing agreement of citizens, 52
Wingenbach, Ed, 65–67, 68–70
Youth Employment and Demonstration Projects, 238